£10·95   Abebo

HI
184773

A REGIONAL HISTORY OF
THE RAILWAYS OF GREAT BRITAIN

General Editors : DAVID ST JOHN THOMAS AND J. ALLAN PATMORE

Volume XI
NORTH AND MID WALES

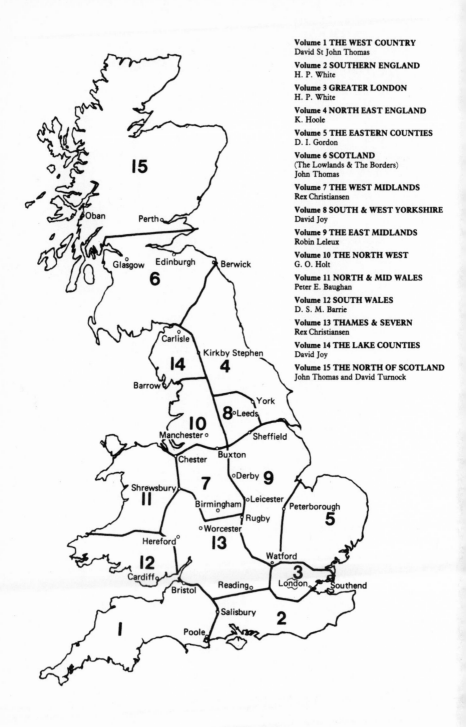

Volume 1 THE WEST COUNTRY
David St John Thomas

Volume 2 SOUTHERN ENGLAND
H. P. White

Volume 3 GREATER LONDON
H. P. White

Volume 4 NORTH EAST ENGLAND
K. Hoole

Volume 5 THE EASTERN COUNTIES
D. I. Gordon

Volume 6 SCOTLAND
(The Lowlands & The Borders)
John Thomas

Volume 7 THE WEST MIDLANDS
Rex Christiansen

Volume 8 SOUTH & WEST YORKSHIRE
David Joy

Volume 9 THE EAST MIDLANDS
Robin Leleux

Volume 10 THE NORTH WEST
G. O. Holt

Volume 11 NORTH & MID WALES
Peter E. Baughan

Volume 12 SOUTH WALES
D. S. M. Barrie

Volume 13 THAMES & SEVERN
Rex Christiansen

Volume 14 THE LAKE COUNTIES
David Joy

Volume 15 THE NORTH OF SCOTLAND
John Thomas and David Turnock

A REGIONAL HISTORY OF THE RAILWAYS OF GREAT BRITAIN

Volume XI

NORTH AND MID WALES

by
Peter E. Baughan

WITH 60 PLATES
12 MAPS
AND FOLDING MAP

DAVID ST JOHN THOMAS PUBLISHER

First published 1980 by David & Charles
This second edition published 1991
by David St John Thomas Publisher

British Library Cataloguing in Publication Data

Baughan, Peter Edwards
  North and Mid Wales. – (A regional history of
  the railways of Great Britain; vol. 11).
  1. Railroads – Wales, North – History
  I. Title   II. Series
  385'.09429'1   HE3019.H/

  ISBN 0–946537–59–3

Printed in Great Britain
by Redwood Press Limited, Melksham
for David St John Thomas Publisher
PO Box 4, Nairn, Scotland IV12 4HU

Contents

       Carmarthen to not quite Cardigan . opening
       Carmarthen to Conwil . trouble at Pencader – open
       to Llandyssul . a change of direction . opening the
       Manchester & Milford . development in GWR
       times . railway to Aberayron . closures – and re-
       openings . Vale of Rheidol Railway

XV   THE 1980S – INVESTMENT FOR THE 'NINETIES   238
       North Wales Coast Line . Celebrations at Blaenau
       Ffestiniog . Shrewsbury & Chester and the Bidston–
       Wrexham line . Cambrian transformation . 'Heart of
       Wales' line . standard gauge main line steam

XVI   TOURIST RAILWAYS INTO THE 'NINETIES   254
       Standard gauge revivals - Llangollen and Gwili . Bala
       Lake Railway . Corris awakening . 'All Change!' on
       the Fairbourne . The Festiniog returns to Blaenau .
       Llanberis Lake Railway . Talyllyn Railway . Teifi
       Valley Railway . 'Roll Up' for the Vale of Rheidol .
       Welsh Highland Railway . Welshpool & Llanfair
       Light Railway

       ACKNOWLEDGEMENTS   265

       SOURCES, BIBLIOGRAPHY AND FURTHER READING   266

       INDEX   269

CHAPTER I

Introduction to the Region

'Night of drama at monument to engineer's genius' ran the headline in the *Liverpool Daily Post* on Monday, 25 May 1970 above a photograph showing the famous Britannia Tubular Bridge in fiery relief against the night sky, flaring pitch streaming from it into the Menai Strait.

Two days before, on the Caernarvonshire shore, I had listened as had so many visitors before me to the rumbling thunder of a train a hundred feet above within the great iron tubes, constructed between 1846 and 1850 by Robert Stephenson, engineer to the Chester & Holyhead Railway Company. Nearby on a stone plinth, hidden amongst trees, stood the broken cylinder press, memento of a near tragedy in 1849 when it failed when lifting one of the tubes. Here Stephenson had accompanied Queen Victoria, Prince Albert and the young Prince of Wales, on a tour of inspection. Were they too, one wonders, awed by the magnificent bridge? Perhaps more so, for we are conditioned now to a diet of bigger and better of everything. I took several photographs that day in 1970 – after all, though the bridge would be there for years to come, one did not know when one would be back. Two days later it came as a shock to hear of its near destruction.

At first pessimism was voiced over the future of the railway. Surely it would be closed, cut back to Bangor or even Llandudno. But Anglesey was still felt to be too important, and Telford's fine suspension bridge could not possibly cope alone. Perhaps a new highway would fling its monstrous self across the Strait, with gangs of men dismantling the Britannia Bridge.

Praise be, this was not to happen. A decision was made, bordering on an act of faith, to rebuild the railway bridge, using architect Francis Thompson's original stone piers to carry a new arched structure. The railway is now safe, and one may happily start this survey of the railways of North and Mid Wales on a refreshing note of optimism.

Of course the Chester & Holyhead is a thing apart, a patrician line unlike any other in Wales. Blessed with engineering marvels, boasting a famous—the first—named train, it has a ring about it denied to more prosaic railways which got on with the job largely unsung, bar local junketing when opened. While the CHR, built for Irish traffic, owing little to local initiative and requirements, received government assistance and was invested in and directed by a major established company, those other railways struggled through often mountainous country dependent largely on the resources of private enterprise. Even so—a measure of the cost of construction—the CHR became as financially insecure as many another Welsh railway, and by 1859 had been absorbed by the mighty London & North Western company, with headquarters at Euston station, London.

With the main grain of North and Mid Wales running east-west, the mountains have dictated the basic patterns of development through the ages, inhibiting intercourse between north and south. In the north, dominated by the Snowdon and Arenig massifs, with the Denbighshire and Clwydian hills to their east reaching to the Cheshire Plain, the river system has carved short valleys northwards to the sea, while a narrow coastal plain affords the only reasonable route for movement westwards out of England. Along this strip mediaeval monarchs built castles at the mouths of the rivers to protect trading posts. Inland, to control the valleys, other fortifications were built, around which grew up small market towns. For centuries travel by land was extremely difficult due to the bad condition of the roads, and a busy coastal trade developed. In the early 19th century the Holyhead Road was built by Thomas Telford. Made for the Irish Mail and other traffic and with little or no intention of benefiting the Welsh people this, and other roads made to Aberystwyth in the west and Milford in the south, did nothing for north-south communication. Canals, even more affected by terrain, were limited to the eastern borderlands of the region. Much of the interior of North and Mid Wales remained isolated until the coming of the railways which, more flexible, were able to follow the valleys, serving and encouraging their agricultural and commercial development.

In the early 19th century industry in North Wales was slight and scattered : mining in the hills for copper, iron and lead;

slate quarrying near Bangor and Caernarvon, at Ffestiniog in
the west and Oswestry in the east; mountain sheep producing
the main export of the area; and thousands of Welsh cattle
yearly driven through the upland passes to English markets. In
Denbighshire and Flintshire there was coal mining and iron
working, soon to expand. The area around Wrexham became
the centre for the Denbighshire industry, and from there, to
carry coal to Chester, the first public railway in North Wales
was projected in 1839; authorised in 1844, it eventually became
part of the Great Western Railway's Paddington–Birkenhead
route.

Once the main lines were established, small branches evolved
serving the valleys. Not all were dictated by strategic requirements or by local need. The Vale of Clwyd Railway, promoted
for local traffic, prospered initially; others, built speculatively
through sparse areas, were always in debt. By the 1870s, most
of these small companies in North Wales had been swallowed
up by the London & North Western.

Speaking at a dinner in 1865, reported in the *Carnarvon
Herald,* Martin Smith, secretary and manager of the Vale of
Clwyd, brought Welsh railway enterprise into focus:

Every year's experience tended more strongly to convince him
that the directors of the Vale of Clwyd acted wisely in secur-
ing terms with the London & North Western Railway at the
time they did. The shareholders enjoyed their 5 per cent . . .
while the connection had enabled their railway to do a good
deal more for the public than would have been possible if
they had been struggling on as an entirely independent concern. If only half the projects talked about at present were
carried out, railways would certainly be plentiful in this part
of Wales. He said if carried out; for they must remember that
the plan or system of making railways was now entirely
changed. Local gentlemen do not now subscribe a penny to
the schemes, indeed if asked to do so they would smile, well
knowing that the lines among these mountains cannot possibly
be worth a fifth or tenth of what they cost, even if made
economically, which is not the case. All the capital is borrowed
from financial associations, and large interest is paid out of
capital, not only during construction but after the lines are
opened, as experience shows that these railways, left to themselves, do not pay working expenses. When the large companies
were bidding against each other for any and every new railway
that came anywhere near them, promoting schemes was no

doubt pretty safe and good business. But these companies appear to have purchased experience, and are now sufficiently cool to sit down and calculate what they can possibly lose in traffic, and what by buying up the competing project, and the result is at most hundreds as against thousands. This mountainous and thinly populated country must depend upon this : the financial associations being got to believe for a few years longer that making railways here is a good speculation, and then, as pointed out, Wales will have a great deal to be thankful for.

This summary explains the troubles behind a company such as the Mold & Denbigh Junction built, after its *raison d'être* had gone, by a contractor who borrowed heavily and put down a double line of rails when most companies, including the Cambrian on its main line, were purchasing land for double but laying only a single track.

Along the southern flanks of the mountains, from Wrexham in the east to Barmouth in the west, are the valleys of the Rivers Dee and Wnion. Here, at Dolgellau, two of the LNWR's neighbours met by end-on junction : the Cambrian and the Great Western. The former branches from the Aberystwith & Welch Coast Railway (*sic*) at Barmouth in the west. The latter arrived from Ruabon on the Shrewsbury–Chester line in the east by absorption of four small companies running via Corwen, where an LNWR branch left for Rhyl, and via Bala, whence a GWR branch climbed north and west to seek slate and join the LNWR at Blaenau Ffestiniog. LNWR vigilance was to keep Great Western influence confined to the Blaenau and Dolgellau branches and to entanglements around the coalfield north-west of Wrexham, shared with another company, the Wrexham Mold & Connah's Quay, which eventually became an outpost of the Manchester Sheffield & Lincolnshire, later the Great Central.

As with the CHR, the Cambrian main line replaced a turnpike road, though its route was formed from several companies serving local communities whose lines butt-ended to each other. The only large, purely Welsh railway in the region, the Cambrian ran from Whitchurch on the LNWR Crewe–Shrewsbury line, westwards across the North Shropshire Plain to the English town of Oswestry, where it chose to have its headquarters, before turning south across the Border to Welshpool and thence through beautiful but difficult country, threading river valleys and cutting through intervening high ground to reach the estuary of the Dovey in Cardigan Bay. There it met and absorbed the Aberystwith & Welch Coast which followed the bay northwards through Barmouth to Pwllheli. At Afon Wen, near Pwllheli, a straggling LNWR branch arrived from Caernarvon.

From Moat Lane, midway between Oswestry and Aberystwyth, the Cambrian ran to Llanidloes, whence the Mid Wales Railway thrust south via Radnor to a junction with the Brecon & Merthyr. At Builth it crossed the Central Wales Railway from Craven Arms, on the Shrewsbury & Hereford, to Swansea, also formed of several small companies, absorbed by the LNWR to get into South Wales. Llanidloes was also the starting point of the northerly end of the Manchester & Milford Railway which aspired to create a through route, much of which entailed running powers over other railways, in an attempt to frustrate Liverpool's 'middle-man' influence on Manchester trade. It became bogged down after only a few miles and ended tamely and unopened in a cutting at Llangurig. The M&M's southerly end, however, was constructed from Strata Florida to Pencader on the Carmarthen and Cardigan line. It became an outpost with the C&C of the Great Western which reached up from South Wales to Newcastle Emlyn, Aberayron and Aberystwyth.

The census returns highlight a trend of de-population in the interior of Wales. Frequently a local peak shows up during the making of a nearby railway, the figures beforehand having been fairly stable. The arrival of the railway in a predominantly rural area, linking hitherto largely inaccessible villages, where pursuits were limited and wages depressed, was a traumatic and liberating event. Nothing like it in living memory could have happened before : a sudden influx of hard-working, hard-living, and often well-paid navvies, whose exploits were wondered at and whose tall tales of distant places lost nothing with re-telling. And when they had gone, there for all to see were the shining rails to a new freedom full of opportunity. Young men moved away to the burgeoning industry of Deeside, Merseyside, and the coalfields, and young women went into service in the growing tourist resorts. Thus, while the population of established market towns like Denbigh, Montgomery and Newtown, for instance, with activities offering reasonable and fairly constant employment, reached a slight peak in the 1870s and 1880s, that of the small Anglesey port of Amlwch, with limited employment potential, halved between 1861 and 1901. In contrast the population of the North Wales coastal resorts increased by considerable numbers. In the heart of the coalfield a small village like Brymbo virtually quadrupled between 1841 and 1901, while on its edge the towns of Wrexham and Ruabon doubled over the same period. Where there was an abundance of a natural resource waiting to be exploited, such as slate at Blaenau Ffestiniog, a new railhead triggered increased production and employment, attracted other railway ventures, and tripled the local population.

Overall, however, the general trend was downwards, and by the first two decades of the 20th century growing competition from the internal combustion engine had further hit any slight remaining profitability of many of the Welsh railways. Those that survived the 1930s—a time of cut-backs—enjoyed an artificial revival during World War II. Post-war austerity kept them in business until the late 1950s and early 1960s. Thereafter an increasing car-owning population, more flexible and reliable bus and carrier services, and the decline of local industries once dependent on the railway, led during the Beeching era to many lines being 'reshaped'—a curious word in the circumstances to describe the holocaust of closures which hit Wales in the 1960s, when cynical stationmasters on rural branches would claim, in black humour, that their secret fear was to see a gang of railway painters descend from a train to bedaub their station—a sure sign it was for the axe. Most of the branches in North and Mid Wales have gone, but their structures often survive, particularly station buildings, turned into 'desirable residences'. Some have suffered unkind fates : Ruthin station site is now a roundabout.

The main lines remain open. Still operating, no longer tenuously, is the Cambrian, from Shrewsbury, not Oswestry, for Whitchurch–Welshpool was an early victim. Also reprieved is the Central Wales line, while the Chester–Holyhead route has a new lease of life. E. G. Bowen, in his *Wales: A Physical, Historical and Regional Geography*, sums up the transport problem:

> It may be said that the evolution of neither the major road system nor the railway network did much to unite Wales as a cultural or economic unit. The way to achieve that would be to build a major routeway, rail or road, through the heart of the country from Rhyl in the north to Swansea in the south. But it is precisely along such a route that the physical

obstacles would be the greatest and the sparse distribution of population such as to render the venture economically impracticable.

Different in intent and style to the public railways were the numerous narrow gauge lines, some of which became absorbed by the main line companies. One of the earliest was the Nantlle· Railway which from the 1820s conveyed copper and slate to the quays under Caernarvon castle walls. Much of its formation was later converted into part of the LNWR standard gauge Caernarvon–Afon Wen line. Serving an area south and east of the latter, and commenced in the 1870s, were the North Wales Narrow Gauge Railways, later renamed as the more romantic Welsh Highland Railway which operated, with breaks in service, until the 1930s. Other narrow gauge lines, born in the days of the slate boom and purely utilitarian, have of late been resurrected as some of Wales' most thriving tourist attractions, 'The Great Little Trains of Wales', consisting (in 1990) of the Bala Lake, Brecon Mountain (in South Wales), Festiniog, Llanberis Lake, Talyllyn, Vale of Rheidol, Welsh Highland, and Welshpool & Llanfair Railways. Operated by a joint marketing panel, some offer journeys of spectacular beauty into the mountains. The Vale of Rheidol, from Aberystwyth to Devil's Bridge, for instance, has gradients and curves of the cliff-hanging, ledge-clinging kind, down which phlegmatic Welsh quarriers once rumbled, but now unexpectedly lit upon by the tourist. After a racketting journey of just one hour, tea and souvenirs may be had at the upper terminus, and the falls visited, before making the return trip—five minutes shorter. And on the way down, to the right-hand side and facing the locomotive, there are vistas which satisfy those who love to capture magnificent scenery on film.

Perhaps the paramount aspect of the Welsh railway scene in its heyday was that of variety : the lordly North Western, with its superb Irish Mail and tourist expresses roaring along a near level main line, through sparkling summer resorts, threading tunnels and the two tubular bridges; the Cambrian, struggling gamely with a heavily-graded single-tracked main line through the mountains but boasting that most marvellous train the Cambrian Coast Express, albeit introduced under GWR auspices; the delightfully individual branches, including the short Holywell, climbing at 1 in 27 to its tiny terminus, the

fussy Vale of Clwyd with its minature 'Crewe Junction' at
Denbigh, the silent heights reached by the Bala–Ffestiniog line,
the rural Great Western south of Aberystwyth, the scenic Central
and Mid Wales lines, and one which gave (and happily still
gives) perhaps most pleasure to tourists—the Llandudno to
Ffestiniog line, passing from seaside resort through sylvan valleys
to modern terminus in the midst of slate mountains. The minor and
narrow gauge railways possessed a wealth of character: the
Welshpool & Llanfair and the Glyn Valley in agricultural setting; the
busy Penrhyn and Padarn slate lines near Bangor.

All were important to the local communities which they
served. Each has, to greater or lesser degree, its own personal
historian, notably in the case of the narrow gauge lines some
marvellously detailed studies by J. I. C. Boyd, Susan and Keith
Turner, and others. Though impossible here to do full justice
to each railway, all will be mentioned in outline. Like others
in this series, this volume reviews the railways in geographical
areas rather than detailing the company histories. The physical
divisions in North and Mid Wales do nevertheless coincide with
the areas served by different and distinct company developments
—thus London & North Western in the north and south,
Cambrian in the middle, and Great Western to east and south.

For this new edition the text has been revised to take it to the end of
the 1970s. The decade just past is covered by a new chapter in which
developments during the 'eighties on the main network are outlined,
as well as that of the two British Rail steam revivals; a final chapter
covers the increasing growth and fortune of the tourist lines.

The railways were constructed under Acts of Parliament, applied
for by boards of directors appointed by shareholders who put up
money to promote and pay for construction. All main authorising
statutes are noted. Footnotes are omitted, but sources are given in a
general bibliography.

A personal note—Welsh readers, I apologise for inconsistencies
with your language; to write of the Bala & Dolgelly's station at
Dolgellau, or the Carnarvonshire company's trains in Caernarvon
station, Betws and Bettws, Conwy and Conway, Porthmadog and
Portmadoc, must raise hackles somewhere. Such are the inevitable
consequences of quoting precisely from mainly English company
board minutes and official documents.

Page 17 (*Top*) Llandudno branch platforms, old Llandudno Junction c.1895; (*centre*) Problem class 2-2-2 piloting a compound on an up express leaving Conwy tubular bridge c.1890; (*bottom*) Conway station, looking east, 1965. (*Collection Roy Anderson; L&GRP; Author*)

Page 18 (Top) Bangor, Francis Thompson's main building, 1970; (centre) Britannia tubular bridge a week before the disastrous fire, May 1970; (bottom) *Hibernia* leaving Holyhead harbour for Dublin, September 1905, Station Hotel in background. (*Author, top and centre; Collection L. Ward*)

CHAPTER II

Chester—Llandudno—Holyhead

Built to secure fast communication with Ireland, the Chester & Holyhead Railway soon became part of the British holiday scene, with Rhyl, Colwyn Bay, Llandudno and Bangor developing into flourishing resorts.

EARLY YEARS OF THE IRISH MAIL SERVICE

The posts to Ireland, started in Elizabethan times, were carried overland by horse and later by coach. The roads were bad, and the sailing packets between Holyhead and Ireland were subject to the tempests of the Irish Sea. From 1800, Irish MPs sat at Westminster. There was soon influential demand for improvement, and Thomas Telford realigned and regraded the Holyhead Road, overcoming the chief delays to the mail coaches at the ferry crossings at Conwy and the Menai Strait with two suspension bridges, both completed in 1826. Concurrently John Rennie improved the Irish port of Howth, and that at Holyhead where the 'Admiralty Pier' was constructed. Steam packets were introduced from 1819, worked from 1821 by the Admiralty on behalf of the Post Office, and using Howth until diverted to Kingstown (Dun Laoghaire) on the opening of the Dublin & Kingstown Railway in 1834. Holyhead lost the London mail service to Liverpool in 1839 after the opening of through rail communication between the latter and the metropolis.

FORMATION OF CHESTER & HOLYHEAD RAILWAY COMPANY

With the coming of railways the government sought to improve the Irish Mail service. In 1836 Charles Blacker Vignoles, civil engineer, surveyed routes to Porth Dinllaen harbour in Caernarvon Bay, through the Welsh mountains from the south, and from Chester along the North Wales coast via Bangor, with

an alternative route across the Menai Strait to Holyhead. The
Great Western Railway engineer, Isambard Kingdom Brunel,
also surveyed a route from Gloucester to New Quay in Cardigan
Bay: though abandoned, it presaged successive GWR forays
into West and North Wales. A projected route from Crewe to
Chester and Ormes Bay (Llandudno), midway to Holyhead,
also failed, but Bills for railways from Chester to Birkenhead
and Chester to Crewe succeeded in 1837. These were opened
on 23 September and 1 October 1840 respectively, the Chester
& Crewe having by that time been vested in the Grand Junction
(Birmingham–Crewe–Liverpool–Manchester). The Chester &
Crewe supported schemes to extend along the coast, and the
Ormes Bay proposal was revived. It did not go far enough. The
mail traffic demanded maximum use of a land route, being
much faster than by sea, and George Stephenson and Francis
Giles advised the Chester & Crewe that a coastal Holyhead line
was feasible and preferable to using Porth Dinllaen; railway
coaches were to be drawn across the Menai suspension bridge
by horses. In May 1840 a government committee favoured
Stephenson's coastal route but trade depression in the early
1840s delayed action. After favourable reports on Holyhead
harbour the government gave its support to the project but a
separate bridge was essential across the Menai. To save time
and permit construction to begin, the Chester & Holyhead Bill
received Royal Assent on 4 July 1844, the Menai crossing
powers being deferred until the next session.

The CHR received support from the two railway companies
linking Crewe with London, the Grand Junction and the
London & Birmingham. But the Grand Junction was suspicious
of the capabilities of George Stephenson and offered its own
engineer, Joseph Locke, (once a Stephenson pupil and who had
replaced him on the GJ when the levels went astray) to aid the
great George. This did not go down well. The CHR, still wet
behind the ears, was also casting acquisitive eyes on the Chester
& Birkenhead, and was involved with another line, the North
Wales Mineral (p 37). Fearing for its investment, the GJ with-
drew. The London & Birmingham may have had similar doubts
– George Carr Glyn, the eminent banker, was its chairman – but
strategic reasons dictated support for the CHR: the rival GWR
was then backing the proposed South Wales Railway, with
designs on Irish traffic. The LBR took half the direction and
£1 million capital in the CHR.

'NOISES OFF'

The success of the CHR Bill did not deter the broad gauge GWR. In 1843 Brunel had arranged further surveys to Porth Dinllaen, resulting in sabre rattling from Paddington which persisted until 1846 when the Gauge Commission advocated restriction of the broad gauge, at which the GWR temporarily lost interest in North Wales. The CHR Bill was passed in the year preceding the great 'Railway Mania' of 1845–46 which spawned an astonishing number of projects. Some were of the most hare-brained description and included several supposed 'direct' lines to shorten the route from the CHR to the south. In 1845 the Ellesmere & Chester Canal and the Birmingham & Liverpool Junction Canal companies (which with others formed the Shropshire Union Canal Company in 1846) considered converting their navigation to a railway, potentially shortening the Irish Mail route north-west of Stafford by about five miles (8km). The Trent Valley Chester & Holyhead Continuation proposed a Stafford–Market Drayton line, with the same object. In 1846 the newly-formed Shropshire Union Canal Company obtained powers for railways, but marginal benefits to the CHR were rendered insignificant by the demise of the GWR's Porth Dinllaen scheme and the amalgamation by Act of 16 July of the London & Birmingham and Grand Junction Railways with the Manchester & Birmingham to form the London & North Western Railway.

In May 1845 the Trent Valley Continuation & Holyhead Junction promoters announced a railway from Stafford via Wrexham, Mold and Bodfari to the CHR near Abergele, cutting the London–Holyhead distance by 21 miles (33.6km). Inaccurate plans led to abandonment of the Bill. Another line, the London & Holyhead Direct, proposed an atmospheric railway leaving the projected Buckinghamshire Railway near Banbury to go by way of Stratford, Kidderminster and Bridgnorth to Shrewsbury where it joined the Shrewsbury Oswestry & Chester Junction (p 37), thence via the Vale of Llangollen and the Holyhead Road to Capel Curig, and on through the Llanberis Pass to join the authorised North Wales Railway (p 92). Of similar intent, the Grand London & Dublin Approximation (a nice touch for the Mania year!) planned an atmospheric line from the capital, northwards through Rickmansworth and Banbury, then via almost the same route as the London & Holyhead Direct, except that it took the Nant Ffrancon Pass to Bangor. Another project was the Direct London & Dublin, from Birmingham via Shrewsbury to Bangor.

OPEN TO BANGOR

During this abortive hubbub, construction of the CHR went ahead. Edward Betts, contractor, took the first eight miles out of Chester, appropriately starting work on St David's Day, 1 March 1845. Betts also had the Anglesey contract, while Thomas Brassey and others took the remaining contracts except at Conwy and Menai. An Act for the Menai crossing was obtained on 30 June 1845, though Robert Stephenson, appointed as CHR engineer, had not then decided on how to span the waters.

Station plans were prepared by architect Francis Thompson who had designed those on Stephenson's North Midland Railway. Chief intermediate station was Bangor, set tightly between tunnels. By August 1846 over 12,000 men were at work. The sea proved troublesome, breaching the works several times. Blasting the tunnels through slate and shale proved 'excessively laborious'. Wooden navvy huts sprang up along the line, some putting to shame local Welsh cottages, and Welsh and English navvies swelled the coastal towns and villages.

Stephenson's first proposal to bridge the Menai envisaged two arches taking the railway 105ft 0in (32m) above the water. Fear of collision between sailing vessels and the bridge spandrels led to unfavourable comparison with the clear headroom afforded by Telford's bridge nearby. The Admiralty demanded a clear 100ft (30.48m) and Stephenson hit upon the alternative of a tubular beam within which the trains would run. He had invaluable help from Eaton Hodgkinson, mathematician and structural engineer, and William Fairbairn, civil engineer and shipbuilder, who perfected the cellular stressing at top and bottom of the tube to keep it rigid. Once the principle was accepted, practice was required, and so the Conwy was tackled first, with a similar but shorter tubular bridge at the safer height of 18ft 0in (5.48m) above the water. Masonry for both bridges, designed by Thompson, was started early in 1846. The wrought-iron tubes were fabricated on the shores of the Conwy Estuary. On completion they were floated on pontoons into position between the bridge towers and raised by hydraulic presses.

At the Chester end of the line, 1¾ miles (2.8km) to Saltney Junction were opened on 4 November 1846 for Shrewsbury & Chester trains (p 38). A cast- and wrought-iron bridge over the Dee collapsed on 24 May 1847 under an S&C train, killing six persons. The inquiry found the bridge to be badly designed and for a time a cloud hung over Stephenson's other works, but the CHR directors continued to express confidence in him. S&C passengers were conveyed by horse bus until the bridge reopened on 26 July 1847.

The first of the two Conwy tubes was floated and fixed by April 1848, Stephenson being aided by his great friend and rival Brunel, and by Brunel's colleague, Captain Christopher Claxton, RN, who took charge of the complicated nautical and signalling arrangements at the floating. A special train first used the up line tube on 18 April. Inspection of the double track from Saltney Junction to the Conwy was made by Captain Wynne of the Board of Trade. Particularly noted was the iron girder Foryd Bridge near Rhyl, with a central opening span over the Clwyd which took 40 minutes from opening, warping a vessel through, to closing. In late April Captain Simmons inspected the Conwy Tubular Bridge and the line on to Bangor, which included several tunnels—that at Penmaenmawr headland had timber avalanche shelters to protect the trains—and two viaducts, over the Rivers Cegin and Ogwen. The down Conwy tube was completed by January 1849.

Chester to Bangor, 59¾ miles (96.2km), opened to passengers on 1 May 1848, with four trains each way daily, and two each way on Sundays. Intermediate stations were Queen's Ferry (latterly Queensferry), Flint, Holywell, Mostyn, Prestatyn, Rhyl, Abergele, Conway (spelt thus until recent times), and Aber. Freight traffic commenced on 1 June, and by mid-1849 there were two daily goods trains in each direction. The CHR virtually put paid to the coastal trade, conducted mainly from Liverpool, passengers deserting the steamers almost immediately.

BANGOR TO HOLYHEAD

While work progressed on the Britannia Bridge over the Menai, two locomotives were shipped to Holyhead, and the 20½ miles (33km) of double track from the first station on Anglesey (Llanfair PG) to Holyhead temporary station opened on 1 August 1848, passengers between Bangor and Llanfair going by coach over Telford's bridge. That day the Irish Mail train started operating, as did the company's steamers, the latter service having been authorised by the CHR Act of 22 July 1848. But the government had perversely given the sea mail contract to the City of Dublin Steam Packet Company—which thereafter ran it at a loss—leaving the four CHR paddle steamers to run a competitive passenger and freight service.

Construction of the Britannia Tubular Bridge was a mammoth undertaking. The central, Britannia, tower, rising 221ft 3in (67.43m) above the water, and two side towers each 18ft 0in (5.48m) less, together with shore abutments, carried two tubes each formed of four sections, totalling 1,511ft 0in (460.55m) either side, with a combined weight of 5,188 tons. The similar but far more complex construction to that at Conwy was under the supervision of Stephenson's assistant, Edwin Clark. The first tube floating on 20 June 1849 was followed two days later by Stephenson laying the last stone of the Britannia Tower. Two months passed while the lifting machinery was prepared; the tube, wedged meanwhile just above high water, was raised between August and November. During the operation the press failed, causing the tube to drop, though fortunately Stephenson had provided support beneath it. The other three up tubes were raised, and on 5 March 1850, to salutes of cannon, Stephenson drove a train headed by three locomotives through the bridge. On 18 March Bangor to Llanfair, 3½ miles (5.6km) opened, and the 2.30 pm Holyhead–Euston express was the first public passenger train to traverse the whole of the CHR. The down tube opened on 19 October 1850. Nineteen lives had been lost during construction of the bridge, which had cost nearly three times the estimated amount.

THE LNWR TAKES OVER

Excessive expenditure and borrowing dashed hopes that the line would be profitable. The CHR abandoned thoughts of running its own trains, and locomotives ordered by the company went instead direct to the London & North Western which worked the CHR from the outset. Through indebtedness to its contractors the CHR board took into its membership Samuel Morton Peto, partner in the largest contracting firm of the time, Messrs Peto, Brassey & Betts. Peto, who became CHR chairman in 1851, was a man of considerable financial resources and a born organiser who did much to develop traffic. Revenue came from the numerous lead, iron and alkali works developing along the Dee Estuary and Flintshire coast, from local colliery sidings, from Caernarvonshire slate traffic, and from fish, Irish cattle and other livestock, Irish goods traffic starting in 1852. In the down direction there was considerable coal traffic to the steamers at Holyhead. Traffic was also developing from the branches then coming into use, and from the budding tourist industry along the North Wales coast.

Nevertheless, the CHR continued in parlous financial trouble, arguing ineffectually with the Post Office over the mail contract, with the LNWR over the working arrangements, and bickering with the City of Dublin company at Holyhead. In 1858 it sought in desperation traffic arrangements with the LNWR's competitors, particularly the GWR. This shocked an acceptable purchase offer from Euston which took effect from 1 January 1859.

ADDITIONAL STATIONS AND THE TOURIST BOOM

As traffic increased new stations were opened : Ty Croes 1848; Bagillt, Colwyn (renamed Colwyn Bay 1876), Penmaenmawr, Gaerwen, Bodorgan, and Valley 1849; Britannia Bridge 1851 (closed 1858); Menai Bridge 1858; Llanfairfechan 1860; Llandulas 1862 (renamed Llysfaen in 1889 when a new Llandulas station opened a mile to the east); Connah's Quay 1870; Sandycroft, Old Colwyn 1884; Foryd 1885; Mochdre & Pabo 1889; Talacre 1903; Shotton, and Rhosneigr 1907. The new stations served established communities, while later improvements, including quadrupling much of the line between Chester and Llandudno Junction, completed by World War I, and the extensive rebuilding of many stations, reflected the growth of tourist traffic. In the 1850s the CHR introduced cheap fares, and 'house tickets' to attract housing developers along the coast. It also dabbled unsuccessfully in hotels, notably at Britannia Park, between the bridges, on the south shore of the Menai Strait. The LNWR more realistically concentrated on extensive tourist arrangements, and the resort towns grew rapidly.

That symbol of importance, a pier, was erected at Rhyl in 1867, and in the next 20 years the town had become 'a cheerful, thriving, fashionable' resort, with aquarium, winter gardens, hot-and-cold water bathing establishment, libraries, billiards and news rooms, a bowling green and other attractions, the chief hotels being the Parade, the Belvoir and Pier, Westminster, Royal and Queen's, with a growing number of seaside landladies catering for the less well-heeled. The resident population for Rhuddlan, which included Rhyl, rose from 3,049 in 1851, just after the opening of the line, to nearly 10,000 by 1901. Actual population for Rhyl proper in 1913—the last full year before World War I—was 9,005. At Abergele, five miles to the west, the main street was half a mile from the beach and development was slower; though by 1885 it was noted as a favourite resort for bathing, it remained altogether a quieter place than Rhyl, and above the town select villas were built. The population of 2,855 in 1851—when Peto toyed with building lodging houses there on learning that bathers preferred it to Rhyl—reached 3,308 in 1861 but then, affected by Rhyl's more powerful attractions, declined to 3,150 by 1901 and 2,121 by 1913. Likewise, Prestatyn, four miles east of Rhyl, was described in 1913 merely as a 'pleasant and salubrious little watering place'. Llandudno (p 27), with the advantage of Ormes Bay and headland, had a similar effect on nearby Conwy, population 1,528 in 1851, where the town walls and the barriers of sea, and high ground at the back, restricted growth to a mere 2,504 by 1901, though it had reached over 5,000 by 1913, just under half Llandudno's 1913 figure. In fact Rhyl, Llandudno, and Colwyn Bay (with Rhos a population of 12,630 in 1913), creamed off the holidaymaker and tripper, leaving the quieter resorts to the less obviously energetic. Penmaenmawr, for instance, five miles west of Conwy, and on a narrow coastal strip beneath high ground, was described in 1885 as 'this delightful and retired watering place', with 'charming walks' as its main attraction, visitors being served by the Penmaenmawr Hotel. By 1913 the population was only 4,042. While Rhyl, Llandudno, and Colwyn Bay (with Rhos) have forged ahead (1971 populations respectively 21,715, 19,009, 25,535), with modern development to match, the coastal towns to the west have retained much of their late-Victorian character.

The cathedral and university city of Bangor is the exception as regards population. Here there was industry, particularly from slate working, and the natural junction for communications with Anglesey. Its position as a principal approach to Snowdonia, and its fine commanding views, brought early tourist development. From a population of just over 7,000 before arrival of the railway, 10,825 was reached by 1871, with a slower growth thereafter reaching 11,237 by 1913 and 14,526 in 1971.

On Anglesey and in Flint development tended to the extremes. Anglesey remained predominantly agricultural, with the notable exception of Holyhead (p 29), while the Flint and Deeside industries steadily increased, though they were to some extent affected by the faster growth of competitive industry in South Wales and the import of cheaper ores. In the 1890s the great John Summers ironworks was established on the Dee Estuary, while Connah's Quay rose in importance following the silting of smaller ports to the west. Flint itself, an ancient town with a castle, had 2,845 souls in 1851 and only reached 4,279 by 1901; in 1971 the figure for the municipal borough was 14,660, that of Connah's Quay 12,296. Two small 'stations' deserve mention: between 1894 and 1927 a platform was in use at Conwy Marsh, a mile west of Conway station, for a nearby volunteer camp—it was also occasionally used for excursions; during World War I platforms for munitions workers were erected at Queensferry.

LLANDUDNO BRANCH

Though not on the main line, Llandudno's importance as a source of traffic cannot be overstated. Its population in 1851 was only 1,131. The St George's Harbour Act of 20 August 1853 authorised a harbour in Ormes Bay, with a railway to join the CHR east of the Conwy Tubular Bridge. Whatever the hopes of the promoters—though a pier was built they had soon to abandon the harbour undertaking—Peto of the CHR saw tourist potential. Speaking to his shareholders in 1856 he stated that the Llandudno line should have priority: 'A remarkable change has taken place at that locality within the last four years. It has become a much frequented bathing and watering-place. . . .' Originally the railway junction was planned for through running from the branch to Conwy. The cramped layout between the castle walls and the tunnel would have made the necessary enlargement of Conway station difficult, so it was decided to exchange passengers at the junction which was replanned to face Chester. A small platform was erected at the junction fork with another, staggered, platform on the down side. The 3-mile (4.8km) branch opened on 1 October 1858.

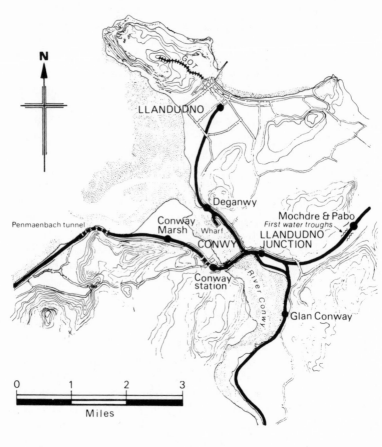

N

LLANDUDNO

Penmaenbach tunnel

Conway
Marsh

Wharf

Deganwy

Mochdre & Pabo
First water troughs

CONWY

LLANDUDNO
JUNCTION

Conway
station

River Conwy

Glan Conway

0   1   2   3

Miles

From Llandudno

LLANDUDNO JUNCTION
1858

Platform

To Chester

From Holyhead

Platform

Based on sketch from 1858 Parliamentary Papers. British Library

By then 'a completed system of drainage had been established at Llandudno, gasworks, waterworks, a spacious market hall, public reading rooms, baths, etc. . . .'. Surprisingly, a report on an accident a year later described some branch trains as working into Conway station, but it would seem this ceased when in 1860 the LNWR built a proper interchange station at the junction. Trains were worked by an LNWR tank engine, hired by the small company, but withdrawn for the first few winters when horses took over.

The branch was leased to the LNWR in 1862. Next August additional clerks were required at Llandudno, 'the duties having increased beyond the capacities of the present staff'. The intermediate station at Deganwy opened in 1866. The branch was vested in the LNWR by Act of 28 July 1873, and doubled and improvements made at the junction, Deganwy and the terminus in 1875, with excursion platforms and sidings at the latter in 1885. By that time Llandudno's population had risen to about 5,000. Apart from specials and excursions, summer weekday arrivals in 1885 totalled 28 trains, with through carriages from Lancashire, the Midlands, and London. With the extension to Betws-y-Coed (p 118) the LNWR improved the river steamer wharf at Deganwy to take timber and slate traffic from the Conwy Valley. The wharf was extended in 1882, requiring earth fill which came from the opening out of part of Belmont tunnel at Bangor. The slate was conveyed between Blaenau and Deganwy in 150 narrow gauge quarry trucks carried on 50 specially adapted standard gauge wagons. The first consignment from the enlarged wharf was loaded on 1 October 1885. In 1891 Llandudno's population reached 6,065, and in Easter 1892 a new five-platform terminus was opened. The junction station, a rambling affair, was demolished and a new one opened on 1 November 1897, some distance to the east, with six through lines, two bays at each end, and improved facilities. Llandudno locomotive depot became redundant with the building of new premises south of the junction in the early 1880s.

HOLYHEAD

The population of Holyhead in 1841 was 3,869. With the arrival of the railway and construction of a government harbour of refuge to the designs of James Meadows Rendel, and later

Sir John Hawkshaw, it rose to 9,689 by 1881—a growth in
startling contrast to the rest of Anglesey. The Great Breakwater,
7,860ft (2.4km), was completed in the 1870s, and a 7ft 0in
(2.13m) gauge railway took stone from Holyhead Mountain for
tipping as a sea defence along the structure. The first, temporary,
Holyhead station was opposite the Porth Dafarch Road. On
20 May 1851—timed to coincide with the Great Exhibition in
London—a ¾-mile (1.2km) single-track extension opened to the
Admiralty Pier, and a new station came into use at the south
end of the railway's inner harbour on 14 September 1851. The
extension, partly on timber viaduct along the harbour water-
front, was worked at first by horses and, until stopped, Holyhead
children would run alongside the trains to retrieve pennies thrown
by passengers. By Act of 13 August 1859 the extension was
improved, and 0–4–0 tank engines took over. Extensive remodel-
ling of the railway harbour was completed with a new station
and hotel opened in 1880. During World War I Holyhead was
a destroyer base, creating considerable supplies traffic. Four
railway steamers were lost on war service, and when other
routes to Ireland were closed due to submarine activity, Holyhead took all the traffic. The hotel closed in 1951. Ordinary
freight traffic ceased in 1968 (but see p 33). Population in 1971
was 10,608; most of the employed would have lost their jobs if
the railway had closed in 1970 (p 32).

CHESTER AND HOLYHEAD SERVICES

At first the express locomotives took water at Holywell, Rhyl,
Conway, and Bangor. To achieve non-stop running for an
improved timetable James Ramsbottom, LNWR locomotive
superintendent, invented the water trough and scoop whereby
tenders were replenished at speed. The first trough in October
1860 on the down line at Mochdre, west of Colwyn Bay, was
followed by its up line partner in November, both moving to
Aber in 1871. Further troughs were installed near Prestatyn in
1885 and Flint in 1895. Their use ceased in the late 1960s.
   The LNWR gained the sea mail contract in 1883, only to
lose it immediately afterwards because of government policy
favouring Irish-based enterprise. Improvements to the mail and
express trains at this time included the vacuum brake in 1882,
8-wheeled carriages in 1883, and proper sleeping cars from
1891. In 1897 day mail trains were made available to third-

class passengers. This apparently gracious move was in fact a clever bit of manipulation, encouraging third-class passengers to use the City of Dublin boats, with which the mail trains connected, thus horrifying first- and second-class passengers into patronising the LNWR's boat expresses and connecting steamers, known disparagingly as 'pig-boats' by disdainful CDSP officers because the LNWR fleet carried livestock. The Dublin company could never truly compete with Euston and in 1920 relinquished the coveted mail pennant to its rival.

Extensive excursion arrangements were organised in North Wales, including circular omnibus tours from various CHR stations. Starting in the 1880s, a fast businessmen's train ran daily between Llandudno and Manchester; from 1908 this sported 'club' coaches—special saloon accommodation in return for a guaranteed number of season tickets. One of the most notable 'foreign' workings was a red-liveried North Staffordshire Railway Llandudno express from the Potteries which first appeared well before World War I. Despite decelerations and official discouragement during that war, holiday traffic remained heavy. The inter-war years saw further increase in passenger traffic and in the mid-1930s there were some 90 weekday passenger trains on some parts of the line, with more on Saturdays. From 1930 the new Royal Scot 4–6–0s took on the mails, sometimes working double-headed with 16 coaches or more. Tourist initiative peaked in 1939 with the opening of a railway-inspired holiday camp at Prestatyn. In the summer of 1951 British Railways ran a daily 'Festival Train Cruise': Rhyl–Corwen–Barmouth–Afon Wen–Caernavon–Bangor–Rhyl, such ventures continuing until closure of the Corwen line. The Royal Scots maintained their dominance on the main line until the early 1950s when Princess Coronation pacifics and the new BR Britannias took over. Local passenger trains went over entirely to diesel multiple-unit (dmu) operation in 1965 but main line expresses kept the diesel at bay for another two years.

THREE DISASTERS

LNWR parsimony toward adequate refuge sidings led to the wrecking of the Irish Mail near Abergele on 20 August 1868. A goods train shunting at Llandulas (later Llysfaen), with an insufficiently long siding, left seven vehicles—two containing casks of paraffin oil—standing on the down main line. During fly-shunting they were projected backwards on a falling gradient, meeting the mail about ¾ mile from Abergele station, engulfing it in flame, and killing 33 persons. On 17 August 1879 flooding swept away the stone Llandulas viaduct. Traffic was diverted over the GWR and Cambrian lines via Afon Wen, but from 25 August passenger trains used a temporary diversion on a low timber bridge over the Dulas. Round-the-clock work at Crewe produced a new steel viaduct, opened on 14 September. The most recent accident of consequence was the collision between the night up Irish Mail and a light engine at Penmaenmawr early on 27 August 1950, mainly caused by the signalman's mistaken belief that the light engine had run clear into the yard. Six people died and some 35 were injured. The signal box was resited to be opposite the goods yard.

RATIONALISATION

Closures of lightly-used stations commenced in the inter-war years: Llysfaen, Foryd, and Mochdre & Pabo on 5 January 1931 (Foryd reopened seasonally as Kinmel Bay Halt in 1938 and 1939). Llandulas and Old Colwyn closed on 1 December 1952, Aber 12 September 1960, and Sandycroft 1 May 1961. Chester station was renovated between 1955 and 1961, with new platform coverings, track-circuiting, and colour-light signalling. Quadrupling was heavily reduced in the 1960s and many more stations closed to passengers from 14 February 1966: Queensferry, Shotton Low Level, Connah's Quay, Bagillt, Holywell Junction, Mostyn, Talacre, Conway, Menai Bridge, Llanfair PG, Gaerwen, and Valley. Happily one of the enamel signs at Llanfair PG (the longest railway station name in Britain —Llanfairpwllgwyngyllgogerychwryndrobwllllantysiliogogogoch) was rescued for the Industrial Railway Museum at Penrhyn Castle. Freight closures commenced with Holywell Junction, 6 April 1959, and Sandycroft 1 May 1961, and then peaked at some 15 stations in 1964. Menai Bridge, closed 4 March 1968, re-opened for freightliner traffic during reconstruction of Britannia Bridge.

THE 1970S

The most expensive disaster on the CHR, thankfully without loss of life, occurred on 23 May 1970 when the Britannia

Tubular Bridge was made unusable by fire. A container service linking London and Eire had commenced in January 1968 and by 1970 a considerable investment had been made at Holyhead in a new automated container terminal served by rail and to be worked by two new vessels. Because of this and the rail business with Rio Tinto Zinc, Associated Octel and the Wylfa Head nuclear power station, not to mention some two million passengers a year between Bangor and Holyhead, it was considered imperative to rebuild the bridge. A steel arched structure using the original masonry towers was opened on 30 January 1972, with single track but provision for two, and incorporating work for a road bridge above the rails, opened on 11 July 1980.

On 21 August 1972 Shotton Low Level, rebuilt for double track and named Shotton, reopened to passengers. Llanfair PG, which had reopened with a nearby single timber platform from 29 May 1970 as a bus/rail interchange for a Holyhead shuttle during the Britannia Bridge rebuilding, closing from 31 January 1972, reappeared from 7 May 1973, named Llanfairpwll, with two new platforms replacing the former demolished ones. Other stations once threatened with closure were retained. Work started which by completion in 1984 would give Chester multiple-aspect signalling and a rationalised track layout permitting two-way working at all platforms. The Holyhead and Shrewsbury lines were combined for two miles (3.2km) to Saltney Junction, the double track using the south side of the former quadruple Roodee viaduct from 4 November 1979 (see also p 43).

Improved car ferry loading facilities were installed at Holyhead in 1975–6 as part of a £2 million redevelopment to take a new vessel which started two daily return crossings with Dun Laoghaire from 2 May 1977. Built by the Danish ferry specialists, Aalborg Vaerft, the 7,836-ton *St Columba* is a two-class, multi-purpose ship with accommodation for 1,600 passengers (2,400 in peak season), and combinations of 335 cars or 36 lorries. The hotel and station (except for the old train departure side) were demolished in 1979 to make way for a modern terminal.

Finally, the early morning up and early evening down 'Emerald Isle Express', popular since the late 1940s because it allowed passengers a reasonable night's sleep on the ferry as opposed to those who arrived at Holyhead on the later down Irish Mail, lost its title from 5 May 1975. (See Chapter XV.)

CHAPTER III

Shrewsbury—Chester

The North Wales coalfield curves from Point of Ayr in Flintshire south-east through Mold, Brymbo, Wrexham and Ruabon to Oswestry. From early times there were opencast coal working and lead and zinc mining on the westerly side of the East Denbighshire part of the coalfield. Furnaces and forges for iron-making operated at Bersham, Plas Madoc and Ruabon in the 17th century. By 1721 a blast furnace was in production at Bersham, using coke from coal mined at Rhosllanerchrugog near Ruabon; the New Bersham Company made munitions during wars of the late 18th century. The early 19th century saw iron production commence in earnest at Brymbo. In 1824 the British Iron Company was founded at Ruabon, where fireclay deposits were exploited for the brick and terra cotta industry.

A decade later, the coal owners and ironfounders in the East Denbighshire field were conscious that because of inferior communications their activity was stagnating compared with their brethren on Deeside and in South Wales. The prime need was to speed their products to the growing industry and shipping facilities on Deeside. Railways were projected south from Chester as early as 1839 but countrywide recession intervened. When by 1843 nearby railway development again encouraged local promotion, some 22,000 tons of coal and 8,000 tons of iron were annually making a slow journey northwards from the coalfield by inadequate roads or circuitously by canal and river. A railway was expected to double existing coal traffic, with 100,000 tons additionally going to Liverpool and Birkenhead, and 20,000 tons of coke to the Merseyside, the Holyhead steamers and the locomotives of the Grand Junction Railway. Passenger potential was considerable: nearly 35,000 people travelled in 1843 by stage coaches taking $1\frac{1}{2}$ hours between Wrexham on the east of the coalfield (population 5,818 in 1841), and Chester; 15,000

Page 35 (Top) GW Hall class 4-6-0 No 4998 on an up passenger train at Wrexham General, June 1963; (centre) Wrexham Central, looking east, June 1963; (bottom) GW 2800 2-8-0 class No 3837 on down mineral train at Ruabon, July 1963. (Author)

Page 36 (*Top*) Mold, 1970; (*centre*) abandoned station at Denbigh, looking south, 1970; (*bottom*) Gwyddelwern, c.1870s. (*Author, top and centre; National Library of Wales*)

others went by private coach, horse, or on foot. Wrexham and Chester carriers conveyed 8,000 tons of merchandise yearly, and Wrexham was the focal point for routes taken seasonally by the drovers with thousands of head of Welsh cattle.

NORTH WALES MINERAL RAILWAY

Encouraged by directors of the projected Chester & Holyhead, who foresaw that trains from such a line (a useful feeder) would pay to use the CHR into Chester, the locally-promoted North Wales Mineral Railway Company was incorporated on 6 August 1844 for a line from Wrexham northwards along the Alyn Valley to Rossett, thence across the West Cheshire Plain to a wharf on the Dee Navigation at Saltney, with a curve nearby to the CHR. By Act of 21 July 1845 the NWM took powers to extend for five miles (8km) south to Ruabon, with a freight branch from Wheatsheaf, north of Wrexham, through the coal-field to Brymbo and Minera; on 27 July 1846 powers were taken for small branches to Ffrwd, Brynmally, Brymbo and Vron colleries. Wheatsheaf Junction to Minera, $6\frac{1}{4}$ miles (10km), opened in July 1847, and the colliery branches, totalling some five miles (8km) by the following November.

SHREWSBURY OSWESTRY & CHESTER JUNCTION RAILWAY

The CHR meanwhile had become enmeshed in a struggle for supremacy between the London & Birmingham and Grand Junction companies. In 1845 it promoted a cut-off route, the Cheshire & Shropshire Junction, to link Chester with forces friendly to the LBR at Shrewsbury. Their livelihood thus threatened, the NWM directors promoted the Shrewsbury Oswestry & Chester Junction Railway from Ruabon to Shrews-bury, authorised by Act of 30 June 1845. The SO & CJ anticipated a profitable future. Parliamentary evidence showed that in 1844 the coach *L'Hirondelle* carried 5,552 passengers (fares, Ruabon–Shrewsbury, 10s od [50p] inside, 6s od [30p] outside); *Royal Oak* and *Nettle* 8,848, Chester–Oswestry–Newtown; the Holyhead Mail 5,000, Llangollen–Oswestry–Shrewsbury; *Accommodation* 5,050, Oswestry–Shrewsbury; and *Liver* 7,384 between Shrewsbury and the Grand Junction's Whitmore station. Over 117,500 travelled by other means. Some

1,000 tons of Cefn Mawr building stone, 20,000 tons of timber, mostly pit props, and 31,000 tons of goods from the Shrewsbury–Llangollen–Wrexham area to Liverpool, went annually by canal. Road freight included 1,040 tons of flour from Oswestry mills to collieries and ironworks near Cefn Mawr, over 12,000 tons of wheat, 300 tons of barley and malt for Llangollen breweries, and 250 tons of Montgomeryshire butter. There was considerable movement of livestock. The Shrewsbury district received some 128,000 tons of coal from the area traversed by the new line; 85,000 tons of Pontcysyllte limestone journeyed to ironworks near Wellington, 3000 tons of burnt limestone went elsewhere, 15,000 tons of iron ore were imported for mixing with Welsh ore, 45,450 tons of Shropshire iron went to Liverpool and Manchester, and 4,000 tons of slates and flagstones came from Llangynog and Llangollen.

SHREWSBURY & CHESTER RAILWAY COMPANY FORMED

By two SO & CJ Acts of 27 July 1846 extensions were authorised: Leaton to Wem; Gobowen via Oswestry to a proposed Shropshire Union branch railway at Crickheath; and into the centre of Shrewsbury to a new joint station with the Shrewsbury & Birmingham, Shrewsbury & Hereford, and SU companies. On the same day the S&CR Act consolidated the NWM and SO&CJ as the Shrewsbury & Chester Railway. After the SU was leased to the LNWR the first two extensions were abandoned by Act of 1851, save $2\frac{1}{4}$ miles (3.6km) of the Crickheath branch, opened as a single line from Gobowen to Oswestry on 23 December 1848.

The S&C engineer was Henry Robertson; Thomas Brassey was contractor. With stations at Saltney, Rossett, Gresford, Wrexham and Ruabon, a stud of four locomotives from Longridge & Co, with more on order from that source and other makers, the $14\frac{3}{4}$-mile (23.7km) NWM section opened on 4 November 1846, together with a length of the CHR into Chester, of which by agreement the S&C took temporary possession. Five trains ran each way on weekdays and two on Sundays. S&C second-class carriages had glass windows and partitioned compartments, luxury in those days. South of Ruabon, the SO&CJ section ran through the eastern foothills of the Denbighshire Mountains, and earthworks were heavy. Where the River Dee emerged from the deep-cut Vale of Llangollen into the North Shropshire Plain Robertson constructed a stone viaduct, 1,508ft 0in (459.6m) long and 147ft 0in (44.8m) high, with 19 spans having brick interior arching. Just $2\frac{1}{4}$ miles (3.6km) to the south he crossed the Ceiriog Valley at Chirk with an 846ft 0in (257.8m) long compound stone and timber structure: two extreme arches of 120ft 0in (36.5m) span constructed of 16 layers of 3in (7.6cm) timber planks (replaced by masonry arches in 1858–9), with ten intermediate stone arches, the highest being 106ft 0in (32.3m). Over these viaducts Captain Wynne of the Board of Trade revealed that beneath the military engineer's exterior there beat an artist's heart. Though he thought Robertson's viaducts 'magnificent', his aesthetic sensibilities were upset by what Chirk viaduct had done to Telford's adjacent canal aqueduct:

It is to be regretted that the two works are necessarily placed so closed (*sic*) together for the more recent one completely degrades the other which has so long given celebrity to the valley and been looked upon as one of its leading features, the two are so mixed up by their close juxtaposition that the proper effect of each is lost, and the scenery which is very beautiful not improved . . .

The $25\frac{1}{2}$-mile (41km) SO&CJ section opened to a temporary terminus at Shrewsbury on 12 October 1848. At noon a special train of 59 carriages hauled by three locomotives left Chester, carrying the S&C board members, their friends, and the Corporation of Chester, all bound for a banquet at Shrewsbury. (According to MacDermot, public traffic commenced on 16 October, but Lewin, revised by C. R. Clinker, gives 14 October.) The extension to Shrewsbury joint station opened in June 1849. Intermediate stations were: Cefn, Llangollen Road (p 44), Chirk, Preesgweene (later Weston Rhyn), Gobowen, Whittington, Rednal, Baschurch, and Leaton.

Two Acts of 9 July 1847 authorised the S&C and CHR to construct a station at Chester, to be managed jointly with the LNWR and the Birkenhead Lancashire & Cheshire Junction. This latter, an 1847 amalgamation of the Chester & Birkenhead with the existing BL&CJ of 1846, now comprised the original C&B and the line from Hooton via Warrington to the Manchester & Birmingham at Stockport with a spur, opened 28 November 1850, from Helsby to the Chester & Crewe east of

Chester. The joint station, designed by Francis Thompson and constructed by Brassey, opened on 1 August 1848. Behind a fine frontage of 1,050ft 0in (320m), there lurked a 750ft 0in (228.6m) departure platform with arrival bays, backed by a large carriage shed, all covered with an iron-and-glass roof. A 270ft 0in by 170ft 0in (82.3m by 51.8m) goods shed was also built. To the west of the station was a triangular junction to the CHR and C&B, also used for turning locomotives. Through movements used the long platform, down trains the north end and up trains the south, a scissors crossing enabling them to pass each other on a through line behind.

UNPLEASANTNESS AT CHESTER

In 1849 the LNWR quarrelled with the Great Western. Originally, the London & Birmingham had supported the S&C as a useful route to thwart the Grand Junction. But now the newly constituted LNWR looked with dismay at what the LBR had aquiesced in: a potential rival route between Birmingham, Chester and Birkenhead. The S&C, and its neighbour the Shrewsbury & Birmingham, were thus to be fought over by Paddington, seeking access to Merseyside, and Euston, determined to stop it.

The Shrewsbury–Wolverhampton–Birmingham line was authorised in two portions in 1846. By 1847 Euston controlled authorised railways approaching the Shrewsbury & Birmingham from the south; it seemed inevitable that both S&B and S&C would fall into LNWR hands. The two small companies, hoping to develop traffic independently between Merseyside, the Black Country and South Wales, made a traffic agreement with the BL&CJ which challenged Euston between Wolverhampton and Birkenhead. Captain Huish, LNWR general manager, reacted in October 1849 with an ultimatum to the S&C. It was rejected. In consequence, the Chester station joint committee, on which the LNWR had a majority, forbade the booking of Wolverhampton passengers via Shrewsbury. When remonstrances followed, the S&C's Chester booking clerk was thrown out of his office. The BL&CJ, cowed by this blunderbuss approach, deterred S&C third-class passengers by operating connections at ungodly hours. The S&C thereupon ran omnibuses to Birkenhead, only to find them barred from Chester station yard where gangs of LNWR toughs defaced S&C timebills and posters.

Though an injunction stopped most of this behaviour, the BL&CJ was 'persuaded' to re-route its southbound traffic via the LNWR. It even ludicrously put the clock back and consigned local Welsh and Shropshire traffic by road or canal to combat an S&C attempt to use the Dee into Chester for freight. In October 1850, BL&CJ shareholders protested at these ruinous actions of their board, and S&C traffic once again went to Birkenhead. Meanwhile Euston was undercutting the Shrewsbury & Birmingham. In desperation, mindful that the Great Western would soon reach Birmingham and Wolverhampton, the two Shrewsbury companies effected a traffic agreement with Paddington in January 1851. Euston retaliated by packing S&B meetings with shareholders who had been buying into the smaller company. Rex Christiansen in Volume 7 of this series has told of what followed. After unbelievable chicanery, including an illegal agreement with Euston under forged seal by an unauthorised second board of S&B directors, the company eventually purged itself and agreed on amalgamation with the GWR. Despite similar intimidation, the S&C also managed to repel a Euston assault and obtained statutory running powers between Saltney Junction and Chester, replacing a former agreement, and over the whole of the BL&CJ. In 1852 a Bill for amalgamation of the GWR, S&B and S&C (henceforth called the 'Associated Companies') was rejected in the Lords. It was re-deposited, and meanwhile a joint S&B and S&C managing committee was extended to include the GWR.

THE GREAT WESTERN REACHES CHESTER AND BIRKENHEAD

Sympathetic to Euston, James Bancroft, BL&CJ chairman, managed a board of directors whose policies swayed to the fortunes of the battle south of Chester. In November 1851, noting Paddington's advance northwards, the BL&CJ offered a lease to the Associated Companies which was postponed following failure of their amalgamation Bill. Concurrently, the LNWR and CHR made a show of promoting lines to Birkenhead, causing Bancroft to about-face, proposing a lease to Euston and increased tolls from the S&C. A court action followed, and from December 1853 S&C Birkenhead trains were withdrawn, ironically causing Bancroft to buy locomotives to work S&C traffic. During 1853 the struggle continued in Parliament, the GWR also (but unsuccessfully) seeking to lay broad gauge between Wolverhampton and Birkenhead. The Associated Companies' amalgamation was at last effected in 1854, bringing the first standard gauge locomotives—34 of them—into GWR possession from 1 September. The Act precipitated a BL&CJ palace revolution and a traffic agreement with Paddington. A GWR Birkenhead goods service started from 2 February 1856, iron ore going via the Shrewsbury & Hereford to South Wales in exchange for steam coal northwards to Birkenhead, while a GWR Birmingham–Birkenhead passenger service began on 1 May 1857. An Act of 1861 confirmed an 1859 agreement between the GWR and LNWR for joint ownership of the BL&CJ, renamed Birkenhead Railway, the companies taking possession of the line and working stock on 20 November 1860. That month GWR shareholders authorised the laying of 'narrow' gauge (really 'standard', but to the GWR authorities 'broad' was standard at that time!), within the broad gauge between Reading and Paddington thus completing, by August 1861, the 'narrow' gauge throughout to the north. Meanwhile, for a new service to Merseyside, some 200 4-wheeled passenger vehicles were ordered, and on 1 October 1861 the first 'narrow' gauge London–Birkenhead through train left Paddington at 9.35 am. On 7 June 1865 there occurred the only serious accident on the S&C, north of Rednal; faulty permanent way derailed a late-running, very long, inadequately-braked, double-headed excursion train, killing two enginemen and eleven passengers.

MAIN LINE SERVICES OVER THE S&C

According to Ahrons, Chester locomotive shed was home during the late 19th century to a 'miscellaneous and assorted lot of old stagers'; some of these GWR locomotives he described as 'paleozoic', others 'as if they had been left by the Roman founders of the city'. They hauled expresses which were quite leisurely until June 1880 when a new fast service, nicknamed the 'Zulu' (confusingly, as there was also a West Country 'Zulu' out of Paddington) left the capital at 4.45 pm, reaching Birkenhead at about 10.00 pm, the up train leaving Birkenhead at 11.45 am to arrive at Paddington at 5.25 p.m. Avoiding Chester via the triangular junction, the down train called at Gobowen and Wrexham, where a Chester portion was detached. Later it ran direct to Chester, reversing to reach Birkenhead, but in 1888 the Chester portion was again detached, in Chester cutting, the up train calling at Wrexham and Ruabon. From 7 March 1892 the Birkenhead service boasted the first GWR corridor train, steam-heated and gangwayed to connect with lavatories, but restaurant cars did not appear until the early 1900s. Sleeping cars operated between the summers of 1923 and 1924, only being reinstated 30 years later. The fastest express timings remained virtually those of the 1880s until just before World War I when, following completion of the cut-off routes in the south, they improved respectively to $4\frac{1}{2}$ hours and 4 hours 50 minutes to Chester and Birkenhead. Only minutes separated these timings from those in force through to World War II.

Though local S&C traffic was important, Paddington's main interest in the line lay in the development of the South Wales–Birkenhead coal traffic, and passenger access to Merseyside. Mention should be made of through workings to the South of England. Between 1863 and 1866 a through carriage operated between Birkenhead and Dover and Hastings, via Reading and the South Eastern Railway, taking some $10\frac{3}{4}$ hours. In 1889 there was a short-lived Birkenhead–Ilfracombe service, via the Severn Tunnel, Bristol, Taunton, and Barnstaple. In the late 1890s a curious new service was started, using the Mersey Railway, of a Liverpool Central–Ruabon–Corwen afternoon train with, for a short period, a Ruabon–Liverpool morning working. In 1898 this venture blossomed into a daily Liverpool–Paddington train with, via Reading and Redhill, a through Folkestone coach which connected with sailings from Boulogne. These Liverpool trains could not compete with the LNWR and were withdrawn after the summer of 1899. Through coaches operated to Dover and Deal in the early 1900s, by way of Reading and Redhill (1903–4) and Southall and Addison Road (1905). In concert with the London & South Western Railway a through Bournemouth train via Reading and Basingstoke started in July 1910, operated alternately with GWR and LSWR (later Southern) coaches. With wartime breaks, and latterly summers-only over the S&C, it ran until the mid-1960s when it was transferred to Liverpool.

STATION IMPROVEMENTS AND ADDITIONS

At Chester in 1890 a new island platform was added and eight through lines provided: up and down slow and up and down fast passenger between the island and the old long (now down)

platform; a reversible passenger line to the north island platform; and to the north again another up through passenger
and two through goods lines. There were five bays at the Crewe
end and three at the Holyhead. Additional buildings, extended
roofing, widened road bridges and two new footbridges and
hydraulic luggage lifts completed the improvements.

New stations were opened at Johnstown & Hafod in 1896
and Balderton in 1901, both north of Ruabon, and in the 20th
century a liberal sprinkling of halts: Old Woods, Stanwardine,
Haughton, Trehowell, Whitehurst (Llangollen Road), and
Rhosymedre, all south of Ruabon; Wynnville, just to the north;
and Rhosrobin between Wrexham and Gresford. They were
extensively used by miners and other workmen and together they
reduced between-station distances to a maximum of $3\frac{3}{4}$ miles
(6km) and a minimum of $\frac{1}{2}$-mile (0.8km).

<h2 style="text-align:center">WREXHAM AND RUABON</h2>

In 1861 Wrexham had a borough population of 7,562, while
nearly 20,000 lived in the parish. It was described in 1866 as
'a lively market town, with spacious streets, and substantial,
well-built houses'. Ruabon was 'a pleasant village, surrounded
by beautiful scenery, parts of which, however, are rendered
dingy and repulsive by numerous iron works and collieries. These
furnish employment to a large population'. In fact, over 14,000
persons resided in the district in 1861. That year Daniel Gooch,
GWR locomotive superintendent, chairman of the company in
1865, and a baronet a year later, was prompted by his board
to buy with others a colliery near Ruabon belonging to Henry
Robertson. Together they formed the Ruabon Coal Company,
with the intention of increasing traffic on the line in return for
preferential rates.

From the mid-19th century the opencast mining in the west
of the coalfield gave place to an easterly movement to the con-
cealed measures. Collieries were sited near the rail network and
attracted new branch lines. Wrexham became the focal centre
for the coal and iron industry in the area. Growth of population
and employment pushed Ruabon's 15,150 population of 1871
to 21,721 by 1901; and Wrexham's from 8,510 to nearly 15,000,
while increasing traffic from the ever busier main line, the Mold
area and the Ruabon–Barmouth line led at Wrexham between
1909 and 1912, to lengthening of platforms, new station build-

ings, an additional up bay, and up and down avoiding lines. In the Edwardian era, for every four Flintshire miners, the East Denbighshire coalfield employed ten. The mid-20th century however saw progressive closure of many pits, and Ruabon's 1971 population was only 5,663 for the civil parish. Employment in Wrexham was encouraged to switch to new industries and by 1971 the town was the main industrial and administrative centre in the area, with a population of 38,955.

ECLIPSE OF THE SHREWSBURY—CHESTER LINE

Of the 22 intermediate stations and halts, only Gobowen, Chirk, Ruabon, and Wrexham remain open. Trehowell Halt closed on 31 December 1951, Balderton 5 May 1952, Rhosymedre Halt 9 March 1959, and remaining closures on 12 September 1960. Gobowen to Oswestry, with intermediate Park Hall Halt opened 1926, closed on 7 November 1966 (passengers had used the Cambrian's Oswestry station since 1924). Intermediate goods stations closed in 1963–4 except Baschurch in 1965, and Wrexham General, 1970. In March 1967, high-speed electric trains began running north of Birmingham on the North Western main line, and the principal London–Birmingham services became based on Euston, the through Paddington–Birkenhead trains ceasing on 4 March. Ruabon became an unstaffed halt in 1974. In 1979 the Shrewsbury–Chester service consisted of some nine trains each way, with five on Sundays. (See Chapter XV.)

GLYN VALLEY TRAMWAY

For many years a single-track narrow gauge railway ran from Chirk up the wooded Ceiriog Valley to slate and granite quarries near Glyn Ceiriog. After early attempts to make a tramway linking the quarries and the S&C, the standard gauge Ellesmere & Glyn Valley Railway was authorised by Act of 6 August 1866, from the Cambrian at Ellesmere to the GWR at Chirk, thence following the Glyn Ceiriog road to the quarries. By Act of 1869 the Ellesmere–Chirk portion was abandoned and the remainder, some 8 miles (12.8km), made to narrow gauge. In 1870 the company was re-incorporated as the Glyn Valley Tramway. Construction started in June 1872, and the 2ft 4¼in (72cm) gauge line, commencing from a wharf on the SU Canal and sidings north-west of the GWR Preesgweene

station, opened to freight by April 1873 and to passengers on
1 April 1874. With ruling gradient (in early years) of 1 in 19,
it was worked by horses, goods and passenger vehicles descending
as far as Pontfaen by gravity, the horse riding in a rear dandy,
a method ended after an intoxicated brakesman caused a
passenger train to be hurled from a sharp curve at Pontfaen
Bridge into the River Ceiriog on 19 December 1874. In 1878
the company was authorised to extend to quarries at Pandy and
to improve the existing line. Horse traction continued until temporary closure (to passengers – freight continuing) from 1 April
1886, the company having been authorised in 1885 to abandon
from east of Pontfaen whence a new extension was made to the
GWR station and the SU Canal at Chirk, and to use steam.

Two locomotives from the Snailbeach District Railways
(p 194) were used during construction, the GVT gauge being
increased by ¼in to suit them. Both companies had Henry, later
Sir Henry, Dennis on their boards and as engineer. Improved
interchange facilities came into use at Chirk when the extension
was opened to freight in mid-1888, probably worked by the
two SD locomotives, for the first of two 0–4–2 Beyer Peacock
tram engines, *Sir Theodore*, built that year, did not arrive until
October. The second *Dennis*, arrived in April 1889, after which
the SD locomotives returned home. Passenger traffic recommenced on 15 March 1891, trains often being mixed, and
worked bunker-first. The terminal stations had small platforms,
with buildings, but the intermediate stopping places at Pontfaen,
Castle Mill, Pontfadog (this did have passing loop and buildings), and Dolywern remained primitive as before. A third tram
engine, *Glyn*, was acquired in 1892 and a 4–6–0 Baldwin tank
in 1921. Road competition forced closure to passengers from
6 April 1933 and freight from 6 July 1935.

Dee viaduct, Shrewsbury & Chester Railway, 1848
(Illustrated London News)

CHAPTER IV

Chester—Mold—Wrexham

Eleven miles west of Chester, the town of Mold lies in the Alyn Valley, with Halkyn Mountain between it and Deeside to the north, the Clwydian Hills to the west, and the Denbighshire range to the south. To north-west and south-east is the North Wales coalfield (p 34). In the late 18th century mining activity was centred east of Mold, around Buckley and Leeswood, with coal used in processing the iron ore, lead, zinc and fireclay found in the valley and surrounding hills. By the 1790s a horse tramway was operating from collieries and brickworks at Buckley, on the low eastern foothills of Halkyn Mountain, down to the port of Connah's Quay on Deeside. According to C. F. Dendy Marshall there were probably earlier and similar tramways, from Ewloe and Mancot, near Hawarden, further to the east; at Brymbo, in the coalfield between Mold and Wrexham, he mentions an 18th-century tramway to the Glascoed Valley, and another serving blast furnaces at Ponkey (Ponciau) between Bersham and Ruabon. To the south of the coalfield, where the Dee emerges from the Vale of Llangollen into the North Shropshire Plain, below Ruabon, the Ellesmere & Chester Canal Company (later part of the Shropshire Union) took powers by Act of 29 June 1804 to construct a horse tramway from its Llantysilio canal branch at Pontcysyllte to Acrefair. The tramway, opened in 1805, was extended to the Plas Madoc colliery by 1808, and thence northwards via Hazeldine's ironworks, and various collieries and brickworks, to Afon Eitha and the Ruabon Brook colliery, south of Rhosllanerchrugog, a total of some $3\frac{1}{4}$ miles (5.2km). These early, isolated tramways, feeders to water routes, were forerunners in the Industrial Revolution which made imperative proper outlets for the wealth of the area. Within the second half of the nineteenth century the coal-field became host to a network of railways.

In 1844 the people of Mold sought a rail outlet, petitioning the Chester & Holyhead directors to bring their line through the valley. The Deeside route being preferable, a branch was planned instead from Saltney, via Bretton and Kinnerton, but the route, criticised by colliery owners, was dropped in April 1845. That year, at the height of the railway mania, several schemes appeared in the district. The Trent Valley Continuation has already been mentioned (p 21). Others included a crossing of the Dee in their proposals: the Manchester & Birkenhead Continuation & Mold Rhuabon (*sic*) & North Wales Railway, from the North Wales Mineral at Ruabon via Minera, Buckley, and Connah's Quay, thence to the Chester & Birkenhead near Sutton; the Birkenhead & Holyhead Junction—which after the demise of the CHR's Mold scheme hopefully added '& Mold Extension' to its title—from Birkenhead to the CHR at Flint, thence through Mold, Hope and Bradley to the NWM near Gresford; the Liverpool Birkenhead Parkgate & Holyhead Junction, from Birkenhead to the CHR at Connah's Quay; and the locally-promoted Mold Junction, from Mold to the C&B at Hooton.

The CHR joined in with a scheme to Mold from its main line at Pentre, with branches to Pontblyddyn, Buckley, Nant Colliery, and the Dee at Queensferry. In January 1846 the B&HJ&M Extension, LBP&HJ, and the Mold Junction were still before Parliament. The Manchester & Birkenhead Continuation however had given place to a Birkenhead Chester Mold Ruabon & Vale of Llangollen Railway, from the C&B at Ledsham, via Queensferry to New Inn Bridge where a branch left for Mold, the main line continuing through Ffrith, Coed Poeth and Ponkey to Acrefair, where a branch went to Llangollen, before joining the SO&CJ (p 37) north of Cefn viaduct. Schemes across the Dee, however, were doomed by Admiralty disapproval. All bowed out, except the Mold Junction and CHR whose directors agreed on formation of a new Mold Railway Company for a line from near Saltney on the CHR, via Kinnerton, Penyffordd and Padeswood to Mold.

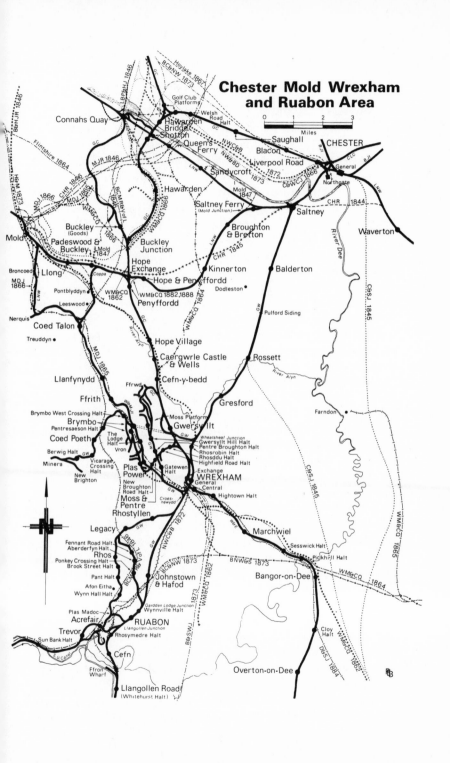

Chester Mold Wrexham and Ruabon Area

Hoylake 1866
BG&NW 1873
B&HJR 1846
Golf Club Platforms
Welsh Road Halt
CHESTER
Connahs Quay
Hawarden Bridge Shotton
Queen's Ferry
Saughall
General
NW&BB
Blacon
Flintshire 1864
GC
Liverpool Road 1872
Northgate
CLC
B&HM 1873
MJR 1846
Sandycroft 1873
LNW
C&WCJ 1866
C&SJ 1845
MDJ 1866
CHR 1846
BCM R&WCo 1896
WM&CQ 1866
Hawarden
Mold 1847
CHR 1844
MDJ 1869
Saltney Ferry (Mold Junction)
Saltney
Waverton
Mold
Buckley (Goods)
WM&CQ 1866
Broughton & Bretton
River Dee
Padeswood & Buckley 1847
Buckley Junction
Mold 1847
CHR 1845
Kinnerton
Balderton
Broncoed
Hope Exchange
Llong
Coppa
Hope & Penyffordd
Dodleston
MDJ 1866
LNW
Pontblyddyn
WM&CQ 1862
WM&CQ 1882,1888
Penyffordd
Pulford Siding
C&SJ 1845
Leeswood
Nerquis
Coed Talon
GC
WM&CQ 1864
Treuddyn
River Alyn
Hope Village
Caergwrle Castle & Wells
Rossett
MDJ 1865
River Alyn
Llanfynydd
Cefn-y-bedd
Ffrwd
Ffrith
GC
Gresford
Farndon
Brymbo West Crossing Halt
Brymbo
Moss Platform
WM&CQ 1865
Pentresaeson Halt
The Lodge Halt
Wheatsheaf Junction
Coed Poeth
Gwersyllt
Gwersyllt Hill Halt
Berwig Halt
GW
Vron
Pentre Broughton Halt
Rhosrobin Halt
Rhosddu Halt
Highfield Road Halt
Minera
Vicarage Crossing Halt
Plas Power
Gatewen Halt
Exchange
WREXHAM
New Brighton
New Broughton Road Halt
General Central
Hightown Halt
Moss & Pentre
Croes-newydd
Rhostyllen
Legacy
Marchwiel
GW
Fennant Road Halt
Sesswick Halt
Aberderfyn Halt
BCM R&WCo 1896
NW&BB 1872
Pickhill Halt
Rhos
WM&CQ 1862
BNW&S 1873
Ponkey Crossing Halt
Brook Street Halt
Bangor-on-Dee
Pant Halt
Johnstown & Hafod
WM&CQ 1864
Afon Eitha
Wynn Hall Halt
Garddon Lodge Junction
Plas Madoc
Wynnville Halt
Cloy Halt
Acrefair
RUABON
WM&CQ 1862
Trevor
Llangollen Junction
Sun Bank Halt
Rhosymedre Halt
S U Canal
B&SW 1873
Cefn
WM&CQ 1884
Ffron Wharf
Overton-on-Dee
Llangollen Road (Whitehurst Halt)

Miles
0 1 2 3

MOLD RAILWAY

In November the Shrewsbury & Chester Railway lodged a Bill
for a Mold branch, quickly killed off by an offer from Edward
Betts, whose work on the CHR Chester-Shotton length was
drawing to a close, to complete the Mold company's line
simultaneously with the CHR opening to Conway. The Mold
Railway Company was incorporated on 9 July 1847 to make
its main line, and a branch via Pontblyddyn to limeworks at
Ffrith. Its financial state reflected that of the CHR, then
extremely grave, and lack of funds threatened stoppage of the
works. With half the company's board wearing Mold and CHR
hats alternately, the directors were at a loss as to what to do.
Despite opposition from shareholders—*Herepath's Journal* of
24 March 1849 said that 600,000 to 800,000 tons of minerals
yearly from the Mold district were too important to be neglected
—the CHR agreed to purchase the line, and to Betts taking as
partner his brother-in-law Samuel Morton Peto (p 24), they to
receive cash and debentures in payment.

The Mold Railway, worked by LNWR trains (p 24) opened
on 14 August 1849 with intermediate stations at Broughton,
Hope and Llong. The first $7\frac{1}{4}$ miles (11.6km) were double track,
the remaining $2\frac{3}{4}$ miles (4.4km) into Mold being single. In June
1849 the LNWR locomotive committee authorised building of
'an Engine and Tender in one for the use of the Mold line';
No 247 *Mammoth*, a Crewe goods 2–4–0, specially built as a
tank engine, started work in October 1849. That month the
branch timetable appeared in *Bradshaw* preceded by the note
'Company's arrangements incomplete—accuracy doubtful',
hardly the thing to encourage passengers. Early in 1851
Padeswood station was opened at the Ffrith branch junction.
Connecting road services operated between Mold and Corwen,
Bala, and Dolgellau. Mixed passenger and goods trains operated
from early days but mineral workings seem to have waited for
the opening of the Ffrith branch which it had been agreed
should extend initially only for $2\frac{1}{4}$ miles (3.6km) from Ffrith
Junction to Coed Talon, whence a private railway served
Nerquis colliery, leaving construction of the remainder of the
line to the lime quarries until required. The branch opened in
November 1849, worked by Edward Oakley, mine and quarry
owner, with his locomotive *Diamond*, until 1852 when the CHR

and LNWR took over. The ruling gradient was 1 in 40, down which loaded coal trains went to storage sidings between Coppa and Ffrith Junction. New coal pits were opened at Coed Talon by 1861; sidings served Leeswood Hill colliery by 1863 and the Coppa Oil Company by 1865. The oil was distilled from locally mined 'cannel" coals. Ffrith Junction to Coppa was doubled a year later. By the early 1860s industrial development in the Mold district had raised the population to over 12,000. In June 1869 a bridge on the nearly-completed Mold & Denbigh Junction Railway (Chapter V) at Mold provided a vantage point for rioters to attack soldiers attempting to remove by train colliers in dispute with the Leeswood Coal Company.

On the Mold line, accidents due to under-powered locomotives stalling on the 1 in 43 incline between Broughton and Hope were partly responsible for an LNWR experimental 0–6–0 goods tender locomotive in 1858, precursor to the ubiquitous DX class. After opening of the Mold & Denbigh Junction, doubling was completed to Mold, apparently by July 1870. To avoid confusion with Broughton on the Lancaster & Carlisle Railway, Broughton station became Broughton Hall in April 1861, and Broughton & Bretton from 1 July 1908. Padeswood gained '& Buckley' from 1 February 1894, and Hope '& Penyffordd' from 16 January 1912 to distinguish it from Hope station in the Derbyshire Peak District. Additional stations opened in 1891: Kinnerton on 2 March, and 'Saltney Ferry (Mold Junction)' on 1 October to serve the new Mold Junction steam shed, opened a year earlier.

WREXHAM & MINERA RAILWAY

South of the Ffrith branch the coalfield was served by minor branches from the Shrewsbury & Chester line, including Wheatsheaf to Minera (Chapter III), plagued by two rope-worked inclines. On 17 May 1861 the Wrexham & Minera Railway was incorporated for a 3¼ miles (5.2km) line from Croes Newydd on the S&C, south of Wrexham, to the Minera branch at Brymbo. The W&M opened for mineral traffic a year and five days after Royal Assent, and the westerly incline on the old Minera line was abandoned. There were now two spurs into the coalfield: LNWR from the north and GWR from the south. Battle was joined for a line throughout.

FIGHT FOR THE COALFIELD

In 1861 George Hammond Whalley, MP, a man of immense drive and considerable local power, with Benjamin and Robert Piercy, engineers, and Thomas Savin, contractor, together promoted the Oswestry Ellesmere & Whitchurch Railway. With David Davies of Llandinam they had planned and constructed, or were completing, railways from Llanidloes in Mid Wales, through Newtown to Oswestry (Chapter X). Euston supported the OE&W for the traffic it would divert from the GWR at Oswestry to Whitchurch on the LNWR Crewe–Shrewsbury line, opened in 1858. Though the O&EW received Royal Assent, a separate Bill for an OE&W branch, entitled the Ellesmere Wrexham & North Wales Mineral, did not proceed. Its route, however, from Ellesmere via Ruabon and Wrexham to the LNWR Ffrith branch, seeking access to the Mold district, served to awaken Paddington to threatened competition in the coalfield. Planned ostensibly to get the GWR to Connah's Quay as an alternative to its rapidly silting port of Saltney, a Bill for a Mold & Wrexham Railway appeared in 1862. This proposed a line from the Mold Railway at Padeswood to the GWR at Wrexham; a branch to the 5¼-mile (8.4km) Buckley Railway (authorised by Act of 14 June 1860 to convert its horse tramway into a proper mineral line, with a curve at Connah's Quay to the CHR); and running powers into Mold, Wrexham, and Connah's Quay. The GWR scheme was opposed by a Bill from the Whalley/Piercy/Savin group: the Whitchurch Wrexham Mold & Connah's Quay Junction, successor to the EW&NWM, but now to link the OE&W with the Buckley Railway so as to improve access to the Dee and outlet to the south, independently of the GWR. Behind its promoters, intent on stopping the Mold & Wrexham, was the LNWR.

Evidence on the Bills was heard in Parliament in May 1862. Henry Robertson (p 37), on the board of the Shrewsbury & Hereford, engineer to the Central Wales, Vale of Llangollen, Wellington & Severn Junction, and Wrexham & Minera, with interests in the Brymbo ironworks and Ruabon Coal Company, destined for a seat in Parliament and eventual knighthood, joined with two other distinguished engineers, John Fowler and John Hawkshaw, in support of the Mold & Wrexham. James Davison, a Connah's Quay brick manufacturer, told of a two-mile bed of fireclay, eight brickworks, eight potteries and several collieries in the Buckley area, served by the LNWR but requiring access to the south. George Bellis, the Buckley's engineer, said that his line would open on 2 June and would be best served by the GWR scheme.

The Mold & Wrexham was attacked by counsel for Euston as an intrusion into LNWR territory. Apparently the destinations of Wrexham coal varied according to how Paddington viewed the matter: 'The coal itself, if it was sensitive, and was in the room either in spirit or in ashes, must be puzzled to know where it was to go'. The GWR boasted about Saltney, yet left it off its map; it was at Wrexham, twice the size of Mold, yet Mold was suddenly the most important. Mold, counsel thought, had enough rail communication, but if the GWR got there the LNWR should be allowed into Wrexham. Support was strong for the WWM&CQJ. Mr Clayton of the Bryn Mally colliery wanted access to Connah's Quay; in 1861 his coal and ironstone had approached 100,000 tons and the GWR, serving his Moss Valley works, complained of wagons blocking the line and kept him waiting. Another witness talked of demand in Wrexham for Caernarvonshire slates and, with perhaps unconscious humour, believed that via the WWM&CQJ they would arrive without break.

Under cross-examination Piercy admitted that several of the Whalley/Savin railways had not been completed. Counsel for local landowners claimed that these three were 'in the habit of going about the country promoting lines as independent ones, without intending to make any, and selling them to other parties after the Acts had been obtained. Piercy agreed that the Denbigh Ruthin & Corwen (Chapter V) was one such, and had first been offered to the GWR. Counsel claimed that Piercy's four completed lines—promoted as independent— had eventually been paid for by Euston: the WWM&CQJ would go the same way, and Piercy's evidence was contradictory and inaccurate: '. . . if he had been asked when the Reform Bill was passed, he would ask to explain – he saw everybody, knew everything, gave pages of argument, but never answered a question'. Whalley's evidence showed he had fingers in many local railway pies, including involvement with Savin and Piercy in Vale of Clwyd developments. Victory went to the WWM&CQJ, so far as related to the line north of Wrexham. Whalley was criticised, one committee member publicly stating his belief that '. . . I am not using a harsh term when I say that he has been dabbling in railway matters in a somewhat questionable form'.

WREXHAM MOLD & CONNAH'S QUAY RAILWAY

The WM&CQR Act of 7 August 1862—Whitchurch was dropped from the title—authorised construction from Wrexham via Gwersyllt, Caergwrle and Hope, where it passed over the Mold Railway, to a junction with the Buckley Railway. Two westerly curves to the Mold Railway were authorised, but running powers into Mold were not. In June 1863 the company agreed to work the Buckley's line as part of its own railway.

The 9½ mile (15.2km) WM&CQ main line, ruling gradient 1 in 70, opened for goods and mineral traffic on 1 January 1866. Land and works were for a double line but the track was single, with small stations at Wrexham, Gwersyllt, Cefn-y-bedd, Caergwrle, Hope Junction (renamed Penyffordd in 1877) and Buckley, a short branch to Ffrwd ironworks, and several colliery sidings. The curves to the Mold Railway and a junction to the GWR at Wrexham were incomplete. The major engineering work was a five-arched stone viaduct over the Alyn. Colonel Yolland inspected the line for passenger traffic in February but required existing passing loops at stations to have platforms. Consent was refused until after a second inspection in April, when the southerly Hope junction was complete, though no arrangement had been made for working through to Mold. The northerly curve was not made. The WM&CQ opened for passengers on May Day 1866 with three trains each way on weekdays and a connecting bus service between Hope and Mold. In 1867 the LNWR and WM&CQ agreed on an interchange station at Hope: two small platforms on each railway, isolated from outside communication and known as Hope Exchange, came into use shortly thereafter and the bus service ceased. In June 1872 a new station opened at Bridge End (renamed Caergwrle Castle in 1898 when Caergwrle became Hope Village).

George Dow, in his *Great Central* volume III, has some delightful descriptions of the early state of the railway, which he described as 'ramshackle': mixed trains, worked with an old 0–6–0 and 4-wheeled tender, by staff without uniforms, and often so packed on market days that passengers perched on the tender coals and even overflowed on to the footplate. For years the WM&CQ service consisted of six weekday stopping trains each way, connecting at Hope with LNWR trains. Mineral traffic, at first poor, picked up from the 1870s.

THE CLC REACHES CHESTER

In 1862 the Manchester Sheffield & Lincolnshire and Great Northern companies formed the Cheshire Lines Committee for management and working of railways including the Cheshire Midland and West Cheshire, together constituting a line from Altrincham to a junction at Helsby with the Birkenhead Railway. The Midland Railway joined the committee in 1865, in which year the Chester & West Cheshire Junction was authorised from Mouldsworth on the WCR to a station at Northgate, Chester, powers being transferred to the CLC in 1866 and the line opening in 1874. A decade before, Edward Watkin, one of the foremost railway figures of the time, became chairman of the MS&L. The arrival, albeit as a partner, of his company at Chester was the first stage in a campaign by Watkin to get the MS&L into North Wales. Before taking that story further, the outcome of the struggle in the coalfield between Paddington and Euston should be noted.

WREXHAM & MINERA JOINT RAILWAY AND GWR MOSS VALLEY BRANCH

In 1865 a Mold–Wrexham Bill lodged by the Mold & Denbigh Junction failed, the Wrexham & Minera Railway obtaining powers instead, on 5 July 1865, to extend from Brymbo to the LNWR Ffrith branch near Tryddyn, south of Coed Talon, with a curve south of Ffrith Junction to Llong on the Mold Railway. An attempt to open the W&M to passengers failed after inspection by the Board of Trade in July 1866 had condemned weak bridges and faulty works. By an Act of 11 June 1866 the Brymbo extension was transferred to the GWR and LNWR, becoming their Wrexham & Minera Joint Railway. Rails were laid on the southerly, unused, end of the Ffrith branch up to the joint line junction by order given to the LNWR engineer in November 1866. The W&MR, Wrexham–Brymbo, vested in the GWR in 1871, and the $2\frac{3}{4}$-mile (4.4km) joint line opened to freight on 27 January 1872. The GWR $3\frac{1}{4}$-mile (5.2km) Moss Valley branch, authorised by Act of 21 July 1873, left the W&M about

$\frac{3}{4}$-mile (1.2km) from its commencement, and terminated at Ffrwd ironworks. According to MacDermot the first $1\frac{7}{8}$ miles (3km) from the W&M, to a connection with the old Ffrwd branch where it left the Wheatsheaf–Minera line, opened to freight on 11 May 1881 (some sources give 20 March 1882). MacDermot states that closure of the now superflous eastern incline between Gwersyllt and the Moss Valley branch did not take place until October 1908.

LNWR MOLD AND TRYDDYN LINE

Because of the Ffrith branch gradients, the Ffrith Junction curve was abandoned in favour of a $4\frac{3}{4}$-mile (7.6km) Mold–Tryddyn line, authorised by the LNWR Act of 16 July 1866 which also empowered purchase of the Nerquis Railway, part of which was to be used for the new line. The single-track railway opened from Tryddyn Junction, Mold, to Oak Pits colliery on 16 March 1869 and throughout to a triangular junction with the Ffrith branch at Coed Talon on 8 July 1870. In 1887 rail connection to Nerquis colliery was removed (reinstated 1923), and thereafter the Tryddyn line seemingly fell into disuse, for during preparations in 1891 to open it for passengers instructions were given for 'works to enable the branch to be reopened', and for refurbishing of 'the existing station at Coed Talon'. A weekday service of four trains each way (three on Saturdays) started on 1 January 1892.

AN EXCESS OF SCHEMES

Returning to the WM&CQ, the early 1860s saw a number of railway projects in the area. In 1862 a Birkenhead Flintshire & Holyhead Bill proposed a Hooton–Queensferry line, with branches to the CHR and Buckley lines, and running powers into Chester. In 1863 the WM&CQ unsuccessfully applied for branches to Whitchurch, Hawarden, the Mold Railway at Kinnerton, and the Vale of Llangollen Railway. The Whitchurch line was approved in 1864, but failures that year included a Flintshire Railway from the WM&CQ to Holywell, and a Dee & Mersey Junction, planned to take the company through the Wirral to Merseyside. Powers for branches in Northop and Hawarden, and a Dee Valley line to Farndon in Cheshire, were granted to the WM&CQ in 1865. In 1866 a North Wales

Birkenhead & Liverpool Railway failed to get powers for a line linking the WM&CQ, Buckley, and CHR with the Birkenhead Railway near Ledsham. The Buckley secured two Acts in 1866, one confirming the 1863 working agreement, and the other authorising passenger traffic, not exercised except for rare excursions to Rhyl. An 1866 WM&CQ Bill, for another shot at a Mersey line, this time jointly with the Hoylake Railway, again failed, along with a link to an extension westwards from Chester by the Chester & West Cheshire Junction, though assent was given to a Whitchurch line deviation and small branches in Hawarden. There the WM&CQ took a breather, exhausted by Parliamentary conflict and expense. Much of it was for nothing; branch powers gained during those years were later abandoned.

The 1866 country-wide financial crisis following collapse of the mid-1860s mania, and poor traffic returns, led the WM&CQ to approach Euston for purchase or working of its line. LNWR records show that Euston was tempted—and to open the Buckley, then also seeking a sale, for passenger traffic. This would have prejudiced the proposed GWR and LNWR Mold–Wrexham scheme and after objections from Sir Daniel Gooch, GWR chairman, the WM&CQ negotiations ceased in 1871, as did in 1877 those for a joint LNWR and WM&CQ ownership of the Buckley, leased to the WM&CQ in 1873.

Projects in the early 1870s included further abortive attempts to cross the Dee. A North Wales Chester & Birkenhead Bill of 1872 for a line from Buckley to Birkenhead via Parkgate and Bidston, and a branch to Chester, was withdrawn, but followed in 1873 by two Bills: a North Wales & Birkenhead Direct line from the WM&CQ to Neston, Birkenhead, and Chester; and a Birkenhead Chester & North Wales, which latter received Royal Assent. The same promoters unsuccessfully lodged Bills for railways from Wrexham: to Whitchurch and on to Stafford (Birkenhead North Wales & Stafford), and to the Cambrian at Whittington, thence by running powers via the Mid Wales and Brecon & Merthyr to South Wales (Birkenhead & South Wales Junction). Despite attempts to interest the WM&CQ the BC&NW, including a high-level Dee bridge, was not made.

Lengthy though this recital of unrelieved failures is, it highlights the lure of traffic through the coalfield, linking output with Birkenhead particularly, and with the Potteries in one instance but otherwise by through running. It was not until the WM&CQ itself extended northwards to the Dee that an

established company, the MS&L, which had bided its time
awaiting a better financial climate, was encouraged into completing by construction and acquisition the alternative routes to
Chester and Birkenhead.

WM&CQ HAWARDEN LOOP, WREXHAM CENTRAL EXTENSION, AND BRYMBO BRANCH

Final impetus for the Dee crossing commenced in 1882 when on
18 August the WM&CQ obtained powers for the double-tracked
Hawarden Loop Line, taking the company from Buckley through
Hawarden, where a station was built, and over the CHR by
girder bridge, with another station—Shotton & Connah's Quay,
to the Dee, with a branch down to the CHR at Connah's Quay
where improved dock facilities were to be made. Clauses in the
Bill for a bridge over the Dee, with two 70ft (21.35m) opening
spans, a short railway to the north to a new dock, and change
of name to 'North Wales Railways & Docks Company' were
not sanctioned. At Wrexham a ½-mile (0.8km) single-line
extension (doubled in 1888) was authorised, passing under the
GWR to terminate in the town centre where a new Central
station was opened on 1 November 1887. The earlier terminus,
now a through station, was renamed Exchange. The Hawarden
and Wrexham works were accompanied by doubling of the line
south of the junction at Buckley. Because of the lingering
possibility of an alliance with Euston, the 1882 Act also provided a connection from Penyffordd to the Mold Railway,
allowing through running between Chester joint station and
Wrexham Central. This was abandoned when in 1889 after
Piercy's death, his holding of more than half the WM&CQ
stock was purchased by the MS&L. Finally, the Act authorised
a 4-mile (6.4km) single line to Brymbo, built in the teeth of
GWR opposition, from a triangular junction south of Gwersyllt.
It opened for freight to Moss & Pentre in 1882; Plas Power,
with a junction to the Wrexham & Minera, in June 1884;
Brymbo in 1887; and was opened for passengers on 1 August
1889, with stations at Moss & Pentre, Plas Power, and Brymbo,
and later halts at Rhosddu and Highfield Road in 1905, and
New Broughton Road in 1906. A ½-mile (0.8km) mineral branch,
opened 8 October 1888, doubled back from Brymbo to parallel
the GWR branch to Vron colliery.

MS&L LINK TO CHESTER NORTHGATE

Realising that the WM&CQ could not afford the cost, the MS&L decided to build the elusive Dee link; powers were obtained by Act of 28 July 1884 for the Chester and Connah's Quay railway, from the end of the Hawarden Loop to a triangular junction with the CLC west of Chester Northgate. The Dee was crossed by the expensive Hawarden Bridge, of two fixed bowstring girder spans and a 287ft 0in (87.47m) hydraulically-operated swing span, the inaugural construction ceremony being performed on 16 August by the Rt Hon W. E. Gladstone, who lived at Hawarden Castle and who had supported efforts to link railways on either side of the river. Meanwhile, on 31 July 1885 the Wirral Railway obtained powers for an extension from Bidston to a triangular junction with the Chester and Connah's Quay line north of Hawarden Bridge while on the same day, to the south, the Wrexham & Ellesmere was incorporated (Chapter X). These moves came at a time when Watkin and the Cambrian chairman were discussing a working union of their Welsh railways. At Watkin's urging, and despite joint GWR and LNWR threats to take over the Seacombe Hoylake & Deeside and the Wirral itself, the Wirral company transferred its Bidston line to the MS&L and WM&CQ by Act of 26 August 1889.

The Hawarden Bridge was opened by Mrs Gladstone on 3 August 1889. Chester to Connah's Quay, 6¾ miles (10.8km), with stations at Liverpool Road (Chester), Blacon, and Saughall, opened on 31 March 1890, on the same day as the 4½-mile (7.2km) Hawarden Loop and the 1-mile (1.6km) Connah's Quay freight branch. A Chester Northgate–Wrexham Central service was started, worked by the MS&L with four trains daily in each direction. A new station—Buckley Junction—was opened; the first Buckley, to the north of the junction and known as Buckley Old, was closed, re-opened as being useful for local workers in 1893 and finally closed in 1895. In 1891 two stations were opened : Connah's Quay & Shotton, and two small platforms, solely for use by Chester Golf Club, east of Hawarden Bridge. That year, seeking further expansion, Watkin suggested to Paddington that the MS&L and GWR should jointly make the Bidston line, the Wrexham & Ellesmere, and lease the WM&CQ, with MS&L running powers into Oswestry. Paddington revealed

all this to Euston, negotiations were stillborn, and construction
started independently on the two lines. The W&E opened in
1895 (Chapter X). The Bidston line involved the reluctant
WM&CQ and further impoverished that company. In 1897 the
Great Central Railway (lately MS&L), by financial pressure,
got the WM&CQ into the hands of a Receiver, and its acquisition by the GCR was then but a matter of time.

The 14¼-mile (23km) double-tracked Bidston line, renamed
the North Wales & Liverpool Railway, offering a new route
between Birkenhead, Chester and Wrexham, opened for freight
on 16 March, and to passengers on 18 May 1896, worked by
the WM&CQ with borrowed MS&L locomotives until the
GCR took over in 1901. The Wrexham, Buckley, and NW&L
Railways were transferred to the GCR from 1 January 1905.
Two more stations were opened : near Saughall at Welsh Road
(a World War I military halt serving Shotwick Park Aerodrome
and Queensferry Acceptance Park), opened to the public in 1919
and renamed Sealand in 1931; and Hawarden Bridge Halt,
two 300ft concrete platforms on the north side of the bridge,
serving some 1,000 workers daily from the nearby John Summers
steelworks and also the Sealand housing estate, and which first
appeared in *Bradshaw* in 1924. Lt Col Mount inspected the
Hawarden Bridge Halt in February 1928 (following instructions
from the Ministry of Transport dated April 1926 !) and remarked
that 20 of each of the 27 up and 26 down daily passenger
trains called at the halt.

MOLD–WREXHAM–MINERA AND MOSS VALLEY PASSENGER SERVICES

The GWR double-tracked W&M line from Wrexham to
Brymbo opened for passenger traffic on 24 May 1882, an intermediate station at Plas Power opening in 1883. In April 1898
Colonel Yorke inspected the Wrexham & Minera Joint Railway
prior to extension of the LNWR passenger service between Coed
Talon and Brymbo. The two single-platform stations, Llanfynydd
and Ffrith, had no passing loops or signals. On 2 May 1898
four weekdays-only passenger trains started running between
Mold and Brymbo. From 1905 LNWR motor buses operated
between Mold and Connah's Quay.

GWR passenger services extended to Coed Poeth on the
Minera branch from 15 November 1897. Halts at Brymbo West

Crossing and Pentresaeson opened in March 1905 and the service, operated from then by steam railmotors, was further extended in May 1905 with halts at Vicarage Crossing and Berwig. The Lodge Halt, south of Brymbo, opened in July 1906. A 'motor'-operated passenger service also commenced on the Moss Valley branch on 1 May 1905, with halts at Gatewen, Pentre Broughton, and Moss Platform; Gwersyllt Hill Halt opened in May 1906.

WREXHAM–RHOS–RUABON BRANCHES

To the west of the GWR's Wrexham–Ruabon railway several small industrial branches developed, which had as their oldest section the Pontcysyllte Tramway of the Shropshire Union system (p 47). After the SU lease, the tramway became an isolated LNWR line, worked for some time by the New British Iron Company. When in 1859 the GWR backed the projected Vale of Llangollen Railway, the LNWR and SU countered with their own proposal (p 137). Success of the V of L, however, left the tramway merely as a canal feeder. In 1863 the LNWR converted it to a locomotive line up to Afon Eitha and also along several branches, to the Wynn Hall colliery and the New British Iron Company, and also to the private Plas Madoc branch. This last-named left the GWR main line about ½-mile (0.8km) south of Ruabon station to run north-west to Plas Madoc colliery; by the 1880s it extended beneath the Llangollen Road, crossed the Pontcysyllte line on the level, turning south-west to serve brickworks north of Acrefair. In 1865–6 the LNWR further extended the tramway northwards to Llwyneinion, about a mile (1.6km) north-west of Rhosllanerchrugog, re-opening it throughout for freight only in January 1867—an LNWR service in an area dominated by the GWR.

In 1861 the GWR opened a 1¾-mile (2.8km) siding from Gardden Lodge Junction just north of Ruabon to furnaces at Ponkey (Ponciau) and Aberderfyn, and in 1871 extended it some 1¼ miles (2km) to Legacy, confirmatory powers being received in Acts of 21 July 1873 and 12 August 1889. (MacDermot gives the Ruabon–Aberderfyn opening as 1 August 1861, and extension of the freight service to Legacy from 27 August 1876.) In 1896 a proposed East Denbighshire Railway, supported by the WM&CQ, sought to make a railway from Wrexham to Rhos (Rhosllanerchrugog) on the Pontcysyllte line,

with running powers over that, the WM&CQ and the Wrexham
& Ellesmere. The GWR countered by purchasing, except for
some 220yd (201m) at the canal basin end which remained
LNWR, the Pontcysyllte line—taking possession of it and its
wagons on 12 February 1896, the LNWR branch locomotive
returning to Crewe. Also acquired was the Plas Madoc branch.
By GWR Acts of 20 July 1896 and 6 August 1897 the Pontcysyllte line was connected to the Ponkey branch at Legacy, and
extended by a new 3¼-mile (5.2km) Rhos branch, opened 1
October 1901, to the GWR main line south of Wrexham, with
intermediate stations at Rhostyllen and Legacy. From 1 May
1905 a railmotor service was put on, extended further along the
Pontcysyllte branch with halts at Brook Street, Pant, and Wynn
Hall, and from 5 June 1905 south from Legacy on the Ponkey
branch, with halts at Fennant Road, Aberderfyn, and Ponkey
Crossing. All the halts were closed from 22 March 1915 and
the Ponkey–Legacy line severed, though its south end remained
busy with freight, but the Wrexham–Rhos passenger trains
continued until 30 December 1930. Special passenger trains still
occasionally used the line, for example in August 1945 for the
National Eisteddfod week at Rhos, and for excursions for
Wrexham football club supporters. Pontcysyllte–Pant closed in
1953, and Pant–Rhos on 14 October 1963.

RUN-DOWN OF SERVICES

The main reason for rail closures in the area was the same as
elsewhere—flexible road competition. But an additional factor
was the decline of many of the quarries, collieries, ironworks,
brickworks, and potteries which had first attracted the railways.
The first passenger closure was the former GCR Gwersyllt–
Brymbo branch, on 1 March 1917. Concurrent with the ending
of the GWR regular Rhos branch service, passenger trains also
ceased over that company's Wrexham–Berwig Halt via Minera
line, and over the Moss Valley branch. The first line to close
completely was the Ffrith branch, effectively from 29 July 1934
when a freight was derailed at Pontblyddyn. The Mold–
Brymbo passenger trains (latterly two each way daily) ceased on
27 March 1950, Coed Talon, Llanfynydd and Brymbo remaining for freight but Ffrith closing completely. From south of
Coed Talon to south of Ffrith closed from 1 May 1952.
  Chester Liverpool Road closed to passengers on 3 December

1951, and Saughall on 1 February 1954. Padeswood & Buckley closed on 6 January 1958, followed by Hope Exchange stations on 1 September 1958. The northerly portion of the Buckley Railway beyond Northop Hall colliery was closed in 1959 and the remainder down to Buckley Junction in 1965. The Chester–Mold–Denbigh passenger service was withdrawn on 30 April 1962, though an unadvertised workmen's service ran between Chester and Broughton & Bretton until 2 September 1963. The Buckley Railway closed in 1965. Closures to freight were as follows: Hope & Penyffordd and Kinnerton in 1955; Padeswood & Buckley 1956; Coed Talon 1963; Broughton & Bretton, Brymbo, Coed Poeth, and Minera 1964; Connah's Quay 1966; and Mold 1972. Two non-passenger lines remained open during the 1970s: the GCR Brymbo branch reached Brymbo steelworks via a new connection to the GWR at Plas Power, 1954–8 and 1965–70, when it finally closed, access thereafter being by way of the Croes Newydd–Brymbo and Vron branches; and the Mold branch, 4¾ miles (7.6km) westward from a spur to the Bidston–Wrexham line at Penyffordd, served the Synthite Ltd formaldehyde factory at Mold.

Chester Northgate closed to freight in 1965 and passenger services thence to Connahs Quay (Dee Marsh Junction) ceased from 9 September 1968. Economies and introduction of conductor-guards from April 1969 justified grant-aided continuation of the New Brighton–Wrexham service. Proposals in 1970 to terminate trains at Wrexham General and do away with Central came to naught. (See Chapter XV.)

The riot at Mold, 1869 (*Illustrated London News*)

CHAPTER V

The Clwyd Area

In 1854 George Borrow, traveller and author, embarked on a walking tour of Wales, parts of which were shortly to be penetrated by the railway—an invention for which he had no liking. He reached the Vale of Clwyd in late summertime:

> I looked and perceived an extensive valley pleasantly dotted with trees and farm-houses, and bounded on the west by a range of hills.
> 'It is a fine valley, sir', said my guide, 'four miles wide and twenty long, and contains the richest land in all Wales. Cheese made in that valley, sir, fetches a penny a pound more than cheese made in any other valley'.

Of gentle contour, unlike the scenery westwards in Snowdonia the vale, carved by the River Clwyd which rises some 20 miles from the coast in the Denbighshire hills, lies nine miles west of Mold, and runs roughly north-west. Seven miles south of the coast a narrow valley cuts eastwards through the Clwydian Range towards Mold. There are three towns in the vale, each with some 3,500 inhabitants in Borrow's time: the ancient cathedral 'city' of St Asaph, five miles inland; the county town of Denbigh, ten miles, clustered around a ruined hilltop castle; and Ruthin, 16 miles, again with a fortified hill. There is another castle, at the village of Rhuddlan – remnant of a once-thriving borough, where the Elwy joins the Clwyd, under three miles from the sea. Between there and the coast lies Morfa Rhuddlan (Rhuddlan Marsh), liable to flood, and the site of an 8th-century battle and massacre. Until the Restoration of 1660, the vale witnessed frequent conflict: Denbigh and Ruthin castles, held for the king, were ruined in the civil war period. Since then, the people have had a peaceful agricultural existence, with the main towns as markets, exporting their produce towards Chester, and to Liverpool by sea, and receiving necessities in exchange.

Beyond Ruthin the vale narrows and curves south-west to the village of Derwen, whence a narrow pass leads to Corwen and the valley of the Dee. The presence of this through route to the south led to considerable local railway activity in mid-Victorian years, the potential link between the Great Western and London & North Western systems leading to confrontation. Two small lines, unconnected physically with the Clwyd area, can also be discussed here, for one was on the local tourist itinerary, while the other attempted to link into the vale.

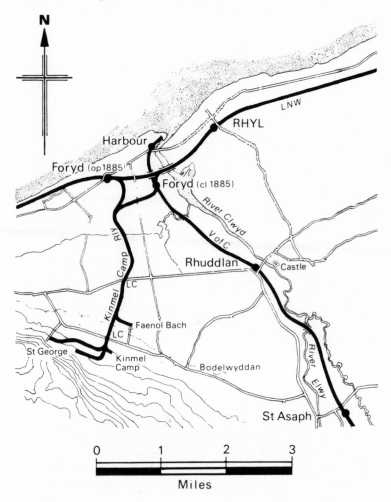

VALE OF CLWYD RAILWAY

In 1845 the CHR sought to tap the vale's agricultural traffic with a Rhyl–Ruthin line but by 1846, with escalating main line construction costs, projected CHR branches were shelved. In 1852 the company encouraged a local Mold–Ruthin venture, which did not proceed. Three railways were projected to Ruthin in 1853–4: from Ruabon via Corwen, from Wrexham via Brymbo, and direct from Rhyl. Late in 1855 another local company proposed a line from Denbigh to the CHR west of the Foryd Bridge over the Clwyd. Townshend Mainwaring, MP for Denbigh, was provisional chairman and the engineer was Benjamin Piercy.

The Vale of Clwyd Railway was incorporated by Act of 23 June 1856. In October the directors forecast a six percent dividend on estimated traffic receipts. Coaches between Rhyl, Mold and Ruthin were stated to carry 25 passengers daily; some 40 travellers went by other means. Obscure arithmetic turned these to potential annual rail receipts of £2,535. Other yearly traffic included 40,000 tons of coal and 4,000 tons of assorted merchandise inwards, and outwards 90 tons of butter, 200 tons of cheese, 300 horses, 2,000 cattle, 5,000 pigs, 5,000 sheep, 1,000 tons of grain and flour, 2,500 tons of Nantglyn blue flagstones from Denbigh, 200 tons of slates, 500 tons of timber, 500 tons of limestone and lime, and 100 tons of bricks and tiles. Including passenger receipts, these produced an estimated £6,829. Fifty percent deduction for working expenses left £3,414 for dividend which, not surprisingly, was six percent on the capital. Nobody mentioned, however that the V of C had no statutory rights into Rhyl, where arrangements were at the whim of Euston.

Construction was let to David Davies, contractor on the Llanidloes & Newtown Railway (Chapter X) where funds had dried up. His partner, Thomas Savin, joined him on the V of C. Despite rain, Denbigh was festive on 7 August when Mrs Mainwaring cut the first sod. Construction was fast. According to the late J. M. Dunn, Davies worked a 16-hour day on the V of C, snatching sleep in the firebox of a dead locomotive. On 22 September 1858 Captain Ross inspected the 10-mile (16km) single track, with works for double line, from Foryd Junction to a temporary station at Denbigh. Intermediate stations were at Foryd, near the junction with the CHR, Rhuddlan, St Asaph, and Trefnant. The line was to be worked with tank engines 'on the principle adopted I believe on some of the LNWR branches, viz, by dividing the line into sections controlled by pilotmen with coloured staves which it is said precludes the possibility of mistake . . .'. Because of unfinished works permission to open was refused, but a week later these were ready and the company promised to work with one engine in steam. 'Train staff' working had been postponed due to the small initial traffic. John Ashbury of Openshaw supplied rolling stock, and three 0–4–2 saddle tanks came new from Sharp, Stewart of Manchester : Nos 1 and 2 named after the Rivers Clwyd and Elwy, and No 3 after Mainwaring's Rhyl home, Galtfaenan. The railway opened on 5 October 1858 with four weekday stopping trains. In November there were complaints of want of lighting in the third-class carriages, 'which gave opportunities of rude conduct to females, and allowed drinking, smoking, and other indecencies with impunity'. Denbigh permanent station opened in December 1860. Until December 1871 Whitehall Dod, a V of C director, had a 'flag' station at Nannerch where he might stop trains.

In 1859 V of C excursion trains necessitated separate sidings and a booking office at Rhyl where from that July only *bona fide* passengers were to be admitted 'as it has become the practice . . . to make the platform a public lounge, to the serious hindrance of the station business'. The company and Davies and Savin sought powers in 1860 for separate rail access to Rhyl via a new river bridge, the two contractors agreeing jointly to lease the railway and work it independently of the LNWR. Parliament, however, insisted on reciprocal LNWR running powers into Denbigh, rejected a proposed V of C steamer link with Liverpool, demanded to see the company's books and the Davies and Savin agreements. To keep V of C affairs private, and the LNWR from Denbigh, the Bill was withdrawn and the lease sacrificed.

TROUBLES AT FORYD

For obtaining ballast, the contractors laid a railway to Foryd beach across land owned by Hugh Robert Hughes of Kinmel Hall, a V of C shareholder. Hughes had wanted the V of C to terminate at his pier on the west side of the estuary, but the

CHR objected, fearing steamer competition to Liverpool. Claiming under the CHR Act his rights of access to the beach, Hughes took possession of the ballast branch and announced he would use it for 'general commerce', exchanging traffic with the V of C at Foryd station. When his workmen were ejected by the CHR, he went to law and was granted an injunction. By August 1859, though fenced off from the V of C, the branch carried transferred freight and passengers to Hughes' pier from where James Napier, another V of C shareholder, operated his steamer *Lion* to and from Liverpool. In May 1860 Napier petitioned against separate V of C access to Rhyl, and in June exposed V of C and LNWR leasing negotiations, both being prejudicial to his steamer traffic. Davies and Savin held most V of C shares as payment for railway works; they rejected the lease, against the advice of V of C directors, currently threatened by Euston with a rival Mold–Denbigh project. Mainwaring and five directors resigned, Robert Gardner of Manchester—an octogenerian—becoming chairman.

By September 1860 Hughes' railway was reconnected to the V of C. A Bill for a proper extension, following Hughes' route, was lodged in November, together with Davies' and Savin's Rhyl Harbour Bridge & Railway Bill, seeking also construction of a tidal harbour, and agreements with the V of C and LNWR. To protect his interests—*Lion* carried 28,700 passengers, 8,632 tons of goods and 2,143 head of livestock in 1859—Napier now turned to the Great Western Railway, then extending feelers towards Rhyl. In view of what followed, we must now introduce Davies' and Savin's Corwen line.

DENBIGH RUTHIN & CORWEN RAILWAY

Projects for 1859 included a Vale of Llangollen Railway, from Ruabon to Llangollen in the Dee Valley, and a similar Ruabon & Denbigh, which went on via Corwen and Ruthin. The V of L succeeded in Parliament, and a year later Llangollen & Corwen and Denbigh Ruthin & Corwen Bills completed a potential GWR route to Rhyl, both receiving Royal Assent, the DR&C on 23 July 1860. Benjamin and Robert Piercy were the DR&C engineers, and Davies and Savin, having put up the Parliamentary deposit for the Bill, were appointed contractors. The first sod was turned by Miss Florence West of Ruthin on 4 September.

Page 69 (*Top*) Dyserth branch steam railmotor at Rhuddlan Road halt, c. 1905; .
(*centre*) Holywell Town, looking down 1 in 27 gradient towards the junction,
thought to be on opening day to passengers, 1 July 1912; (*bottom*) Red Wharf
Bay & Benllech, shortly after opening, 24 May 1909. (*Clwyd Record Office;
Collection L. Ward; Courtesy County Librarian, Anglesey Area Library, Gwynedd*)

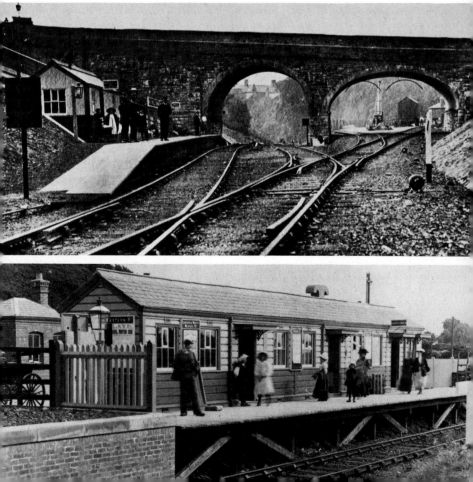

Page 70 (*Top*) Standard and narrow gauge at Port Dinorwic, c.1870s; (*centre*) Caernarvon, looking south, October 1965; (*bottom*) Late 19th century at Peny-groes, with one of the LNWR's numerous DX class 0-6-0 locomotives. (*National Library of Wales, top and bottom; Author*)

In November 1860 the DR&C board, prompted by Savin, sought powers to extend from Denbigh eastwards to Mold and, in opposition to other parties, south-west from Corwen to Bala, whence the projected Merionethshire Railway continued to Dolgellau. That month Davies parted from Savin (p 152), who continued the construction and also negotiations for agreement with the GWR. Thus though the DR&C would serve local purposes as an extension of the V of C, its role as a pawn in strategic railway politics was already defined.

THE GREAT WESTERN AIMS AT RHYL

Chocolate-and-cream at Rhyl—it could have been! In August 1860, noting that Davies and Savin were 'promoters' of the DR&C and virtually controlled the V of C, the GWR decided to make an offer to them to lease both lines. The object was a Great Western express service to a new station at Rhyl. In December, John Williams, a GWR director living on Anglesey, reported on negotiations with Savin over the V of C: '. . . he told me that he and his Friends hold so heavily in the Line that they can control the Company . . . and as a consequence they can put the Screw on them for any purpose . . . they are at daggers drawn and the [V of C] Board are disinclined to do anything which . . . may tend to his advantage'. Williams' separate meetings with Savin and V of C directors and officials were conducted in an extraordinary cloak-and-dagger atmosphere. Telegrams to Williams went under the pseudonym 'Higgins'; other GWR participants took code numbers, so that Euston's minions at Bangor, through which the telegrams passed, would not guess at the intrigue. For the V of C it was deadly serious: 'They are bona fide most desirous to come to terms with us, but feel that they are pinioned by the LNWR at Rhyl . . . if we are obliged to break off with the Corwen the LNWR will assuredly take it up and will thus have them in hand at both ends!' On December 28 Williams reported on projected railways between Mold and Denbigh, one from Savin for the DR&C, and one backed by Euston, either of which would divert the vale's traffic towards Chester, and would interfere with that going south, lessening the DR&C's value to Paddington. Meetings continued, but by February the GWR had mixed feelings. Savin as vendor of the DR&C and power behind the V of C could be the means of getting GWR trains to Rhyl;

his Mold–Denbigh line could render them unprofitable. But it was the V of C which determined the outcome, requiring protection from Euston's wrath and traffic guarantees which Paddington withheld while uncertain of Savin's motives. Growing GWR indifference and promotion of the LNWR-backed Mold & Denbigh Junction Railway resulted in Savin withdrawing his Mold Bill and the whole business was over.

LNWR TAKES CONTROL OF THE V OF C

Though the Mold–Denbigh Bill was before Parliament for the 1861 session (p 76), Euston decided to gain control of the V of C: Denbigh was already linked with the CHR, and further GWR advances would be scotched. In April 1861 the *Railway Times*, sniping at the LNWR's empire-building proclivities, was outspokenly vitriolic on what followed: '. . . the authorities at Euston Square have contrived, through the facile agency of our not over-fastidious negotiator Mr Alderman Bancroft (a gentleman always at Hand when a questionable stroke of business is to be transacted) to embark the company in the Vale of Clwyd to the extent of £21,000 . . .' Bancroft had privately bought out Gardner's V of C holding of £21,000 without telling his bewildered colleagues. The V of C's Bill now went ahead, but without the extension. Savin's Bill passed merely as the Rhyl Bridge Act. Next the LNWR undertook to work the DR&C and V of C as one undertaking, with option of perpetual lease. LNWR directors joined the V of C board in September 1861, Bancroft becoming chairman. To square Hughes, the Foryd extension plans were re-deposited.

FORYD EXTENSION

The V of C Act of 30 June 1862 authorised extension to the Clwyd west shore, an improved junction, and a new pier at the terminus. The $\frac{3}{4}$-mile (1.2km) single track was inspected by Captain Tyler in August 1864. A terminal station, signalling and turntables were lacking, so permission to open was withheld. The V of C August report noted that goods traffic had started. By October 1865 a passenger station had been built, north of the road level-crossing, but the Board of Trade still required a pier platform. Assent to passenger opening came in 1866 but the branch never had regular passenger services; it was retained for freight until closure on 6 April 1959.

OPENING DENBIGH TO CORWEN

LNWR working of the DR&C was confirmed by Act of 1863. From 1 March 1862 V of C trains worked over the $6\frac{3}{4}$ miles (10.8km) from Denbigh to Ruthin, with intermediate stations at Llanrhaiadr and Rhewl. In March 1863 Captain Tyler approved the $9\frac{3}{4}$mile (15.7km) length on to Gwyddelwern. This included gradients of 1 in 50 and heavy works at Eyarth rock cutting where river, road and railway ran closely confined within a gorge, leading to the line's summit 620ft 0in (189m) above sea level where, skirting the westerly flank of Llantisilio Mountain, it crossed the watershed between Clwyd and Dee. Opening, however, fixed for 12 May, was postponed, pending a working agreement with Euston, for reasons apparently attributable to Savin. His ability to 'put the screw on' the V of C now extended to the DR&C. He had paid the Parliamentary deposit, had constructed the line, and had received a heavy shareholding as payment. Though never on the board he exerted an overriding influence; it was mainly with Savin that Euston had negotiated on DR&C matters. But now the DR&C directors were talking of leasing to the LNWR, an eventuality against Savin's interest in controlling this link between the LNWR and GWR. What better retaliation than to prevaricate, to fulfil the contract yet not to the standard—apparently higher than that of the Board of Trade—required by Euston for a branch to its system? Thus not until August 1864 did Captain Tyler report on the remaining 2-mile (3.2km) single line from Gwyddelwern to a temporary terminus at Corwen, near the junction with the Llangollen & Corwen. The principal work was the Corwen viaduct, six 50ft 0in (15.24m) lattice girder spans 30ft 0in (9.1m) above the Dee. The captain required 'the temporary engine shed over the passenger line at Gwyddelwern' to be removed, and refused permission to open. The DR&C shareholders' meeting on 19 September was informed by the frustrated directors of their inability to state when the line would be opened to Corwen, contradicting the prepared half-yearly report which pronounced that it was already in operation. Apparently opening to Corwen temporary station took place on 6 October 1864 (PRO Rail Archives, map of opening dates; *Bradshaw's Shareholders' Guide* for 1865 gives, improbably, 22 September on one page and merely October on another). The ¼-mile (0.4km) through connection to Corwen GWR station (p 138) opened for all traffic on 1 September 1865. Intermediate stations between Ruthin and Corwen were Eyarth, Nantclwyd, Derwen, and Gwyddelwern. Savin used at least two locomotives during construction: an 1860-built Manning Wardle 0–4–0 tender locomotive *Ruthin* (later Cambrian Railways No 2), and the same maker's 1862 0–6–0 saddle tank *Nantclwyd* which eventually ended up on the London & South Western Railway! Denbigh shed was built about 1864.

In October 1864 Savin—not the DR&C board—broke off the leasing negotiations, bringing prompt response from Euston that 'temporary working of the line by the Vale of Clwyd Company until Mr Savin can find his own stock is carried on entirely at Mr Savin's own risk'. But Savin refused to name a date when he would take over, and on the basis of its engineer's report that the DR&C track was in a 'decayed state', the LNWR gave notice in July 1865 that V of C trains would cease working the line. Savin therefore worked the traffic from 1 August, with two hired LNWR locomotives, until 6 February 1866 when, following his bankruptcy, the DR&C board took over. In May the Cambrian sought return of 0–4–2 tender locomotive No 7 *Llanerchydol*, also used by Savin; it reappeared later on the Carnarvonshire Railway (p 99).

In 1866 the DR&C purchased locomotive No 11 (DR&C No 3) from the Mid Wales Railway, a Kitson 0–6–0 goods with 4-wheeled tender. Rolling stock was acquired to replace hired Cambrian vehicles, and a locomotive shed was erected at Ruthin. The Cambrian now threatened action for repayment of hire charges. To avoid seizure, DR&C rolling stock was conveyed to trustees, and in April Thomas Cartwright, DR&C 'Traffic Manager', was appointed Receiver. The company was ripe to fall into the LNWR net, and by this time Euston had full control of the V of C.

LAST YEARS OF THE V OF C . . .

In December 1862 the *Oswestry Advertiser* reported that the V of C was attaching passenger carriages to goods trains, giving 'much increased accommodation, making . . . six trains daily between Rhyl and Denbigh, and five between Ruthin and Rhyl . . . the company do not of course guarantee exact time with the goods trains, having made these arrangements at the request of several inhabitants . . . in the vale'. By 1863 the electric telegraph was installed, and a day mail was conveyed. In 1864 Euston's working and management were put on a statutory basis; amalgamation was effected by Act of 15 July 1867. Taken into LNWR stock were 60 goods wagons and the three locomotives.

. . . AND OF THE DR&C

In January 1867 James Ashbury, influential DR&C shareholder, and Frederick Adolphus Fynney, solicitor and accountant who had acted for the GWR in the 1861 negotiations, set about removing Savin's nominee directors. They also urged repudiation of a proposed amalgamation between the DR&C and the insolvent Mold & Denbigh Junction, to be known as the Mold Denbigh & Corwen Railway, and advocated friendship with Euston. Savin's directors were ousted; by July 1868 Ashbury had control. The opening of the Corwen & Bala and Bala & Dolgelly Railways that year brought an increase in traffic. In 1870 Euston learned that some DR&C trains were entering Denbigh station drawn by GWR engines, resulting in choleric instructions for the practice to cease, coupled with a loan to the DR&C, and beneficial mileage rates. By 1871 the DR&C was out of Chancery. A working agreement from July 1878 brought LNWR directors on to the board. Full vesting was authorised by Act of 3 July 1879. The LNWR took eleven coaching and 55 freight vehicles into stock, as well as four DR&C locomotives (earlier ones had been replaced) viz No 1, a Sharp, Stewart 0-6-0 (originally built for the Furness Railway); No 2, a Wilson 2-4-0 (ex-Shrewsbury & Hereford); No 3, the Mid Wales 0-6-0; and No 4, a Jones & Potts 2-4-0. No 1, as LNWR No 1881, went later to the Cambrian in payment for help when the Llandulas viaduct on the CHR main line failed in 1879 (p 32).

MOLD & DENBIGH JUNCTION RAILWAY

The Mold–Denbigh project supported by Euston in late 1860 was planned for some 17 miles (27.3km) along the narrow valleys of the Alyn and Wheeler, to a 'Y' junction with the V of C near Trefnant, together with a 3¾-mile (6km) cut-off from Bodfari to Denbigh, there to join the DR&C. Once the

LNWR had gained influence over the V of C the scheme lost its appeal, and Euston insisted that the cut-off be abandoned. Shorn of its bargaining counter, the Mold & Denbigh Junction Railway was incorporated by Act of 6 August 1861, its board including the chairman and two directors of the Buckley Railway. The Act required a station at Caerwys, and works connected with the estate of William Barber Buddicom of Penbedw Hall, including artificial cuttings, a carriage drive, and a station at Nannerch. In 1861 Buddicom, one-time locomotive superintendent of the Grand Junction, joined the Buckley board.

Forsaken by the LNWR, the MDJ remained inert throughout 1862–3 while Euston and Paddington battled for the Mold–Wrexham district (p 52). Fearful of its powers lapsing, the MDJ accepted an offer from Richard Samuel France, Shrewsbury mineowner, railway promoter and contractor, to construct the line. George Bellis, MDJ engineer, already acted for the Buckley Railway. France, backed by the Warrant Finance Company, started work in August 1864, receiving preference shares as payment. Rashly, the MDJ promoted several branches in 1865, mostly proving abortive, though a line to Hawarden and altered junctions with the V of C—obviating the need for running powers, then opposed by Euston—were passed; for the 1866 session a 22-mile (35.4km) line to Llandudno was planned by John Ashdown who was also engineer to the Shrewsbury & North Wales (in which France was involved). The Llandudno Bill was withdrawn but the 1866 MDJ Act authorised a line parallel with the Mold Railway to join the WM&CQ, and a branch from Rhydymwyn to near the Loggerheads Mill on the Mold–Ruthin Road. Not authorised were plans for a loop, east of Denbigh, from which a 5½-mile (8.8km) line was to snake south-west to Nantglyn; and a branch from Mold to the Nerquis colliery.

France, who enjoyed the same relationship with the MDJ as did Savin with his companies, suggested completing the doubling of the Mold Railway and inviting the LNWR to work the MDJ. He was however caught short by the 1866 financial crisis and in July the works, almost completed, were suspended. Of £432,000 MDJ capital raised, France had received £430,640. Reporting this, and referring to France, the *Railway Times* rejoiced 'that the collapse will leave the more daring of the speculators thoroughly broken down as well as efficiently exposed'. With works stopped, money short, and appeals to landowners not to press for payment, by Act of 1867 the MDJ nevertheless obtained running powers to Denbigh and over the WM&CQ from the 1866 authorised line, the Wrexham company gaining reciprocal access to Mold. An MDJ Bill to effect amalgamation with the DR&C was withdrawn in March 1868 when London parties appeared willing to put up money to complete construction. June saw negotiations with Euston for working the line, and in October France's contract ended.

A working agreement, dated 12 November 1868 (scheduled to the LNWR Act of 1869), also authorised sale of the partially-built MDJ 'Trefnant branch' between the V of C junction and Denbigh to the LNWR which would, at MDJ expense, double the parallel V of C length instead. That month the tender of Scott & Edwards of Rhyl was accepted for completing the MDJ, and in January 1869 that of Hughes & Son for the stations. March 1869 saw LNWR agreement to the MDJ completing the V of C doubling, instead of paying for it. By August the original line was complete, the Board of Trade inspector commenting that it occupied 'the curious position of being a double line connecting two single ones'. LNWR records state that the company's trains worked the MDJ from 12 September 1869. *Bradshaw's Shareholders' Guide* for 1870 gives 6 September on one page and 11 September on another. The new line, which curved for 15 miles (24.1km) through delightfully sylvan valleys dominated by the Halkyn and Clwydian ranges, gave improved access from Chester to the Clwyd area, with intermediate stations at Rhydymwyn, Nannerch, Caerwys, and Bodfari. The short V of C doubling took five Board of Trade inspections before being pronounced fit for passenger traffic in March 1870. Powers in 1906 and 1914 for a northerly junction curve near Trefnant for through running to Rhyl were not exercised. The MDJ remained independent until passing to the London Midland & Scottish Railway at the 1923 Grouping.

LATER YEARS IN THE CLWYD AREA

Down loops at St Asaph and Trefnant stations received platforms in 1877, and at Ruthin in 1893. At Denbigh the old locomotive shed was replaced in 1870 by one taking four locomotives, while from 1885 a north bay, longer platform, and altered layout permitted an up train to run to one end while a down train ran past to the other. That year the V of C Foryd station closed on the opening of a new Foryd station on the main line. As traffic increased, with trains jockeying for position at Denbigh station, the local council, feeling the county town slighted by the provision of only one-and-a-half platforms, complained. In 1907 Colonel Yorke of the Board of Trade found the station inadequate for traffic, and condemned the practice of backing passing trains into the station alongside the platform in rear of trains already there. The LNWR had a blind spot where Denbigh was concerned; the fine stone exterior (now demolished) remained at variance with the paucity of facilities beyond, and the method of working remained to the end.

On the MDJ, Star Crossing Halt opened in 1914. Sidings were laid serving local industry: at Rhydymwyn in 1873, Nannerch in 1874 and 1877, the Alyn Tin Plate Works near Mold in 1878, Halkyn Lime Works at Rhydymwyn in 1884, Ruby Brick and Tile Works at Rhydymwyn in 1895, North Hendre Lead Works in 1897, Caerwys Cement Works in 1901, and the Partington Steel & Iron Company at Bodfari in 1924; and on the DR&C to the Nantclwyd and Penygraig Lime Works in the 1860s, Dee Clwyd granite quarries at Gwyddelwern in 1891, and in 1924 to the Graig Lelo quarry, south of Derwen.

KINMEL CAMP RAILWAY

An unusual siding was the 3-mile (4.8km) single-track Kinmel Camp 'railway', southwards from the 1885 Foryd station on the CHR to a military camp west of Bodelwyddan church. It opened in 1915 but in 1916–17, to avoid gradients at the St George terminus at the south end, a branch was made to just north of Faenol Bach, terminating with two tracks at a wooden platform whence a lane ran to the camp. Sometime before 1918 the northerly end was diverted to join the V of C near Foryd Junction, providing through running from Rhyl. Mr Roland Parry, who lives nearby, has told how his father recalled an 18-coach train full of soldiers passing through the fields in 1918, when the line was in heavy use. After World War I it was worked by a quarry company near St George, with a green-liveried Hunslet 0–6–0 saddle tank *Margaret*. From 1956 a diesel worked the traffic until closure in 1964.

RUTHIN & CERRIG-Y-DRUDION RAILWAY

For the 1873 session a 16½-mile (26.5km) narrow gauge railway was promoted from Ruthin, via Clywedog Valley, Cyffylliog and Clocaenog Forest, to the unauthorised branch of the North Wales Narrow Gauge Railways (Chapter VII) at Cerrig-y-Drudion. The Bill was withdrawn but powers were obtained by Act of 27 June 1876. Work started in March 1879, but the company failed financially and the line was abandoned in 1884.

CLWYD AREA SERVICES AND CLOSURES

With variations, eight trains ran daily over the V of C, though not all went down to Ruthin or Corwen. One freight worked each way when required, and there were various livestock trains. Fast and slow connecting trains ran between Chester, Mold, Denbigh, and Corwen;. out of nine each way in 1900, five traversed the whole line. Peak services came with the 1930s; in 1934, for instance, 17 trains ran each way on summer weekdays over the V of C and over a dozen on the MDJ. Chester–Mold–Corwen trains mainly changed locomotives at Denbigh.

The picturesque Ruthin–Corwen line closed to passengers from 2 February 1953, though during 1951–1961 it was used by 'Land Cruise' trains operating a tourist circular service, returning via Barmouth and Caernarvon. Denbigh shed closed and Rhyl–Denbigh passenger services ceased on 19 September 1955, intermediate signalboxes and loops being removed a year later. The Chester–Mold–Ruthin passenger and the Ruthin–Corwen freight services lingered on until 30 April 1962. Denbigh to Ruthin closed to freight on 1 March 1965. By then all freight services had ceased except Mold Junction–Rhydymwyn which, with a Rhyl–Denbigh freight, lasted until 1 January 1968. Used again in 1974 for transport of oil line piping, the track was lifted early in 1979. (See also p. 63 and Chapter XV.)

DYSERTH OR CWM BRANCH

In 1864 a 4½-mile (7.2km) freight line was unsuccessfully promoted from Prestatyn on the CHR up the Prestatyn Valley to terminate opposite Cwm church. By Act of 16 July 1866 the LNWR received powers for a branch to the Rhuddlan–Holywell road at Dyserth, serving lead and haematite mines in the valley, which at that time sent their products by the nearby River Clwyd. Thus a further incentive would be the closure of the troublesome Foryd Bridge (rebuilt as a fixed structure in 1880–81). In December 1867 orders were given to complete the first two miles (3.2km), including a long 1 in 45 gradient, to the Talargoch lead mine, and in March 1868 the remainder 'up to Cwm' (the line was called 'Prestatyn and Cwm' though terminating some distance from Cwm village). The 3-mile (4.8km) single track opened for freight on 1 September 1869, with a goods station at Meliden shortly after.

From 28 August 1905 a steam railmotor service took tourists up to the ruined Dyserth castle and the Cwm waterfalls. At Prestatyn, the railmotor ran from the platform to the signalbox, collected the train staff, and reversed onto the branch. Short platforms were provided at Rhuddlan Road (renamed Woodland Park, after a nearby housing estate, in 1923), Meliden, and Dyserth, others opening at Chapel Street in 1906, St Melyd Golf Links 1923, and Allt-y-Graig 1928. Authorised in 1908 and 1915, but not made, was a light railway extension from Dyserth along an old tramway to the Pandy and Marian Mills, thence towards Newmarket village (now Trelawnyd). Passenger services ceased after 20 September 1930, Meliden closed to freight on 1 April 1957, and the whole branch on 4 May 1964. Dyserth quarry traffic reprieved the line as a private siding until 8 September 1973. The rails were lifted in 1980 and Rhuddlan Borough Council later purchased the trackbed. North Clwyd Railway Association has ceased to attempt a reopening.

HOLYWELL RAILWAY

Midway between Flint and Mostyn on the CHR a station was opened in 1848 to serve the town of Holywell, 1½ miles (2.4km) to the south-east and 550ft (167.6m) up on Halkyn Mountain. East of the station the CHR crossed on the level the Holywell Limestone Company's tramway which ran down to the small harbour at Greenfield. In early years the local combination of rich ores, coal and limestone, bad roads and the proximity of the harbour, led to intensive industry of smelting and chemicals. Textiles were produced from the late 1770s, and by the mid-1830s over 800 persons were so employed, with mills powered by steam engines and water wheels. The 5,000 population of 1801 more than doubled by 1851. Thereafter an industrial decline set in as cheaper ores were imported into South Wales and as the benefits of the CHR over the previous advantage of

Holywell's harbour promoted industrial growth further east along Deeside. In 1871 a marked drop in population was noted after transfer of a textile works to Lancashire.

By Act of 29 July 1864 the 2-mile (3.2km) Holywell Railway was authorised along the tramway to a new pier, with connection to the CHR which was to be crossed by bridge, replacing the level-crossing. In 1865 powers were sought for extension to the MDJ at Nannerch to convey Wrexham coal via Holywell harbour. The Bill met successful LNWR opposition. In 1866 and 1867 a 2½-mile (4km) Port of Holywell Railway, with 'wildly erroneous plans' engineered by Charles Crockford, was rejected by the Board of Trade.

The original line was complete by June 1867, when Crockford's crossing on the CHR was closed. Although Euston agreed in 1868 to a platform adjacent to Holywell main line station, the HR was used merely as a lime and cement stone tramway until the 1870s when it lay derelict. There was brief excitement in 1873 when directors of the Mersey Railway promoted two lines: the Liverpool & North Wales from Birkenhead, over the Dee to the HR at Greenfield; and the Holywell & Mold, from Holywell, via Halkyn to the MDJ near Mold. There was Great Western interest in these, and Euston managed to stop them. Royal Assent went instead to the rival Birkenhead Chester & North Wales (p 57).

Choked by undergrowth, the HR was purchased in 1891 by the LNWR. Not until 1902 did it receive further but indecisive consideration, for conversion into an electric tramway. From 5 June 1905 LNWR motor buses had operated between Connahs Quay, Flint, Northop and Mold and on 11 October buses were introduced between Holywell station (soon to be 'Junction') and the town; their success justified reconstruction of the railway. LNWR Acts of 20 July 1906 and 26 July 1907 authorised alterations, and a new curve to the CHR. The 1½-mile (2.4km) single line, with 1 in 27 gradient, and one halt at St Winifride's (sic)—for visitors to the famous well—opened for passengers and freight to the small Holywell Town station on 1 July 1912, passenger trains being worked by a tank engine and two picnic saloons converted to form an auto-train. Sixteen weekday trains ran each way. By World War II there were as many as 29 on Saturdays and 17 on Sundays. Decline set in with road competition; the line closed on 6 September 1954, except to Crescent Siding which served textile mills until 11 August 1957.

CHAPTER VI

Anglesey Branches

Before discussing the Anglesey branches we must dispose of a myth : that there was a railway on the island before the coming of the Chester & Holyhead. Though the Anglesey Railway Company was incorporated in 1812 for a mineral line from Holland Arms to a proposed dock at Red Wharf Bay, research by the late Kenneth Brown (*Railway Magazine* July 1940 and January 1941) proved that it was not constructed.

ANGLESEY CENTRAL RAILWAY

In the 1860s the port of Amlwch on the north coast of Anglesey had a population of some 6,000. To the south lay Parys Mountain, where silver, copper, zinc, alum, and sulphur had been mined since the 1760s, while south again were the small towns of Llanerchymedd and Llangefni. In 1852 the CHR surveyed a branch to Llangefni, but nothing came of the idea, nor of a local scheme in 1858 for a railway from Gaerwen on the CHR through Llangefni to Amlwch, thence to Cemaes and Llanrhyddlad to rejoin the CHR at Valley. Promoters of an Anglesey Central Railway, from Gaerwen to Amlwch, approached the LNWR in 1862 as to working the line but were rebuffed. Nevertheless, they obtained Parliamentary powers on 13 July 1863; in 1864 a deviation was authorised at Gaerwen. By October 1864 the contractors, Dickson and Russell, had almost completed work as far as Llangefni; the LNWR engineer was then authorised to form a junction at Gaerwen, at ACR expense, and in December Euston approved a 'temporary arrangement for the use of Gaerwen station and supply of stock'.

The first 4½ miles (7.2km) opened on 16 December 1864, though not for public use; according to *Herepath's Journal* a special train, carrying directors and friends, left Bangor at

10.00 am, reaching Llangefni—12 miles (19.3km) from Bangor
—in 37 minutes. The contractors gave luncheon to 100 guests
in the Bull Hotel, Llangefni, with further refreshments at the
British Hotel, Bangor, after arriving back at 5.30 pm. Captain
Rich inspected the line to Llangefni in February and March
1865. Single throughout, with an intermediate station at Holland
Arms, it left the CHR up line at Gaerwen; though 'the junction
is only intended for goods', passengers used the north side of the
up main line platform.

Passenger services commenced from Gaerwen to a temporary
station at Llangefni on 12 March 1865, worked by an LNWR
locomotive and carriages on loan. Apparently the contractors
had a stake in the ACR, whose minute books cannot be traced,
for in August 1865 Russell fruitlessly asked the LNWR to adopt
the line. In November the ACR sought powers to lease or sell
to the LNWR, or to Russell's partner, John Dickson. Included
in the Bill, but dropped later, was a 4⅛-mile (6.6km) branch
from Rhosgoch to Cemaes Bay, west of Amlwch. Traffic returns
for six months to December 1865 were satisfactory: 18,839
passengers and 3,866 tons of freight had been carried, exclusive
of livestock.

On 26 January 1866 Captain Rich inspected the 3½ miles
(5.6km) to Llanerchymedd, single throughout, with sidings.
Llangefni temporary station was abandoned, the new station
being ½-mile (0.8km) further on. The ruling gradient was 1 in
67 and the curves sharp. 'I would, therefore, recommend that
the line is worked at moderate speed. There are no turntables,
and the Company propose . . . to work only with tank engines
to Mr Fairlie's patent and to put up the turntables when the
line is completed.' The section opened to all traffic on 1 February
1866. Though the captain noted only the two end stations on
the section as existing in January, by April–June 1866 *Bradshaw*
showed the intermediate one, Llangwyllog, to be open, the
service then being of four trains each way on weekdays, connecting with main line trains at Gaerwen. The ACR Act of
1866 authorised agreement with Dickson for lease or working,
or with the LNWR for lease or sale. In September Dickson
informed Euston that he would work the traffic; his request to
be allowed to run trains through to Bangor was not granted.

The last 6¾ miles (10.8km), again single with sidings, and an
intermediate station at Rhosgoch, was inspected by Major Rich
in January 1867. He found it incomplete. The necessary works

having been done, the section opened to passengers on 3 June 1867, final approval being confirmed by fast-rising Lt-Col Rich on 31 August. According to reminiscences of Mr O. Dew (*LMSR Magazine* 1926) who worked, so he claimed, a 20-hour day as first stationmaster at Amlwch, the line carried freight as early as 10 September 1866, two wagons of coal and two of flour being the first arrivals at Amlwch, the flour being discharged on the ground as there were no facilities for dealing with it! From the first there was considerable copper ingot traffic from Parys Mountain to Birmingham, only terminated on closure of the smelting works. For years there was a regular traffic in artificial manures.

During construction, Dickson employed an 0–4 + 4–0 Fairlie locomotive, *Mountaineer*, built by James Cross of St Helens in 1866, in use on the ACR as early as April that year, and probably moved to the Neath & Brecon Railway by October 1867, or earlier. (Dickson also worked, for a short time, the Neath & Brecon whose chairman, William Laurence Banks, was on the ACR board, as was Richard Hanbury Miers, the N&B's first chairman.) Dickson failed financially in 1868, and that July the N&B noted interest in a Hawthorn 0–6–0 well tank *Miers* which, as *Anglesea* (*sic*), the N&B had been trying to get returned from the ACR. According to Dew, it was this locomotive which worked the ACR trains, 'but there was continuous trouble with her'. After further negotiations for the LNWR to work the line had failed, hire was resumed of an LNWR locomotive and carriages. During 1871–3 up and down refuge sidings were put in at Gaerwen with a crossover for freight workings between the down LNWR line and the siding at the back of the ACR platform.

THE LNWR TAKES OVER

The hiring arrangement continued until January 1867 when, following a court case concerning sale or hire of rolling stock, the ACR was informed that the LNWR could no longer lend locomotive power. Three alternatives were offered: outright purchase by Euston; a proper working agreement; or the ACR might buy 'the Engine and Carriages now on the line'. Purchase was agreed for £80,000, an LNWR Act of 1876 giving Euston possession on 1 July. The state of the line reflected the ACR's longtime financial troubles: bridges and culverts were in 'fair' condition, the stations dirty, the fences decayed, rails required replacing, sleepers were rotten, and the ballast was soft and shaley. In contrast the telegraph, erected by the Post Office, which had a right of way for its line to Ireland and allowed the railway one wire, was brightly modern.

In 1877 a loop line and station building improvements were approved for Llangefni, while in 1878 a refuge siding went in at Llanerchymedd, a locomotive shed and sidings at Amlwch. Tragedy struck in the early hours of 29 November 1877 : during the night a thunderstorm had rumbled over Anglesey and heavy rains swelled the Caedro woollen mill dam beyond bursting point, the torrent sweeping away a culvert and part of the line at Caermawr Bridge, about a mile (1.6km) north of Llanerchy-medd. The 4.25 am from Bangor (locomotive, composite, three thirds, brake third, and brake van) fell into the gap, killing the driver, stoker and a ganger. A direct double junction at Gaerwen, and new station buildings at Holland Arms, Llangwyllog, and Rhosgoch, 'in lieu of the existing wooden sheds', were ordered in 1882. A new waiting shed, waiting room, lamp room, and an extension to the platform, with covering, were built at Amlwch in 1883–4. The train staff-and-ticket system was superseded by absolute block working in 1886 and by the electric staff in 1894. Platforms were extended at Llangefni in 1887, Holland Arms, Llangwyllog, and Rhosgoch in 1890. A footbridge was ordered for the Bangor end of Gaerwen station in 1911, while in 1914 Llangwyllog received a new passing loop and up platform.

PROPOSED BRANCHES 1883–1909

In 1883 a proposed Anglesey & Caernarvon Direct Railway, from Gaerwen to Caernarvon, via Newborough and a ferry crossing, failed in Parliament, as did an 8½-mile (13.6km) South Anglesey Light Railway from Gaerwen to Newborough in 1909.

The castle town of Beaumaris just missed being connected to the railway system. A private coach operated to Bangor station, and in the late 1870s Euston investigated a branch line, only to be disappointed by a traffic survey. In 1880 a proposed steam tramway also came to nothing. Seven years later, at local insistence, the LNWR again considered a branch, but engineering problems at the proposed Beaumaris station site caused its abandonment. Between 1 June 1901 and 30 September 1910 the LNWR operated a Bangor–Beaumaris omnibus service.

RED WHARF BAY LINE

In 1897 the LNWR planned two new railways on Anglesey. One, from Menai Bridge to Beaumaris, was dropped in favour of a tramway—the Llanfair & Beaumaris Light Railway—which was rejected by the Light Railway Commissioners on the grounds that the road was too narrow. The other was for a line from Llanfair PG to the northerly end of Benllech Sands. Tourist traffic was prospering, and on Anglesey's east coast Red Wharf Bay and Benllech Sands, unsullied by development which might have been their lot had the 1812 colliery railway been built, stood open and inviting, safe for bathing and boating, and within a short distance from Bangor. W. Jones, MP for North Caernarvon urged a connection to Llangefni on the ACR. A compromise resulted in the junction at Holland Arms, the route between there and Pentraeth closely following that of the 1812 scheme. When by the LNWR Act of 1 August 1899 the 6¾-mile (10.8km) Red Wharf Bay Railway was authorised, however, the terminus was not the thriving village of Benllech, but near the Ship Inn at Red Wharf, of tourist interest only, but saving a mile (1.6km) of construction. Even this might have brought some commercial success but, to save money, and in an ineffective attempt to serve both Red Wharf and Benllech, a 1¾-mile (2.8km) deviation was authorised in 1900 whereby the railway terminated merely at a lonely crossroads, over ½-mile (0.8km) west of Red Wharf and a mile (1.6km) south of Benllech. The consequences were to be felt as soon as the railway was challenged by the motor vehicle. In the early 1900s, however, the LNWR was heavily involved in expenditure elsewhere, particularly on the North Wales main line, so Red Wharf had to wait. In 1905 it was agreed the line should be more cheaply built as a light railway. Connections went in at Holland Arms in June 1907 for construction trains. That year saw archaeological discoveries in a cutting near Pentraeth : 'two human skeletons, one doubled up and the other outstretched', some urns and 'a bronze spear or dagger-head'. The relics were sent to Bangor University, at which the LNWR solicitor became rather pompous : the finds were the company's though he doubted 'whether there can be any legal property in human remains, however ancient'. The dispute was resolved by donating the lot to the new county museum.

Page 87 (*Top*) Fairlie locomotive *Merddin Emrys* on Festiniog Railway workmen's train at Duffws, c.1880. Incline in background; (*centre*) Turn of the century on the Bala-Festiniog line. 517 class 0-4-2 tank at Trawsfynydd; (*bottom*) Class 25 diesel No 25156 on freight at Blaenau, August 1979. Line to Trawsfynydd, and North Western hotel in background. (*National Library of Wales, top and centre; Robert H. E. Baughan*)

Page 88 (*Top*) Llangollen, looking south, July 1963; (*centre*) Approaching Bala Junction from Ruabon, May 1963; (*bottom*) 5700 class 0-6-0PT No 4683 running round junction shuttle train at Bala station, May 1963. (*Author*)

June 1908 saw inspection of the 4¾ miles (7.6km) from Holland Arms to Pentraeth, single track with a ruling gradient of 1 in 88. There was a new passing loop at Holland Arms with a second platform for the branch train, passengers crossing the line on the level from the Amlwch branch platform, and three low, short, single platform halts with shelters: Ceint (near the home of the Tudors); Rhyd-y-Saint, and Pentraeth, the temporary terminus. The line opened to Pentraeth on 1 July 1908 with five weekdays trains each way, an additional one each way on Thursdays, and a daily goods. Colonel Druitt described the branch train:

> For the present an engine and one or two coaches as required are to be used on the line with a centre gangway and only one entrance and exit, as the platforms are short ones. To avoid having to run the engine round the train a compartment is provided for the driver at the rear of the end carriage and means provided for him to regulate the steam and brakes from that end.

It was not a railmotor, as on other branches, but an auto-train (or 'motor train' in LNWR timetables) consisting of a Webb 2-4-0 tank, and either one or two coaches converted from old picnic saloons. (A photograph of the train, reputedly taken at Holland Arms on the opening day, was reproduced in the *Railway Magazine* of May 1914.)

Pentraeth to Red Wharf Bay, with intermediate halt at Llanbedr Goch, opened on 24 May 1909. Red Wharf Bay & Benllech station had a single platform and the only signal on the branch, a fixed distant to warn drivers that they were approaching the terminus. There were six trains each way on Thursdays, five each way on other weekdays only, later increased to seven up and down, with an extra one on Mondays and Fridays.

LATER YEARS AND CLOSURES

The Red Wharf Bay passenger service succumbed to road competition on 22 September 1930. Mr R. Dyson (*Railway Magazine* 1930) has described how stopping trains frequently merely slowed at the halts, continuing on their way if there were no passengers to set down or pick up. 'Several of the trains take a diversion to the market town of Llangefni, after calling at Holland Arms, to which latter place they return and then continue their journey forward, an extra mile or two with no excess fare!' Others occasionally ran through to Gaerwen. For some time there was a thrice-weekly goods service, but the line was closed completely on 3 April 1950 and the track lifted three years later.

As for the Amwch branch, in the late 1880s some six trains ran each way on weekdays only, the branch train occasionally backing to the Gaerwen down main platform after departure of a Holyhead connection for ease of loading. Through trains from Bangor would run onto the branch and set back into the bay for the up connection. In early years only one train operated but later the traffic required two; from July 1914 trains passed at Llangwyllog, the only other station where there were two platforms. Much of the motor-train work was between Gaerwen and Llangefni only. At peak holiday times ordinary passenger trains supplemented the service. Amlwch shed closed in 1931.

The Anglesey branches did not attract any new development, and as in many other small Welsh towns the population trend was downwards. Llangefni, with 1,696 in 1861, fell to 1,563 by 1881, though rising to over 1,700 by 1901 and thereafter holding fairly steady. Amlwch, which had grown with the winnings from Parys Mountain, declined from the 1850s following scarcity of ore in the copper mines, many of the men finding employment on the railway and harbour works at Holyhead. Thus the population of 6,285 in 1831 was down to 5,949 by 1861 and under 3,000 by 1901. The 1971 figure was 3,681.

In October 1952 a ¾-mile (1.2km) light railway for Associated Ethyl opened from the end of the Amlwch branch to a new factory. On 4 August 1952 Holland Arms station closed to all traffic. The Amlwch branch was one of those selected for trials of a prototype AEC lightweight diesel train in May and June of 1953. Diesel multiple-units were introduced from 28 May 1956 and for a time seemed to prove popular. Steam working was reinstated from Christmas 1961, remaining—with occasional dmu workings—until inevitable closure to freight and passengers on 1 and 7 December 1964 respectively. The branch remains open to serve Associated Octel at Amlwch (See Chapter XV.)

CHAPTER VII

North and West Caernarvonshire

The setting for the railways described in this chapter is the most beautiful in Wales: a dramatic mixture of mountain, valley, and pasture. To the north is the Menai Strait with Bangor and Caernarvon, whence south-westwards, interrupted by three great outliers of the Snowdon chain—Garnedd-goch, Bwlch Mawr, and Yr Eifl—the coastal plain runs by Porth Dinllaen to the Nevin Peninsula. To the south lie Tremadoc Bay and the coastal towns of Pwllheli, Criccieth and Portmadoc; and in the east the great barrier of Snowdonia, cut by the north-west to south-east passes of Nant Ffrancon from Capel Curig to Bangor; Llanberis from Beddgelert and Capel Curig via the Nant Gwynant to Caernarvon; and the more hilly route from Beddgelert via Betws Garmon. South of Caernarvon the country rises gently to the saddle at Pant Glas between Garnedd-goch and Bwlch Mawr to provide a route through to Tremadoc Bay. In the early 1800s slate quarrying near Bangor and Llanberis, slate and copper in the Vale of Nantlle lying east-west on the northern flank of Garnedd-goch, was a rapidly growing industry, output being shipped from the Menai to provide paving and roofing for the swelling population of industrial England. An early trickle of tourists, intent on the grand tour of Snowdonia, were patronising Bangor and Caernarvon, while the increasing importance of Irish communication was focussing sharp London eyes upon the quiet, natural harbour at Porth Dinllaen. In the mountains and hills were forestry, and sheep by the hundred thousand, and in the gentle lands south of Caernarvon cattle and crops.

FIASCO OF THE NORTH WALES RAILWAY

A projected railway in the 1830s along the North Wales Coast to Porth Dinllaen did not mature, but November 1844 saw two

schemes: a Porthdynllaen Carnarvon & Bangor Railway (sic);
and a Bangor & Carnarvon Railway, with a branch to a pier
in the Menai Strait at Bangor. Less the pier, these united as the
28½-mile (45.8km) North Wales Railway, engineered by Sir John
Rennie and Thomas Page, from Bangor to the east side of
Caernarvon, thence by the expensive coastal route on the sea-
ward side of Yr Eifl to Porth Dinllaen. Its object was to develop
Irish traffic through the port, making unnecessary the continuation of the CHR to Holyhead. Unperturbed, the CHR proceeded with its Holyhead line, supporting the NWR as a useful
feeder, and counter to a Bill backed by the GWR in November
1845 for a broad gauge Worcester & Porth Dynllaen Railway,
surveyed by Brunel. The W&PD progressed in Parliament and
frightened CHR shareholders, but was withdrawn after the
Gauge Commissioners had advocated restricting spread of the
broad gauge. Also abortive was a standard gauge Great Welsh
Junction Railway, engineer Sir John Rennie, with lines from
Bangor and Porth Dinllaen joining to continue through Harlech
and Dolgellau to Shrewsbury, Hereford and Monmouth,
followed by a sweep through South Wales to Pembroke.

The North Wales Railway received Royal Assent on 21 July
1845, but within a year the company had lost credibility, after
deputy chairman William Chadwick had saucily loaned NWR
money to the Richmond Railway, of which he was chairman. A
general deterioration of NWR affairs led to wide and severe
criticism, and in 1849 Chadwick was forced to produce the
company's books. They were found to be, illegally, in code, which
when deciphered revealed gross financial manipulation. The
CHR refused to help, and the NWR was finished.

BANGOR & CAERNARVON RAILWAY

The CHR now showed interest in other projects for a Bangor–
Caernarvon branch, but the LNWR opposed CHR financial
involvement and insisted construction should be by private
parties. By December 1849 the scheme was restricted to a branch
to Port Dinorwic – on the Menai Strait midway between
Bangor and Caernarvon – to collect slate from the Padarn
Railway (p 100). Not until after August 1850, when Peto joined
the CHR board, were independent promoters encouraged to
plan a line to Caernarvon, leaving the CHR some ¾-mile
(1.2km) east of the Britannia Bridge. The Bangor & Caernarvon

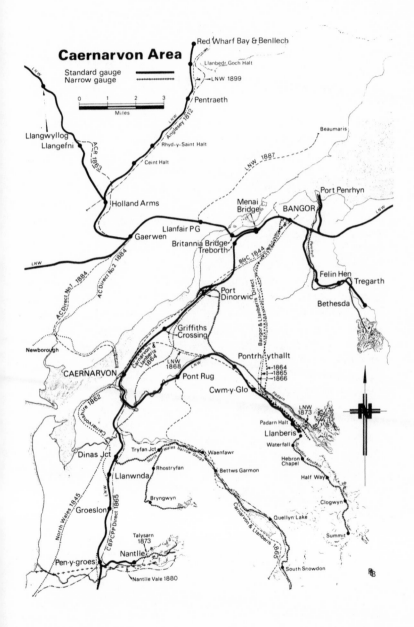

Caernarvon Area

Standard gauge
Narrow gauge

0   1   2   3
Miles

Red Wharf Bay & Benllech
Llanbedr Goch Halt
LNW 1899
Pentraeth
Anglesey 1812
Rhyd-y-Saint Halt
Ceint Halt
Beaumaris
LNW 1887
Llangwyllog
Llangefni
A.C.R 1863
Port Penrhyn
Holland Arms
Menai Bridge
BANGOR
LNW
Llanfair P.G
Gaerwen
Britannia Bridge
Treborth
B&C 1844
Felin Hen
Tregarth
A.C Direct No.1 1884
A.C Direct No.2 1884
LNW
Port Dinorwic
Bethesda
Bangor & Llanberis Direct
Newborough
Griffiths Crossing
Carnarvon & Llanberis 1864
LNW 1868
Pontrhythallt
1864
1865
1866
CAERNARVON
Pont Rug
Cwm-y-Glo
Padarn
LNW 1873
Carnarvon 1852
Padarn Halt
Llanberis
Waterfall
Dinas Jct
Tryfan Jct
North Wales Narrow gauge
Waenfawr
Hebron Chapel
Llanwnda
Rhostryfan
Bettws Garmon
Mouldas
Half Way
Bryngwyn
Clogwyn
North Wales 1845
Groeslon
C&BP/CPP Direct 1865
Carnarvon & Llanberis 1865
Quellyn Lake
Summit
Talysarn 1873
Pen-y-groes
Nantlle
South Snowdon
Nantlle Vale 1880

Railway Act of 20 May 1851 authorised the CHR to work the line. The contractors, M'Cormick and Holme, also principal B&C shareholders, were responsible for construction of the CHR's ill-starred and uncompleted Britannia Hotel and Park, overlooking the Menai Strait. In November 1851 they offered to extend the branch to the Caernarvon quays but instead the terminus was sited at the north end of the town, 8½ miles (13.6km) from Bangor. Work concentrated on reaching Port Dinorwic; an LNWR locomotive first reached the port, and slate traffic started, on 1 March and 10 March 1852 respectively. The branch, single track on land bought for double, had one large work, the 497yd (455m) Vaynol tunnel. The remaining single line to Caernarvon opened to passengers on 1 July, and freight on 10 August, 1852, leaving a mile (1.6km) of the Port Dinorwic line as a branch: 'Port Siding'. In 1854 the B&C was leased to the CHR, and later to the LNWR which absorbed it in 1867.

During 1853 there were four weekday trains each way and two on Sundays, with one intermediate B&C station at Port Dinorwic. Mail trains started from 1 October 1854, leaving Bangor after arrival of the London night mail, and returning before departure of the up mail. In 1854 a station opened at Griffiths Crossing; and Treborth in 1855, only to close about the same time as Britannia Bridge station on the CHR, and then re-open in 1858. By the 1860s there were six weekday trains each way, and three on Sundays. In 1861 the population of the Caernarvon district, administrative centre for the area, was 8,512. The railway promoted growth; a decade later it was over 11,000. Thereafter the population increased slowly over the years, the town becoming a tourist centre of importance, passengers travelling from Bangor being treated to fine views of the Menai Strait and Anglesey.

Avoidance of main line facing points led to an unusual layout at Menai Bridge station which opened at the junction in 1858: the single-track branch ran to the south face of the southerly platform, and then crossed over the CHR down line on the level to make a trailing junction with the up. A trailing cross-over west of the station from the down main to the branch permitted Bangor to Caernarvon trains to run through and then set back into the branch platform. On 9 May 1865 a Caernarvon to Bangor train (locomotive, van and four carriages) left the branch platform against the signal, and while crossing to the up

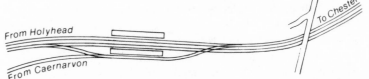

Sketch reconstructing trailing junctions from description in Board of Trade report on accident on 9 May 1865

main line collided with the locomotive of an approaching down Holyhead passenger train. Twenty-five passengers were injured. Not until 1870 was the track layout altered, with a direct double junction and an additional platform. In 1871 powers were obtained to double the B&C: Menai Bridge–Treborth, and Port Dinorwic–Caernarvon, were completed in 1872; the block system followed in 1873; and Treborth–Port Dinorwic, including a second bore for Vaynol tunnel on the down side, and a new station at Port Dinorwic, south of the old, opened in 1874.

SOUTH OF CAERNARVON

By Act of 20 May 1825 the Nantlle Railway Company was incorporated for a tramroad down the valley from copper mines and slate quarries in the Vale of Nantlle to Penygroes, and then north to the quays below the walls of Caernarvon castle, where the River Seiont reaches the Menai Strait. The line, engineered by George Stephenson and his brother Robert, was some nine miles (14.4km) long, of 3ft 6in (107cm) gauge, and opened in 1828.

In 1852 there were plans for a Carnarvon & Pormadoc Railway, but it was not until 1857 that Edward Preston, lessee of the Nantlle Railway, sought support for a Carnarvonshire Railway linking the two towns, using some of the Nantlle formation. With dangerous curves and steep gradients, the Nantlle then operated four passenger trains each way daily, worked by eight horses; four others performed duties including the connecting Portmadoc–Penygroes omnibus. Despite Preston's assurances that the LNWR and CHR were not financially involved in his Carnarvonshire Railway, worried shareholders of both publicly probed his influence with the CHR board. In

the *Railway Times*, March 1858, *Old Suffering Shareholder*
asked 'whose are the horses and carts used during the winter
months (when the passenger traffic on the Nantlle is reduced
to almost nothing . . .) to convey parcels, goods, and empty
packages to and from the Bangor and Carnarvon station to the
shops and private houses of the inhabitants of Carnarvon?'.
And 'will he explain', demanded *Scrutator* that month, 'who
the Mr Preston is who is reported . . . as defending the Chester
and Holyhead in an action brought against them for damaging
a leg of mutton and five fowls – whether it is himself or another
Mr Preston who is thus doing the legal business of the Company . . .'.

On 15 May 1858 the *Railway Times*, its knife into the LNWR
and CHR, made a prediction startling for its accuracy, and
worth quoting as a cynical summary of the inaugural proceed-
ings of many a new railway scheme.

The denoument of the plot is at hand. A public meeting is to
be held at Criccieth on the 25th instant, in pursuance of
resolutions passed at a meeting of the 'Directors of the
Carnarvonshire Provisional Company!' held at Port Madoc
on the 28th April. This will be a farce with . . . a few Joneses
and Williamses, local celebrities of good standing in the
county, of highly respectable character, and of an agricultural
and unsuspicious turn of mind; next, a few master-minds –
just one or two – of directorial experience in railway matters,
and influence with adjoining companies, sufficient to keep the
board in hand, and *manage* the concern; we shall next have a
staff of officers ready to do their master's business, and keep
his counsel; and, lastly, two or three contractors, immense
capitalists, although unknown in the moneyed world, who will
appear in the share list as (normal) contributors for £20,000,
£30,000, or £50,000, a piece! We need not doubt, under
these circumstances, that the line will be made, or that the
London and North-western shareholders will, in due time, be
called upon, for the sake of the 'connexion', to make the most
costly part of the line – the 'Junction', as Mr Preston calls it –
through the town of Carnarvon, and ultimately to lease the
whole concern.

While this was coming to the boil, November 1858 saw a
Llyfni Vale Railway and Harbour Bill, for a 3ft 6in (107cm)
line from the Nantlle quarries to a new harbour at Pont Llyfni,
west of Penygroes. The scheme was rejected, and again in 1860.

For the 1861 session the Aberystwith & Welch Coast Bill included a railway from Afon Wen to the B&C at Caernarvon. This was dropped by agreement with the Nantlle in January 1861, and a Portmadoc & Porthdynllaen Bill, with a Penygroes branch, was withdrawn. A Nantlle Bill for 1861, aiming to thwart the West Midland's Shrewsbury–Portmadoc scheme (p 141) with improvements including change of gauge and use of locomotives, was withdrawn when the WM line failed. The Nantlle was still running trains: on 15 June 1861 the *Railway Times* reported a recent derailment when a train and two horses had fallen down an embankment, killing a woman and injuring several people. In November Thomas Savin and Benjamin Piercy, who had signed the agreement not to trespass towards Carnarvon, nevertheless promoted a Bill for the $27\frac{5}{8}$-mile (44.4km) Carnarvonshire Railway, from a junction with the B&C, and running south-west across the harbour mouth before turning south-east to join the Nantlle route at Llanwnda, thence through Penygroes to the coast at Afon Wen, and on to Portmadoc. The incensed Nantlle accused them of bad faith, re-deposited its Bill, and in March 1862 additionally suggested an A&WC extension to Penygroes and withdrawal of the Carnarvonshire's Bill. But the CR measure, with greater local support, received Royal Assent on 29 July 1862.

Because A&WC directors could not agree on priorities, the Carnarvonshire works were delayed until 1864 when Savin undertook to construct the line. North of Penygroes was to be on the Nantlle formation, and in 1865 the newly formed Cambrian Railways Company, into which the A&WC had amalgamated, and then constructing the Aberystwyth–Pwllheli line, agreed to make the Afon Wen–Portmadoc section. That year saw rejection of a Carnarvon Beddgelert & Portmadoc & Carnarvon Penygroes & Pwllheli Direct Bill, for two lines totalling 44 miles (70.8km): from the B&C at Caernarvon via the Nantlle to Bontnewydd, Betws Garmon and Beddgelert, whence the Glaslyn was followed to Portmadoc; and from Bontnewydd along the Nantlle to Penygroes, then west to join the old North Wales route and south to Pwllheli. By February 1866 the Carnarvonshire line was advanced such that 'an engine runs over it from Afon Wen to Penygroes'—possibly *Enterprise* (p 150)—and the Nantlle's gauge had been converted between Penygroes and the River Seiont. Failure of the banking house of Overend Gurney & Company, and Savin's bankruptcy, compelled the board in October to seek amalgamation with the Cambrian and Nantlle Railways. In fact, Savin was still active; on 6 September 1866 he ran an excursion from Portmadoc to Caernarvon when the line was still awaiting Board of Trade inspection. There was a derailment at Brinkir, killing six passengers. Points had been tampered with, but the coroner's jury found the company not to blame.

Major Rich inspected the Carnarvonshire Railway in October 1866. The line, $17\frac{1}{8}$ miles (27.5km), was single, with works for double. The Caernarvon terminus was at Pant, just south of the Seiont. Intermediate stations were at Pwllheli Road, an isolated site with self-explanatory title but later renamed Llanwnda; Groeslon, on the Portmadoc Road, serving Groeslon village and Glynllifon Park, the seat of Lord Newborough; Penygroes, for the Vale of Nantlle; and Brinkir (Bryncir), where the railway turned away from the Portmadoc Road to follow the little River Wen to the station on the seashore which took its name. Because of incomplete works consent was withheld, and again in December. By that time the Cambrian's affairs were in chaos and the company was bankrupt, leaving in question the Carnarvonshire's hopes of amalgamation.

As with other companies run by his nominees, Savin remained in control, and on 9 April 1867 the Carnarvonshire board offered him the working of the line. Complaints by Nantlle quarry owners of delays due to break of gauge again postponed the opening while Colonel Rich inspected the Nantlle. He learned that Savin had purchased Nantlle shares and worked that line up to 1864 when he commenced altering the gauge. He had given notice in June 1865 of withdrawal of passenger services; and from 6 August 1866 the freight horse haulage had been replaced by locomotive power between Tyddyn, $\frac{3}{4}$-mile (1.2km) north of Penygroes, and Coed Helen, near Pant. With the Nantlle now in three sections, two short lengths of 3ft 6in (107cm) gauge at either end of just under five miles (8km) of standard gauge, and with narrow gauge trucks aboard standard gauge wagons between Tyddyn and Pant, delays, breakages and pilfering were rife, and traffic was reverting to road. The colonel recommended standard gauge throughout, though eastwards of Talysarn depot in the Vale of Nantlle it should remain 3ft 6in, within which the quarry owners might lay a third rail so as to make a 2ft 0in (61cm) gauge tramroad – the quarry system's gauge. The Nantlle, however, had no funds.

On 25 July 1867 two Carnarvonshire Acts together confirmed deviations made in the line, granted reciprocal running powers with the Cambrian between Caernarvon, Portmadoc, and Pwllheli, and vested the Nantlle in the Carnarvonshire undertaking. Two Carnarvonshire debenture holders agreed to finance a 5-year hire-purchase agreement for locomotives and rolling stock, during the currency of which they would control the board. The Carnarvonshire Railway opened on 2 September 1867 between Pant and Afon Wen, and until 10 October, when the Cambrian opened to Pwllheli the CR trains, three each way on weekdays only, continued over that company's line on to Criccieth, Portmadoc and Penrhyndeudraeth. There was a new station at Chwilog; stations were ordered for Pant Glas and Llangybi in December 1869, and Ynys in July 1872.

Services were worked at first with Cambrian locomotives by agreement dated 14 September 1867 : 0–4–2 tender locomotive No 7 *Llanerchydol* (p 153) was hired from 11 September, and 2–4–0 tank No 59 *Seaham* (built in 1866 by Sharp, Stewart) from 16 September; it is not clear what hauled the trains for the first nine days or so. The hire-purchase agreement provided for four carriages, four vans, and 58 wagons, already in use; and two locomotives, eight carriages and four cattle trucks on order. The first CR locomotive, apparently named *Glynllfni*, a Sharp, Stewart 2–4–0 tender type arrived about May 1868. In June the CR board noted that hire of *Llanerchydol* had ceased, and in July that *Pioneer*, seemingly on private hire, was no longer required. A second, similar, Sharp, Stewart was delivered in December 1868, after which a further locomotive, presumably *Seaham*, return to the Cambrian.

THE LNWR TAKES CONTROL

Following the *Railway Times* prediction, by 1868 Euston was involved with the link to the B&C at Caernarvon. Early in March 1869 three CR directors resigned, transferring their shares to LNWR directors. The LNWR's Hedworth Lee was appointed engineer, and Martin Smith (ex-V of C) became manager of the Carnarvonshire and Llanberis lines (p 102). By Act of 1870 the reciprocal running powers were cancelled and the CR vested in the LNWR after which CR vehicles, repainted in LNWR livery, were confined to the Carnarvonshire lines until going into general stock in August 1871. Locomotives Nos 1 and 2 received respective LNWR numbers 1790–1; in 1872 they were sold to the Malines–Terneuzen Railway.

In 1870 powers were obtained for a new junction at Penygroes, while the remainder of the Nantlle was converted to standard gauge. By December 1871 a single-platform station, goods shed, and turntable (removed 1901) were being erected at Talysarn, henceforth known at Nantlle. The 1¾-mile (2.2km) single-track branch opened for minerals from 1 August, and passengers on 1 October 1872, with six weekday trains each way and two extra on Saturdays and Caernarvon fair days. The Penygroes station was that which had stood at Pant, now redundant (p 103); a permanent station opened in 1878, with a footbridge in 1883. Eastwards of Nantlle the old quarry line remained horse-worked, eventually passing as such into ownership of British Railways! In 1893 up freight loops at Brynkir and Dinas Junction (p 108) were lengthened and given platforms, while a loop and up platform went in at Llangybi in 1914–15.

PADARN RAILWAY

Either side of Elider Fawr in Snowdonia, lie two vast slate quarries: the Penrhyn at Bethesda, and the Dinorwic above Llyn Padarn in the beautiful Llanberis Pass. In 1824 the Assheton Smiths, the Dinorwic quarry owners, built a 7-mile (11.2km) 2ft 0in (61cm) gauge tramroad, with inclined planes, via Deiniolen to Port Dinorwic on the Menai Strait. To avoid the inclines, a 6⅝-mile (10.6km) 4ft 0in (122cm) gauge line, known as the Padarn Railway, running alongside the lake and then by Pontrhythallt and Bethel to Port Dinorwic, opened on 3 March 1843. From December 1849 horse traction was ousted by Horlock 0–4–0 tender locomotives *Fire Queen* and *Jenny Lind*, replaced by Hunslet 0–6–0 side tanks *Dinorwic* (1882) and *Pandora* (1886). Another Hunslet, *Velinheli*, arrived in 1895. Quarry and port had its own 1ft 10¾in (58cm) gauge tramroad system, worked by a fleet of little 0–4–0 locomotives, narrow gauge slate trucks travelling between Dinorwic and the Menai two abreast on flat wagons of the Padarn main line. From early years workmen used manually-operated velocipedes, but between 1895 and 1947 a workmen's train ran daily, calling at Gilfach Ddu (Dinorwic), Quarry, Penllyn, Pontrhythallt, Crawia, Pensarn, Bethel, Cefn Gwyn, Penscoins, and Port Dinorwic. The

Padarn line closed completely on 27 October 1961, though much of the lakeside route has been re-opened by a tourist enterprise.

RAILWAY TO LLANBERIS

Early in 1863 slate owners in the Vale of Llanberis approached the LNWR for a branch from Caernarvon. Euston was cold towards the idea, but by November there were three independent schemes: the Carnarvon & Llanberis No 1, from Caernarvon station, paralleling the B&C for a mile towards Bangor, thence through Pontrhythallt to Llanberis, with running powers over the B&C and authorised Carnarvonshire route to the Caernarvon quays; Carnarvon & Llanberis No 2, from the Carnarvonshire near the Menai Strait along the later constructed C&L route for $9\frac{1}{2}$ miles (15.3km) to Llanberis; and the Bangor & Llanberis Direct, backed by Colonel Pennant of the Penrhyn quarry, $8\frac{5}{8}$ miles (13.9km), from the west end of Bangor station, south to Cwm-y-glo to join the route of the C&L No 2 Bill to terminate close to the Royal Victoria Hotel. The C&L No 1 and B&LD Bills were rejected, Royal Assent on 14 July 1864 going to the No 2 Bill.

On 15 September 1864 the Hon Emily Wynn cut the first sod at Llanberis, accompanied by music from military bands and salvoes from some 18-pounders which echoed along the mountain ranges for several seconds. The *Illustrated London News* noted that 106 houses had been built in the Llanberis area within the past year, and that the railway would reduce the carriage rate of between 4s od (20p) and 9s od (45p) per ton for the district's slate, ironstone, sulphur and copper to between 1s od (5p) and 1s 6d ($7\frac{1}{2}$p), while coal from Caernarvon would travel at only a 1s od per ton, saving 6s 6d ($32\frac{1}{2}$p).

By November 1864 Charles Rolfe, C&L engineer, had prepared junction plans with the B&C at Caernarvon essential, he said, to defeat another attempt from the Bangor & Llanberis Direct, and to effect a working agreement with Euston. 'Your line', he informed his directors, 'is too short a one to be worked economically by itself'. The B&LD reappeared in 1865 but Euston disliked the proposed Bangor junction—for through running in the Holyhead direction, entailing reversal inside Belmont tunnel to reach Bangor station—and the Bill failed. Also thrown out was that mouthful of a line, the CB&P&CP&PD (p 97), which threatened the C&L's proposed $9\frac{3}{4}$-mile (15.7km)

Betws Garmon branch from Llanrug along the south shore of
Llyn Cwellyn to slate quarries near Llyn Gader. This was
authorised by C&L Act of 5 July 1865, along with the
'Carnarvon Town Line', linking the C&L at Llanbeblig with
the B&C. A last attempt by the B&LD in 1866 again failed.

The 1866 financial crisis hit the C&L and works were
suspended. The LNWR offered to purchase and complete the
line, or take a share in the Llanberis end, to which it would
make a link from Griffiths Crossing on the B&C; there was also
a threat to resurrect the B&LD if the C&L proved awkward.
Thus Euston became joint owner of 4⅛ miles (6.6km) at the
Llanberis end, with running powers over the remainder in
return for allowing C&L use of Caernarvon station. Construction was transferred to an ex-C&L director, S. L. Seckham, and
his partner, S. C. Ridley. (In passing, an 1867 Carnarvon &
Llandwrog Bill, 6½ miles (10.4km) from the C&L at Llanbeblig
to the Vron colliery at Llanrug, did not proceed.) Though construction recommenced, negotiations between the LNWR, CR and
C&L as to junctions between them became so protracted that
Euston ceased payments, and as a precaution deposited plans
for the Griffiths Crossing cut-off, known as the Llanberis Junction Railway. Early in 1868 agreement was reached for Euston
to own jointly the whole C&L and to work the traffic. The
Betws Garmon branch was abandoned, and the junction with
the Carnarvonshire Railway was authorised, by the C&L Act
of 1868.

In June 1869 Colonel Rich inspected the 8-mile (12.8km)
single line, with sidings, and stations at Llanberis, Cwm-y-glo,
Pontrhythallt (not ready), and a temporary one at Seiont Bridge,
known as 'Morfa'. The railway was opened by the LNWR on
1 July with five trains daily each way, working stock having
arrived via the Cambrian and Carnarvonshire lines. Pontrhythallt first appeared in *Bradshaw* in October 1869; Pont Rug
station opened on 1 June 1880. An LNWR plan in 1873 for a
⅝-mile (1km) semi-circular curve between Llyn Padarn and
Llyn Peris, to terminate at the quarries, was objected to by
Assheton Smith and dropped a year later.

In building the Carnarvon Town Line, the LNWR was under
obligation to Caernarvon Corporation to make a station at
Segontium Terrace, south of the tunnel under Castle Square,
where an island platform was planned, with offices at street
level. Space was tight, and the corporation waived its claim in

return for a contribution towards construction of Bridge Street. Works ordered for the B&C station in 1869 included removal and re-erection of the goods shed, a longer station platform, with bays, a scissors crossover in the centre, and additional sidings. A new two-road locomotive shed (extended in 1875) and turntable were constructed at the Bangor end. The Town Line had connections of 17 chains (342m) and 28 chains (564m) respectively from the C&L at Morfa and the CR at Pant to Llanberis Junction, whence nearly a mile of double track passed along the rear of the quays – giving a fine view of the castle, bored through a 163yd (149m) tunnel, and then climbed in cutting at 1 in 40 up to Caernarvon station, before which it merged into a single line with the platform on the down side. It opened for freight on 5 July 1870, in which month, by Act, the C&L vested in the LNWR. Alteration to standard gauge of the remaining Nantlle line down to the quays was completed by December 1871. Orders were given in August 1870 to remove the Morfa station, and the Pant station, goods shed and turntable, though not until January 1871 was permission received for opening throughout for passenger traffic.

EARLY ACCIDENTS

Combination of tunnel and gradient soon produced a bad accident. In the early morning of 5 May 1871 an Afon Wen train arrived at Caernarvon. After running round the train, the locomotive performed some shunting preparatory to moving to the south bay to await the return trip. As several vehicles had been attached, the driver took the train through the tunnel, and up the bank beyond, so as to get a run at the gradient up to the bay. Meanwhile, a Llanberis train (tank engine, passenger brake, third-class, composite, third, and brake van) arrived on the up line, due to return on the down almost immediately. After running round the train, the driver whistled for the signal to leave; the signalman, forgetful of the first train, complied; and at a speed of about 14mph the Llanberis locomotive met the rear of the Afon Wen train being propelled up the incline. A porter was mortally injured and there was severe damage. At Chwilog on 1 April 1872 twenty-two passengers were injured in two evening excursion trains. The first was stopped for ticket collection when the second, following, ran into it. At Llangybi, north of Chwilog, the 'man in charge' had no watch and the station no clock. The driver of the second train, though cautioned about the first, nevertheless departed so fast that the guard barely got aboard. On seeing the Chwilog distant at danger he screwed down the brake, but this proved insufficient for the 15 vehicles on the 1 in 60 decline. Though the Board of Trade called for block working, this was not introduced on the Carnarvonshire until 1880.

LATTER DAYS ON THE 'CARNARVONSHIRE LINES'

In 1894 an up loop, island platform, footbridge, and more sidings went in at Caernarvon; the Afon Wen and Llanberis lines junction was advanced to the south end of the station, the double track being henceforth worked as independent single lines. Two temporary platforms at Caernarvon served special trains on 13 July 1911 for the investiture of the Prince of Wales, the royal train using Griffiths Crossing. For the 1969 investiture of Prince Charles a platform was constructed north of the station.

Llanberis tourist traffic increased following opening of the Snowdon Mountain Railway (p 105) and the LNWR ran observation cars (p 134) from Rhyl and Llandudno. From 2 March 1914 an auto-train worked the branch. A loop and up platform went in at Llangybi in 1915. Early that year the LNWR's only petrol-electric railcar—a Westinghouse 38-seater—worked the Nantlle branch until withdrawal from 12 August 1916, 'due to the embargo on petrol', steam trains continuing thereafter. On 1 January 1917 Pont Rug and Nantlle closed to passengers. Pont Rug reopened in July 1919 and Nantlle from 5 May 1919. Road competition forced withdrawal of Llanberis passenger services on 22 September 1930, and Penygroes–Nantlle on 8 August 1932. Excursion trains continued on both lines, however, and on 21 November 1936 Padarn Halt was opened west of Llanberis station. Caernarvon locomotive shed closed on 14 September 1931 and was later demolished. Immediately after World War II there was heavy tourist traffic, particularly to 'Penychain – for Pwllheli Holiday Camp' on the Cambrian line; in 1947 the loops at Dinas (p 108), Brynkir, and Llangybi were lengthened to accommodate 10-coach trains. In 1949 London Midland Region trains commenced working through to Pwllheli from the Carnarvonshire line.

Griffiths Crossing closed to passengers on 5 July 1937, and Dinas completely on 10 September 1951 (re-opened on 9 August

1963 for use that day by the Queen during a tour of Wales).
Pant Glas closed on 7 January 1957, Treborth 2 March 1959,
and Port Dinorwic 12 September 1960. During this time the
Llanberis excursions still proved popular, advertised as 'The
Snowdonian', with tourist traffic on the Afon Wen line becoming
ever busier, trains following one another in quick succession on
summer days. It was the last flicker of life. The Nantlle branch
closed completely on 2 December 1963; the Llanberis freight
service last ran on 3 September 1964 (official closure 7
September); intermediate Carnarvonshire line stations closed to
freight during 1964 (Pant Glas 1952), and passenger services
ceased—to intense local feeling, for the railway had been much
a part of local life—on 7 December 1964. Track was lifted in
1968. Following closure of the Padarn Railway on 27 October
1961, Port Siding closed three days later. The B&C, singled in
1966, closed to freight on 4 August 1969 and passengers from
5 January 1970, only to be temporarily re-opened between 15
June 1970 and 5 February 1972 for a freightliner terminal at
Caernarvon in place of Holyhead while the Britannia Bridge
was being rebuilt. B&C. track was lifted in 1972. At Caernarvon
and Llanberis the old trackbeds have been used for road
improvements.

LLANBERIS TOURIST RAILWAYS

Llanberis was not without rail interest by closure of the standard
gauge branch, for since 1896 it has been the starting point of
Britain's only rack railway. The 2ft 7½in (81cm) gauge Snowdon
Mountain Railway, with steepest gradient of 1 in 5½, climbs
from a small station at the south end of the town, 353ft (107m)
above sea level, for 4⅝ miles (7.4km) to Snowdon Summit station,
at 3,493ft (1,065m). Apart from the termini, the line is single,
with passing loops at the intermediate stations of Hebron, Halfway, and Clogwyn. Trains consist of a bogie coach propelled
by a locomotive but not coupled to it. The return trip takes
some 2½ hours. Operating from Easter to October, on clear days
the railway offers unrivalled views beyond North Wales and
Anglesey to the Lake District peaks and Snaefell Mountain on
the Isle of Man. There is no guarantee of a clear view, and no
matter how warm down in Llanberis, things can get pretty
chilly at the summit!
Though Bills for a Snowdon Railway from Llanberis were

lodged in 1872 and 1875, not until 1893 was the Snowdon Mountain Tramroad & Hotels Company formed, with the route's landowner, Assheton Smith, as chairman. A Swiss-pattern, Abt system rack railway, with several viaducts and unusual construction problems, the SMR opened on Easter Monday, 6 April 1896. The day was marred by derailment at Clogwyn of the locomotive *Ladas* which fell into a ravine. The coaches, automatically braked above 5mph (8km), halted safely, but a passenger died after jumping from the train. *Ladas* was not replaced. The railway reopened in April 1897 since when, barring two minor derailments, it has worked safely. A wooden summit 'hotel' catered in early years for guests wishing to watch the sunrise. The present restaurant replaced it in 1936 and was an experimental radar station in World War II. The locomotives are o–4–2 rack tanks, built by the Swiss Locomotive & Machine Works, Winterthur. Nos 1, 2 *Enid* and 3 *Wyddfa* arrived in 1895, Nos 4 *Snowdon* and 5 *Moel Siabod* in 1896. Three more, slightly different, came from the same makers: 6 *Padarn* (at first *Sir Harmood*) in 1922, and Nos 7 *Aylwin* and 8 *Eryri* in 1923. In 1978 *Aylwin* became *Ralph Sadler* (just *Ralph* now), commemorating that true gentleman who was the SMR's consulting engineer from 1964 to 1977. There are two Hunslet o–4–o diesels: 9 *Ninian* and 10 *Yeti* (both 1986). With passing loops at Hebron, Halfway and Clogwyn, it has been possible with radio control to work nearly 50 train movements daily. The railway is unique and deservedly popular, though through inherent operating restrictions which limit capacity passengers sometimes have a wait in high season. Unavoidably, a ride is not inexpensive.

Across the road from the SMR's Llanberis station is the entrance to another of 'The Great Little Trains of Wales'. The 1ft 11½in (60cm) gauge Llanberis Lake Railway opened to the public on 19 July 1971 for just over a mile from Gilfach Ddu along the route of the old Padarn line to a temporary terminus at Cei Llydan. Trains were worked by a Hunslet locomotive from the Dinorwic quarry, o–4–o saddle tank *Dolbadarn* (built 1922), and a Ruston Hornsby four-wheeled diesel *Chwarelwr* (1949). These were joined later by ex-Dinorwic Hunslets : *Elider* (was *Red Damsel* built 1889), *Maid Marian* (see p 146) and *Wild Aster* (1904); and two German locomotives, a 1937 Jung o–4–o well tank *Cyclops* (now *Ginette Marie*), and 1948 Henschel o–4–o tank *Helen Kathryn* (from Bala Lake Railway). On 10 June 1972 the LLR was extended to Penllyn. From September 1974 the railway was used off-season for laying

underground power cables alongside the lake in connection with the
CEGB Dinorwic hydro-electric pumped storage scheme. Additional
diesel locomotives were acquired, the CEGB providing wagons, an
earth-moving trolley, and a 330yd-long (302m) cable-laying train of
87 single-axle articulated vehicles. Though CEGB work largely
ceased late in 1980, a siding serves a water pumping station between
Cei Llydan and Penllyn. Some CEGB vehicles remain, including a
contractors' small passenger vehicle for lineside cable maintenance.
During 1978–9 the CEGB built a ½ mile (.8km) 'Stabla Railway'
between Penllyn and Pinisarwaun (Stabla), not connected to the
LLR, from whom two diesels and rolling stock were hired; this line
was subsequently removed. (Gilfach Ddu, and developments since
1980 are noted in Chapter XVI.)

DINAS JUNCTION AND NORTH WALES NARROW GAUGE RAILWAYS

Success of steam working on the narrow gauge Festiniog Railway
(Chapter VIII) encouraged similar ventures. By Act of 6 August
1872 the North Wales Narrow Gauge Railways Company was
incorporated for 1ft 11½in (60cm) gauge lines for slate, freight,
and passengers, within the sparsely populated and mountainous
area between Snowdon and the Carnarvonshire Railway. The
22¾-mile 36.6km) 'General Undertaking' was planned from a
junction with the proposed narrow gauge Betws and Festiniog
line (Chapter VIII) at Betws-y-Coed, to run via Capel Curig
and the mountain passes to Beddgelert, thence to join the
Croesor & Port Madoc Railway. A separate 'Moel Tryfan Undertaking' consisted of two lengths: a 5⅛-mile (8.2km) line from
Dinas, north of Llanwnda on the Carnarvonshire Railway, ran
east, skirted the northern foothills of Moel Tryfan to isolated
Tryfan Junction, then doubled back south to quarries near
Bryngwn; and a 7¼-mile (11.6km) extension continued eastwards
from Tryfan Junction to the Caernarvon–Beddgelert road,
thence via Waenfawr and Betws Garmon and alongside Llyn
Cwellyn—dominated to the north by the steep flank of Snowdon
and to the south by that 'bleak and frowning mountain' Mynydd
Mawr—before terminating at Rhyd-ddu, near Llyn Gader at
the eastern end of the Vale of Nantlle. Not authorised were
lines from Betws-y-Coed to Penmachno and Corwen, and
Pwllheli to Porth Dinllaen. The General Undertaking was
abandoned, unbuilt, in 1876.

After various delays, the single-line NWNG opened to freight on 21 May and passengers on 15 August 1877, from Dinas to Bryngwyn—intermediate stations Tryfan Junction and Rhostryfan, and from Tryfan Junction to Quellyn (*sic*), with intermediates at Waenfawr and Betws Garmon. Quellyn to Quellyn Lake (soon renamed Snowdon Ranger) opened on 1 June 1878 (when Quellyn closed) and on to Rhyd-ddu (later Snowdon and then South Snowdon) on 14 May 1881. A coach connected with Beddgelert. Over the years mine and quarry sidings and some halts came into use. Locomotives, all 0–6–4s, were two Vulcan single-boiler Fairlie tanks *Snowdon Ranger* and *Moel Tryfan* (delivered 1875), Hunslet saddle tank *Beddgelert* (1878) for the Bryngwyn branch, and Hunslet single-boiler Fairlie tank *Gowrie* (1908).

On the Carnarvonshire Railway a passing loop was put in at Dinas in 1877 to relieve congestion of LNWR goods trains; LNWR passenger trains used a new exchange station, 'Dinas Junction', from September. To avoid transhipment at Dinas, the NWNG obtained powers in 1885 to extend to Caernarvon harbour, but these were not exercised. An Order of 1900 authorised a 4½-mile (7.2km) extension from South Snowdon to Beddgelert (p 125). In 1904 the Portmadoc Beddgelert & South Snowdon Railway was empowered to construct the Dinas–Caernarvon line, it being intended that the PB&SS and NWNG should unite and be worked electrically. Next the PB&SS took over the NWNG's Beddgelert extension powers, but despite further Dinas–Caernarvon powers in 1908 and engineering works between South Snowdon and Croesor Junction, all remained as before. Instead of expansion, NWNG passenger traffic ceased to Bryngwyn on 31 December 1913, and to South Snowdon on 31 October 1916. Meanwhile *Beddgelert*, scrapped in 1906, had been replaced by a new Hunslet 2–6–2 tank *Russell* (p 126). In 1917 *Snowdon Ranger* was withdrawn, parts going towards keeping *Moel Tryfan* running, and in 1918 *Gowrie* was sold to the government.

With the backing of local authorities, by Order of 30 March 1922 the NWNG and PB&SS merged as the Welsh Highland Light Railway. Dinas Junction–South Snowdon re-opened to passengers on 31 July 1922; an 8¾-mile (14km) extension to Croesor Junction, using near-completed works of earlier attempts, and the old Croesor Tramway to Portmadoc, opened on 1 June 1923 (p 126). A new link between the WHL and the Festiniog

at Portmadoc, authorised by the Festiniog Light Railway Order of
30 January 1923, opened a week later. Thereafter interworking of
the two systems' trains started, *Moel Tryfan* being altered so as
to negotiate the Festiniog's tunnels. A similar exercise with
Russell, spoiling what had been an elegant design, proved
unsuccessful because of the locomotive's overall width. At this
time shortage of motive power led to Festiniog locomotives
working the WHL, and in 1923 the latter company purchased
an ex-ROD 1917 Baldwin (USA) 4–6–0 side tank No 590.
April 1923 saw Colonel Stephens (p 200) appointed as civil
engineer and locomotive superintendent to both railways.
Despite the WHL route passing through beautiful mountain
scenery, with tunnels, rock cuttings, and a ruling gradient of
1 in 40 down to the Aberglaslyn Pass and the estuary, which
it had been hoped would attract tourists, the new combined
operation was not a success. In November 1924 Colonel
Stephens became a director, and in January 1925 chairman and
managing director. From 15 December 1924 the WHL passenger
service was suspended, henceforward to be summers-only. All
traffic ceased for a time in the autumn of 1931, but from 2
November a twice-weekly goods train worked the line. The
WHL suspended all services from 31 December 1933 but the
Festiniog took a lease of the line, effective from 9 July 1934.
Between then and October passenger trains operated daily each
way between Portmadoc and Beddgelert, with some continuing
to Dinas Junction. The hoped-for traffic did not materialise; the
summers-only passenger service ceased after 26 September 1936,
and freight after 19 June 1937. In 1938 Dinas Junction was
renamed Dinas; the days when standard and narrow gauge
trains stood either side of the platform were over. The Festiniog
lease ended on 31 December 1941 and the WHL was dismantled
soon after. *Moel Tryfan* had been withdrawn in 1936; the
Baldwin was cut-up at Dinas in 1942. *Russell* survived, to work
in Oxfordshire and Dorset before retiring, saved for preservation
by the Birmingham Locomotive Club and going to open store
at Towyn, on the Talyllyn, in 1955.

In 1961 the Welsh Highland Railway Preservation Society
was formed and negotiations started, which were to be seemingly endless, to convince the local authorities that the re-
opening of the line was viable. After reconstitution as the Welsh
Highland Light Railway (1964) Ltd, at a time when a rival
project seemed set to scotch the new company's primary

objective, it was decided to restore *Russell* which was acquired
and transferred to the new WHL workshops in Kinnerley,
Shropshire. By 1969 negotiations with the county council had
been resumed. At first it was hoped to restore the section north
of Rhyd-ddu, with the possibility of reaching Caernarvon over
the old LNWR route, but after objections from the county
council work started instead at Beddgelert Siding, motive power
being provided by a 1936 Ruston & Hornsby diesel *Cilgwyn*.
In 1975 a 1924 Orenstein & Koppel o–6–o well tank *Pedemoura*
was acquired. Track was relaid to Pen-y-Mount, with a run-round, in
1976, and in 1978 work started on a station and car park at
Porthmadog. That March reopening from Porthmadog to between
Beddgelert and Rhyd-ddu was approved in principle by the county
council, the remaining trackbed to be a public footpath. The 1970s
ended with the company seeking a Light Railway Order, with the
first intention of reopening to Pen-y-Mount. Stock included
carriages, built and under construction; and locomotives *Russell*,
awaiting a boiler, a 1953 Ruston & Hornsby diesel *Kinnerley*, which
worked, and *Pedemoura*, a 1942 Peckett o–4–2 tank *Karen*, and a 1918
Barclay o–6–o tank *Gertrude*, all being restored. (See Chapter XVI.)

PENRHYN, PORT PENRHYN AND BETHESDA

The Penrhyn quarries are situated at Bethesda—a town founded
by the quarrymen—on the Holyhead Road five miles (8km)
south of Bangor. The 6¼-mile (10km) Penrhyn Railway, first of
the narrow gauge lines in Caernarvonshire, a horse tramroad
with inclined planes, was built to the design of Benjamin Wyatt,
agent to the first Lord Penrhyn. Completed by July 1801, it
replaced carriage of slate by pannier to Port Penrhyn, just east
of Bangor. By 1861 an average of 200 tons of slate went daily
to the port, and some 3,000 men were employed at the quarry.
The first Lord Penrhyn died in 1808; during construction of
the CHR the quarry and tramroad were owned by Col Douglas-
Pennant, a Penrhyn by marriage, who in 1866 was to be created
Baron Penrhyn of Llandegai. With CHR approval, the colonel
constructed a standard gauge branch to Port Penrhyn, opened
early in 1852, the slate traffic from this and the Dinorwic quarry
(Port Siding) going via the CHR to a distribution depot at
Saltney. The single track 1½-mile (2.4km) Port Penrhyn branch,
from Penrhyn Siding on the main line west of Llandegai tunnel

to Quay Siding at Port Penrhyn, was never railway owned. It passed through the fields and woods of the Penrhyn estate until meeting the River Cegin and the tramroad, alongside which it reached the port. The 'branch' became a 'siding' in 1954 and was closed on 2 March 1963.

A Bangor–Bethesda road coach service operated for some years. In 1866 the LNWR staked claim to the town (population nearly 6,000) by opposing a branch of the Bangor & Llanberis Direct scheme. Plans in 1871 for a station to serve Bethesda at Talybont, east of Llandegai tunnel, were deferred when Lord Penrhyn was considering a narrow gauge Bangor–Bethesda line, presumably also to take passengers. Euston was interested, as witness a letter from the LNWR chairman, dated 26 July 1872:

> My Lord,
>   I have had a Line surveyed from Bangor to Bethesda by the route which you suggested but . . . it is so circuitous that I cannot see that it would be of any value to the district.
>   Did I understand correctly that your Lordship had some intention of improving and converting the existing tramway line into a 4ft 8½in gauge railway? and could we make a junction and so have the use of it either jointly or by laying our rails alongside your own road and so accommodate the whole neighbourhood? . . .

But nothing happened; with Euston increasingly involved with the Blaenau line, the Bethesda scheme faded. In 1877 Lord Penrhyn altered the tramway to avoid the inclined planes and permit locomotive working. Retaining the former gauge of 1ft 10¾in (58cm), it took a new westerly course via Tregarth and Felin Hen, and was apparently opened by December 1878, worked by one engine in steam, from the three ordered from de Winton of Caernarvon: 0-4-0s, *Edward Sholto* (saddle tank), and *Hilda* and *Violet* (side tanks). An 0-4-0 Hunslet saddle tank *Charles* arrived in 1882, and two similar, *Blanche* and *Linda*, in 1893, the de Wintons being relegated to the quarry. Three Baldwin tanks purchased in 1923 were unsuccessful, being withdrawn by 1928. The Penrhyn also owned a number of smaller locomotives for quarry and port workings.

Local people continued to call for a standard gauge branch, at last authorised by the LNWR Act of 6 August 1880. The entire route passed through the Penrhyn estate, and there was a clause against interference with the Penrhyn Railway which the

new line passed over once and under twice, running close alongside it for some distance. In February 1884 Francis Webb,
LNWR locomotive superintendent, inspecting the works, found
a powerful spring of water producing 800 gallons a minute. The
new Bangor steam shed was nearing completion and the LNWR
was paying Bangor Waterworks £220 annually for 9,270,000
gallons. Approval was given to lay pipes to get an independent
supply. The 4⅜-mile (7km) single line, with ruling gradient of
1 in 40, commenced at the east end of Bangor tunnel. There were
two viaducts, Cegin (seven arches) and Ogwen (five) the 297yd
(272m) Tregarth tunnel, and stations at Felin Hen, Tregarth,
and Bethesda. Public traffic started on 1 July 1884.

In early years six weekdays-only trains ran each way, increased
in the summer, and in 1908 an auto-train service started;
Bethesda's 42ft (12.8m) turntable was removed to Caernarvon
in 1911. By the 1930s some 16 trains ran in each direction, with
additional ones on Saturdays, and nine on Sundays. These were
cut by half during World War II, and the Sunday service ceased,
until withdrawal of passenger services on 3 December 1951.
The Penrhyn Railway's workmen's service ceased on 9 February
1951. The estate was then owned by the National Trust. The
quarry passed to a private company, but the ageing Penrhyn
Railway, doomed by falling traffic, closed on 24 July 1962,
some of its track and two of its locomotives surviving to continue
in service with the Festiniog Railway. The Bethesda branch
goods service lingered on, and occasional excursions worked the
line—attractions being the vast quarry and the magnificent Nant
Ffrancon Pass—but complete closure came on 7 October 1963.
Many railway relics are displayed at the National Trust's
Penrhyn Castle Museum. The collection includes ex-BR standard
gauge items, and a number of industrial locomotives, but
particularly interesting are the ancient Horlock *Fire Queen*,
the Hunslet 0–4–0 saddle tank *Charles*, the velocipede *Arthur*,
Lord Penrhyn's saloon , a quarrymen's coach, and Penrhyn open
wagons.

Railways to Blaenau Ffestiniog and Porthmadog

During the Welsh slate boom one of the main producing areas was in the mountainous district of northern Merionethshire where some mining, as distinct from quarrying, was necessary. The centre of this industry was at Blaenau Ffestiniog, to which two major English railway companies built expensive branches, following the success of the most famous of Welsh narrow gauge lines.

Blaenau is the industrial offshoot of the village of Ffestiniog (parish population 4,553 in 1861), three miles (4.8km) to the south, and lying at a height of 700ft (213m) above sea level at the head of the beautiful Vale of Ffestiniog through which, between the Snowdon and Arenig ranges, the Afon Dwyryd flows to its estuary at Traeth Bach in Cardigan Bay. The estuary links with another, Traeth Mawr, of the Afon Glaslyn, flowing south from Snowdon. Blaenau is overshadowed by bleak mountain landscapes, and 'enjoys' some 90in (228cm) annual rainfall. To the north, beyond the mountains, is the steep-sided valley of the Lledr which flows through Dolwyddelen—birthplace of Llewelyn the Great—to Betws-y-Coed where it joins the River Conwy on its 16-mile (25.6km) journey northwards to the sea.

W. A. MADOCKS AND PORTMADOC

Quarrying began at Diphwys, Blaenau, in the 1760s, slate going by pannier or waggon down the Vale of Ffestiniog to quays on the tidal Dwyryd. The two estuaries were then marshland and sandbanks. In 1798 William Alexander Madocks commenced reclamation of the larger estuary; by 1800, using a horse tramway, he had constructed an embankment containing the westerly

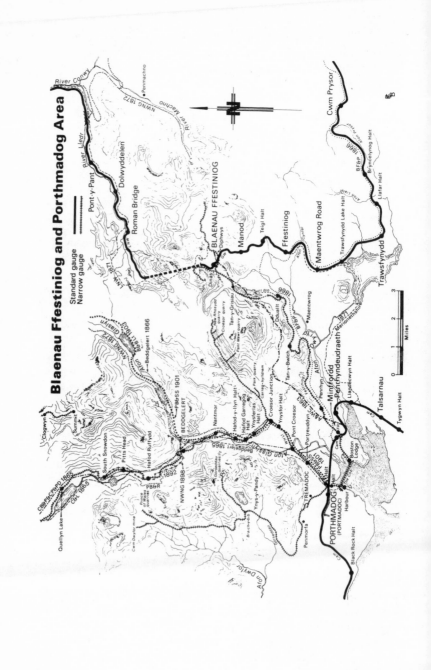

Blaenau Ffestiniog and Porthmadog Area

Standard gauge
Narrow gauge

area of marshland on which he founded the town of Tremadoc. In 1807 Madocks obtained an Act for a much larger embankment, the 'cob', across to the east shore (now Boston Lodge), enclosing some 8,000 acres and completed by 1811. Another tramway was made, and though lifted for a time it was replaced and retained for maintenance purposes after the sea breached the cob in 1812. Where the Glaslyn passed by a narrow exit through the cob a deep scour was formed, and in 1821 Madocks took powers to make a harbour there, named Portmadoc (now Porthmadog), whence slate was shipped from 1824.

FIRST RAILWAY TO BLAENAU

In about 1818 Madocks lived near and was much interested by the newly opened Hay Railway in Herefordshire; soon he planned his own line from Blaenau down to Traeth Bach. Two Bills were lodged in 1824, one for Madocks' Festiniog Railway (here we first meet the anglicised single 'F'; likewise Betws was for some years 'Bettws' and Diphwys was 'Duffws'), from the quarries, running south of the later-constructed railway, via three inclined planes to the east end of the cob; and a rival Festiniog & Port Madoc Railway, north of the later line, surveyed by William Alexander Provis, resident engineer on Telford's Menai Bridge. Both Bills were rejected. In 1825–26 new parties appeared, including the Welsh Slate Company, which had as chairman Lord Palmerston. Another concern, the Royal Cambrian Company, preposterously claimed the right to all minerals in Wales and planned a line on the west side of the estuary, commencing north of Moelwyn Mawr Mountain where slate was found at the head of the Croesor Valley. A Moelwyn & Port Madoc Railway Bill in 1825 was successfully petitioned against by the F&PMR promoters, to whom Madocks had transferred allegiance. After Madocks' death in 1828, James Spooner, engineer to the abortive Moelwyn scheme, surveyed a regularly graded line between Blaenau and Portmadoc with only one short double-inclined plane. After two failures in Parliament his plans and accompanying Festiniog Railway Bill received Royal Assent on 25 May 1832. The 13¼-mile (21.3km) line followed a sinuous course, with some heavy works, and was apparently constructed to a gauge based on 2ft 0in (61cm) between rail centres, now 1ft 11½in (60cm) between rails. It opened on 20 April 1836, with an incline at Tan-y-Grisiau and some quarry branches uncompleted. Thus, Lewis believes (*How Ffestiniog got its Railway*), 'some temporary system must have been used' at the incline where a water wheel, to draw trains up the north side, was not fixed until September 1836. Delays at the incline led to a deviation, including the 730yd (668m) Moelwyn or 'long' tunnel south of Tan-y-Grisiau, completed in 1844; another deviation, east of Tan-y-Bwlch, including the 60yd (55m) 'short' tunnel, came into use in 1851. At Blaenau output increased quickly, from 18,000 tons of slate in 1835 to nearly 90,000 by 1865, with over 2,000 men at work in the quarries. Meanwhile, to the north, the first probes had been made towards Blaenau from the Chester & Holyhead line.

CONWY VALLEY – EARLY PROPOSALS

The River Conwy separates Denbighshire from Caernarvonshire. Ten miles (16km) from the estuary at Conwy lies the village of Trefriw, to which the river is tidal. To the east across the flood plain is the market town of Llanrwst, once famous for the manu- facture of harps and later for woollen spinning and knitting. Four miles (6.4km) south of Llanrwst, where the river has narrowed to flow through a gorge, is Betws-y-Coed, close by the junction of the Holyhead Road with the Portmadoc–Blaenau– Llandudno road and the road (now B5106) to Conwy.

One of the CHR's abandoned 1846 schemes was for a branch leaving the main line under the castle walls at Conwy to run along the Gyffin Valley and via Dolgarrog and Trefriw to Llanrwst. November 1853 saw a proposed Conway & Llanrwst Railway along the east bank of the river; the Bill was withdrawn following a stated CHR preference for the west bank route. In 1857 Edmund Sharpe, engineer and contractor of Lancaster, approached the Board of Trade advocating narrow gauge light railways for secondary routes. The Conwy Valley seemed a likely choice, and in July 1858 he suggested a 3ft 3in (98cm) gauge railway to Llanrwst along the flat west side of the valley, with stations at the Bedol Inn, Tal-y-Bont, and Tal-y-Cafn ferry. The cost, £44,000—of which he would put up £11,000 —compared with £72,000 estimated for a standard gauge line. The *Railway Times* thought CHR shareholders would profit from Sharpe's scheme which by a moderate outlay would bring traffic 'to their improvidently-constructed and miserably- developed line', but at the CHR's meeting in September 1858 the project was dismissed for being to narrow gauge, and Sharpe for being both engineer and expectant contractor. Sharpe thereupon joined the east bank standard gauge parties, and a Bill for a Conway Llanrwst & Bettws-y-Coed Railway, soon shortened to Conway & Llanrwst, received Royal Assent on 23 July 1860.

OPENING CONWAY TO BETWS-Y-COED

The first sod of the Conway & Llanrwst was cut on 25 August 1860 on Lord Newborough's land at the Abbey, near Llanrwst. In October all C&L shares were allotted to Sharpe. This was too much for the LNWR (now amalgamated with the CHR). The Euston directors, with Savin's nearby branch line machinations much in mind, decided that, statutory powers or not, they would take control of the C&L; it was not to be another contractor's line. Thus, in October the LNWR special committee resolved to buy the necessary land, 'deducting £7,000 from the purchase money', and 'that the shares be registered in the names of the members of the [LNWR] Board'. In December C&L shareholders Admiral Moorsom and James Bancroft, both LNWR directors, replaced two original C&L directors. In partnership with Edward Preston of Caernarvon, Sharpe now assumed his role of contractor, resigning the chair to Moorsom, and in August 1861 the LNWR's Hedworth Lee was appointed C&L engineer. By early 1862, after further directorship changes, the C&L was for all intents and purposes part of the LNWR, confirmed by Act of 1863.

On 9 June 1863 Captain Rich inspected the line, 'about 11¼ miles long' (18km), single throughout, with sidings at Llanrwst, and intermediate stations at Llansaintffraid and Tal-y-Cafn. At Llandudno Junction '. . . the passenger traffic is not to be worked into the main line. A separate line and a separate platform have been constructed . . . for the passengers from Llanrwst'. According to the *Illustrated London News*, at 12.30 pm on Tuesday 16 June 1863 a special train left Llandudno, reaching Llanrwst at 1.30 pm, where a *band*, be it noted, gave 'a Welsh rendering of *Rule Britannia*'. Public services started on the following day, with three trains each way on weekdays.

Press reporters on the special train waxed lyrical over the scenery. The man from the *Railway Times*, noting 'well-timbered cliffs' on one side, 'picturesque reaches of grass and cornfields' on the other, the Tal-y-Cafn ferry which took tourists across into Caernarvonshire, and the 'salubrious mineral waters' of Llanrwst, whence a steamer plied to the coast, reminded his readers that Edmund Burke had thought the valley 'the most charming spot in North Wales'. That month a name-board was ordered: 'LLANDUDNO & LLANRWST JUNC-TION'. On station names: Llansaintffraid became Glan Conway in 1865; some 20 years later Tal-y-Cafn acquired '& Eglwysbach', and Llanrwst '& Trefriw'. In 1974 these last two reverted to their original names.

By Act of 5 July 1865 the LNWR was authorised to extend the railway to Betws-y-Coed, 'a favourite haunt of the angler and artist'. Single throughout, $3\frac{3}{4}$ miles (6km), and with sidings at Betws, the extension left the C&L just north of Llanrwst station, superseded by a new structure south of the junction and immediately north of the 86yd (78.7m) Llanrwst tunnel. There were two viaducts, each with six openings. On 18 October 1867 the LNWR special committee ordered that the line be opened for goods traffic 'at once'; in February a crane was ordered for loading slate at Betws. Passenger services started on 6 April 1868; Betws refreshment rooms opened that summer.

FIRST STEAM TO BLAENAU

On the other side of the mountains there had been a trans-formation of the Festiniog Railway. James Spooner was succeeded as engineer by his son, Charles Easton Spooner, who oversaw the introduction of steam traction on the line to cope with the increasing traffic. In October 1864, prior to steam haulage of public passenger trains, Captain Tyler reported on the line, noting that it was single, descending 700ft (213m) at a ruling gradient of 1 in 80 from Dinas, at Blaenau, to the cob, with sidings at eight locations. At Blaenau a $\frac{3}{4}$-mile (1.2km) mineral branch ran to Diphwys. In the previous eleven months two 0–4–0 side tank tender locomotives, No 1 *The Princess*, and No 2 *The Prince*, both from George England & Co, had together clocked up nearly 36,300 miles without derailment. Though speed was generally restricted to 10mph, the captain relished personally testing them at up to 30mph! Trains descended by gravity for $12\frac{1}{4}$ miles (19.7km) to within $\frac{3}{4}$ mile (1.2km) of Portmadoc, loaded slate wagons in advance of and detached from the passenger vehicles. The carriages returned behind the empty wagons, hauled by the locomotives. Though the four-wheeled carriages rode easily and steadily around the many curves, Captain Tyler thought the company might with profit adopt longer vehicles, with bogies, as then used in America and on sharply curved lines in parts of Germany and Switzerland :

> The adoption of locomotive power upon this little line is very important, and has evidently been a very successful experiment. The cheapness with which such a line can be constructed, the quantity of work that can be economically performed upon it, and the safety with which the trains run over it render it an example which will undoubtedly be followed sooner or later in this country, in India, and in the Colonies, when it is desired to form a cheap line for small traffic.

Passengers had been carried free for some months, but public use was prohibited until the carriage windows were barred as a protection against limited structure and formation clearances, and a telegraph installed in the long tunnel, all completed at the time of re-inspection in March 1865, though a passenger service of five weekday trains each way had commenced from 6 January with Board of Trade permission. Two more locomotives were obtained : No 3 *Mountaineer* and No 4 *Palmerston*. Trains worked between Portmadoc and Dinas with one intermediate station at Penrhyn (later Penrhyndeudraeth). Stations at Hafod-y-Llyn, Tan-y-Grisiau, and a second Blaenau terminus at Diphwys (named Duffws) were opened by the summer of 1866, both northern termini remaining in use until Dinas closed in August 1870. In 1867 two more slightly larger locomotives arrived : No 5 *Welsh Pony* and No 6 *Little Giant*. Increasing traffic, however, and the LNWR's growing interest in Blaenau (see later), soon necessitated either an expensive doubling of the line, or longer trains with more powerful locomotives. Thus No 7 *Little Wonder*, first of the celebrated double-boilered Fairlie locomotives, was delivered in the autumn of 1869. The Festiniog was the subject of experiments in February 1870, attended both by the Board of Trade and British observers, and by foreign engineers and missions, the most exalted being that led by Count Alexis Bobrinskoy (Bolrinskey in the Board of Trade report) as emissary of the Russian Emperor. *Little Wonder* excited admiration, hauling long trains up to Blaenau with ease, compared with the slowness and even stalling of the other locomotives. In March 1871 a gold medallion and silver shield were awarded to Spooner by the Emperor. Other Fairlies were ordered: double-boilered No 8 *James Spooner* in 1872, single-boilered No 9 *Taliesin* (1876), No 10 *Merddin Emrys* (1879), and No 11 *Livingston Thompson* (1886 – renamed *Taliesin* in 1931); the last two, both double-boilered, were erected at the Festiniog's Boston Lodge works. Early passenger stock was spartan, though bogie carriages appeared by the early 1870s. A most remarkable vehicle was Spooner's inspection car which had a sail and a ship-like prow for opening level-crossing gates on freewheeling downward journeys. In 1872 an interchange station with the Cambrian opened at Minffordd, and (replacing Hafod-y-Llyn) a station and loop at Tan-y-Bwlch. In later years halts opened at Boston Lodge (for Port Meirion) and at Moelwyn. Dduallt station opened in 1880, in which year a connecting loop went in at Glan-y-Pwll or Dinas Junction (see map of Blaenau), but in 1899 the old Dinas Junction layout was abandoned and replaced by a new junction further east. Duffws station closed from 1 January 1923, re-opened from 1 January 1925, and finally closed completely from 31 May 1931. For the most detailed account of the line, works and locomotives, including those which came later, see J. I. C. Boyd's two-volume history *The Festiniog Railway*.

GORSEDDAU RAILWAY

North-west of Tremadoc, between the mountains of Garnedd Goch and Moel Hebog, lies the valley of the Dwyfawr which reaches the sea near Criccieth. In the late 1850s the Bangor & Portmadoc Slate and Slab Company built an $8\frac{1}{8}$-mile (13km) 3ft 0in (91cm) gauge horse tramway from the Gorseddau quarries 900ft (274m) up on the slopes of Moel Hebog, running via Ynys-y-Pandy—where the company had a large water-powered slate mill, still a spectacular ruin in bleak surroundings —to Penmorfa, whence it used the formation of the early Tremadoc Tramway, opened some time before 1845 from the Llidiart Yspytty iron mine to a wharf at Portmadoc. The A&WC main line (Chapter X) later crossed the Gorseddau Railway on the level, west of the Croesor Tramway's similar crossing.

On 25 July 1872 the Gorseddau Junction & Portmadoc Railways Company was incorporated to take over the tramway, convert

Page 121 (*Top*) Dolgellau, looking west, May 1963; (*centre*) *Seaham* with train passing Cambrian goods warehouse at Dolgelley, c.1882; (*bottom*) Barmouth viaduct, May 1963. (*Author, top and bottom; National Library of Wales*)

Page 122 (*Top*) Aberdovey harbour branch, c.1890s; (*centre*) Train for Aberllefenni at Corris; (*bottom*) Kerry branch terminus, c.1930s. (*National Library of Wales, top and centre; L&GRP*)

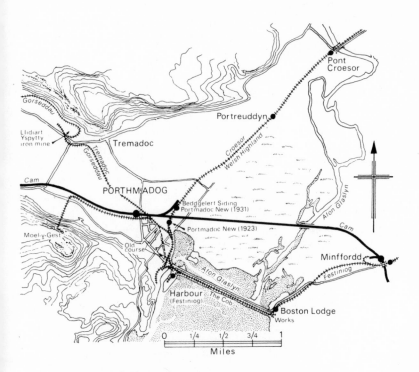

it to 2ft oin (61cm) gauge—actually 1ft 11½in (60cm) as made
—and to extend northwards from Braich-y-bib (north of Ynys-
y-Pandy) some five miles (8km) up the Dwyfawr Valley to the
Cwm Dwyfor (*sic*) Copper and Silverlead mines and the New
Prince of Wales quarries, and to use locomotives. At Portmadoc
the Gorseddau was to extend to join the Croesor Tramway on
the north side of the Cambrian, thus abolishing one of the level-
crossings, but this did not happen; the Gorseddau joined the
Croesor on the south side, and the Gorseddau's improved
Cambrian level crossing was passed by the Board of Trade in
1875. Both crossings remained until, becoming unprofitable, the
Gorseddau closed in the mid-1890s.

The extended and improved railway re-opened to freight on
2 September 1875. Excluding two miles (3.2km) of original tramway between Braich-y-bib and Gorseddau quarries, the line as
completed was some 11 miles (17.7km) long. There appears to
have been one locomotive, an 0–4–0 vertical-boilered de Winton,

sold on closure of the Gorseddau to the Borth Stone Company which worked a quarry on the north slope of Moel-y-Gest, whence an incline ran to a level mile-long stretch alongside and south of the Cambrian into Portmadoc.

CROESOR TRAMWAY AND SCHEMES TO REACH BEDDGELERT

After failure of the 1820s Moelwyn scheme, some 40 years passed before rail connection was made with the quarries. The 4-mile (6.4km) 1ft 11½in (60cm) gauge Croesor Tramway, built by Hugh Roberts, opened on 1 August 1864 from Carreg-hylldrem, in the Croesor Valley, whence it crossed the reclaimed Glaslyn Estuary to Portmadoc, exchanging traffic at Beddgelert Siding with the Cambrian which it then crossed on the level, ending alongside the Festiniog Railway. North of Carreg-hylldrem a separate tramway extended the Croesor line for a further four miles or so, with several branches and inclined planes, to the Park, Croesor, Pant Mawr, and New Rhosydd slate quarries.

In 1865, which saw rejection of the CB&P&CP&PD scheme through Beddgelert (p 97), two Acts were passed on 5 July incorporating the Croesor & Port Madoc and Beddgelert Railway Companies. The C&PM was promoted by Hugh Roberts and the other Croesor directors, with C. E. Spooner (p 118) as engineer, to take over the Croesor Tramway, adapt it for passengers, and make mixed-gauge extensions at Portmadoc (not done) over which the Cambrian (Chapter X) and the Beddgelert Railway might run. The standard gauge Beddgelert Railway was to run northwards from Portmadoc, following the Glaslyn through Beddgelert to terminate just north of Llyn Dinas. *Black's Guide* (1866) described Beddgelert as 'a charming picturesque village . . . at the junction of three vales, and closely surrounded by mountains', at the height of the tourist season 'not infrequently excessively crowded . . . as undoubtedly the cream of Welsh scenery is concentrated here . . . There are some copper mines in the neighbourhood, but the works are not conducted with much energy or success. Coaches, running between Carnarvon and Barmouth, pass through this village daily during the greater part of the year . . .'. The Beddgelert's chairman was David Williams of Castle Deudraeth, Portmadoc, chairman of the Carnarvonshire Railway and a Cambrian director. The Beddgelert got nowhere: though by March 1866 two-thirds of the nine authorised miles (14.5km) were said to be completed, and in the following July an extension was authorised towards Llyn Gwynant, the works were not finished. The company appeared regularly in *Bradshaw's Shareholders' Guide*, with 'works in progress' hopefully appended, but it sank into oblivion after 1869.

There followed several equally unsuccessful attempts to reach Beddgelert, which deserve but an outline here. The first was the 1872 North Wales Narrow Gauge, whose abandoned 'General Undertaking' would have linked the Croesor & Port Madoc, via Beddgelert, with the 'Moel Tryfan Undertaking' (Chapter VII). In 1879 the Portmadoc Croesor & Beddgelert Tram Railway Company was incorporated to absorb the Croesor & Port Madoc convert it to standard gauge, and make a branch to Beddgelert. Within three years, with no work done, the PC&BT was in the hands of a Receiver; an attempt to interest the Festiniog Railway in the line failed. The session of 1882 saw a standard gauge Portmadoc & Beddgelert, terminating near Gelert's Grave (of the faithful and tragic hound of Welsh legend), a magnet to Victorian tourists. In 1890 a narrow gauge Beddgelert & Rhydddu Railway proposed to link the NWNG at South Snowdon with the Croesor line, via Beddgelert, an attempt repeated by the Portmadoc Beddgelert & Rhyd-ddu in 1892. A standard gauge Portmadoc Beddgelert & Snowdon Light Railway of 1897 and a narrow gauge Beddgelert & Rhyd-ddu Light of 1898 both failed, the latter having been trounced by a NWNG scheme for a 4½-mile (7.2km) South Snowdon–Beddgelert extension introduced that year, authorised by NWNG Order of August 1900, but destined not to be made under those powers. By Act of 17 August 1901 the Portmadoc Beddgelert & South Snowdon Railway was incorporated to take over the PC&BT and extend seven miles (11.2km) from Croesor Junction through Beddgelert to terminate at the westerly outlet of Llyn Gwynant, the line to be worked by steam or electricity. The PB&SS—in reality still just the little horse-worked Croesor Tramway—took further powers: by Act in 1904 to extend from the NWNG at Dinas Junction (p 108) north to Caernarvon harbour; and by Orders in 1906 and 1908, respectively to link the termination of the NWNG authorised 1900 Beddgelert extension with the PB&SS 1901 Beddgelert extension, and to adopt the North Wales Power & Electric Traction Company's lapsed 1903 scheme for a light railway from the termination of the 1901 Beddgelert extension along

part of the route of the old NWNG's 'General Undertaking' to
Betws-y-Coed. Optimistically, the PB&SS ordered a locomotive,
Hunslet 2–6–2 tank *Russell*, which on arrival passed its time
while awaiting greater things by working on the NWNG (p
108). Part of the 1906 line only was built, including a cutting,
an underbridge and embankment south of Beddgelert, but the
powers lapsed in 1909.

Affected by so many projects, Beddgelert (parish population
in 1861 of 1,375 and hardly any increase thereafter) seemed
high in the running as the town least likely to succeed. Following the 1922 Welsh Highland Light Railway Order (p 108),
the elusive South Snowdon–Beddgelert–Croesor Junction link
was opened on 1 June 1923 to a station at Portmadoc south of
the crossing with the Cambrian (GWR). At the same time the
Festiniog constructed a short connection (p 109) so that from
8 June 1923 its trains could use the WHL station. This arrangement ceased in about 1929 when to save costs WHL trains
terminated north of the main line, passengers walking down to
the Festiniog trains. By 1931 a new 'station' had opened north
of the crossing, the Festiniog having returned to its original
Portmadoc Harbour terminus. (As to leasing and closure see
p 109.)

While the LNWR was constructing towards Betws-y-Coed, the
slate owners—concerned over delays on the horse-worked
Festiniog—urged Euston to extend to their Blaenau quarries.
South of the Lledr Valley, pointing more directly towards
Blaenau, is the Penmachno Valley. Up one of these the extension
would run as far as the mountains, where a long tunnel was
inescapable. The LNWR surveyed alternative 2ft 0in (61cm)
and standard gauge lines via both valleys to join the Festiniog
Railway, for purchase of which concern negotiations were
started, only to terminate in November 1865. The general
financial troubles of the late 1860s inhibited further progress
but it was not lost on Euston that during 1869 the Festiniog
carried 125,524 tons of slate and considerable local supplies.
Of course the FR was now steam-worked and an entirely
different proposition from when the slate owners first approached
Euston. Now, with reviving LNWR interest, they consistently
refused to guarantee traffic. In October 1870 the LNWR again
prepared plans for a narrow gauge line via the Lledr Valley.

No agreement being reached as to the junction with the Festiniog, however, the extension clauses were withdrawn from the LNWR Bill. When that hurdle was surmounted a new narrow gauge line was surveyed, slightly to south and east of the first and to terminate by a junction with the FR Dinas branch. Bitten by the slate 'bug', but also with the motive of establishing their company in a strategic position to thwart any Great Western aspirations towards North Wales (though still with no guarantee of traffic), the LNWR directors again deposited plans in November 1871, letting themselves in for an expensive and largely unprofitable undertaking. In January 1872 they learned of, but were not dissuaded by, the Welsh Slate Company's intention 'to send all traffic by the Festiniog route for a long term of years'. The Betws and Ffestiniog line—to be to the FR gauge, or wider, but not to exceed standard—received Royal

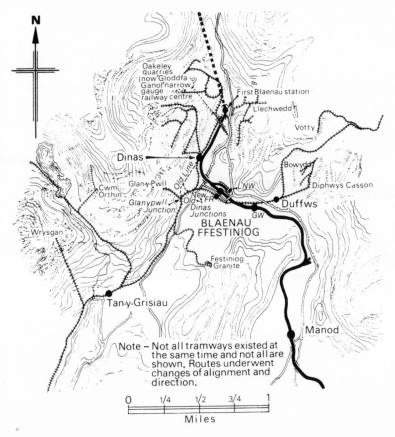

Assent on 18 July 1872. Meanwhile, undeterred, the Great Western had backed an independent company to get it to Ffestiniog, whence a narrow gauge line already ran to Blaenau.

FESTINIOG & BLAENAU RAILWAY

In May 1868 Captain Tyler inspected a new 3½-mile (5.6km) railway with a gauge of 2ft 0in, 'or, more accurately, 1' 11¼" in the clear', built without statutory powers between Ffestiniog and a junction at Blaenau with the FR. The major work was a viaduct, originally with four 80ft (24.4m) timber lattice girder spans on masonry piers, but strengthened subsequently with intermediate trestles. The F&B—promoted by Samuel Holland, MP for Merioneth, and a Blaenau quarry owner—opened on 29 May 1868 with six weekday trains in each direction and two additionally on Saturdays, worked with 4-wheeled coaches hauled at first by FR locomotives, but from August 1868 by new Manning Wardle 0-4-2 saddle tanks, No 1 *Scorcher* and No 2 *Nipper*. Besides 'Festiniog' there were stations at Tyddyn-gwyn, Tan-y-Manod, and 'Duffws', beyond which the line joined the FR Diphwys branch at Dolgareddu Junction, where freight traffic was exchanged.

PROPOSED MERIONETHSHIRE RAILWAY

We must digress to dispose of an interloper. Not to be confused with its namesake (Chapter IX), the Merionethshire Railway, promoted by Samuel Holland and incorporated in 1871, was a 10-mile (16km) mixed-gauge line from the F&B at Ffestiniog planned to run southwards to the Maentwrog–Harlech road which it followed to an interchange station with the Cambrian at Llandecwyn. It duplicated the Festiniog, with whom Holland and other owners were arguing over rates for slate carriage. Though not built, the MR was not abandoned until 1887, after both the GWR-backed Bala & Festiniog (of which Holland was a director), and the LNWR, had reached Blaenau. Euston arrived first, by a short head.

THE NORTH WESTERN REACHES BLAENAU

The LNWR Betws and Ffestiniog line climbed steeply and sinuously along the southern slopes of the Lledr Valley before swinging south to plunge into the long tunnel beneath Moel Dyrnogydd. In August 1872 it was decided to bore the tunnel for standard gauge. Tenders so exceeded estimates that William Smith, recently appointed engineer to the LNWR Chester and Holyhead district, was instructed to do the work; in May 1873 it was decided to construct throughout to standard gauge. Work started at the northern end of the line to facilitate carriage of materials to the tunnel, with four shafts, where hand boring started in January 1874. That year the LNWR's curiously titled Bettws Extension Railway was authorised, continuing the new line by about ¾-mile (1.2km) to terminate north of the Festiniog's Diphwys branch; also the separate, short Dyffws Junction Railway, for interchange traffic, from the Diphwys branch to a point near Blaenau market hall. In April 1875 the LNWR directors gave Bibles, prayer books, and £50 to the vicar of Dolwyddelen for his ministry to the navvies, a hospital fund was started, and a surgeon retained. Contracts were let in January 1878 for small single-platform stations at Pont-y-Pant and Roman Bridge, and for a loop and island platform at Dolwyddelen. Amidst explosions, rock falls, and various mishaps, with death too often attendant on the men inside the tunnel, the boring and hacking, shovelling and carting, seemed endless. Hard rock required special drills. There was severe flooding; by early 1878 some 87,000 gallons a day were creating chaos. Nevertheless, on 4 April 1878 there was open communication throughout. Improvements were made in the Conwy Valley: Llanrwst and Tal-y-Cafn stations received passing loops and second platforms; at Betws, inspected by Colonel Rich in July 1878, there was only one platform and he was emphatic that if trains were to pass each other there should be two, a requirement ignored for some years.

By February 1879 the line to Dolwyddelen was 'being used for the traffic of the locality', freight only, for signalling was incomplete until April. At Blaenau a temporary station was erected at the south end of the tunnel so that the line might open while work continued on the permanent station, built alongside the FR for interchange. Colonel Rich inspected the 11½-mile (18.5km) line in June 1879. George P. Neele, LNWR superintendent of the line, was present, and wrote in his *Railway Reminiscences* (1904) that the colonel (demoted to captain in Neele's account) 'determined to test the width of the single line tunnel, by travelling through it on foot, having a carriage, with its doors open on both sides, propelled by an engine at walking speed all through the tunnel . . .'. The tunnel length was noted as 3,726yd (3.4km)—British Rail's LMR civil engineering department has it as 3,861yd. Within it, about ¼ mile (0.4km) from the Ffestiniog end, the summit of the line is reached, 790ft (241m) above sea level. There were four other tunnels: Beaverpool, Pont-y-Pant, Bertheos, and Roman Bridge, all fairly short; the Lledr viaduct with seven stone arches; and 17 other bridges. Colonel Rich took exception to the masonry work, of large undressed local stone; he was able to insert his arm for depths of 2ft 0in (61cm) without finding mortar, 'beyond small lumps which were as friable as dry road mud' :

> I consider this class of masonry . . . to be very objectionable in Railway Construction as it is almost impossible to detect settlements and bad work. I am informed that it was adopted to please the frequenters of the valley, who thought the beauty of the scenery would be affected by the construction of a Railway, but good rustic rubble work, with fitted joints filled with mortar, toned to a proper colour, would have been more in accordance with old established building, pleasanter to the eye, and more secure.

After re-inspection, the railway between Betws and the Blaenau temporary station opened on 22 July 1879. The exchange sidings with the FR and extension to the permanent station opened on 1 April 1881, after which the temporary station was removed. A year later the GWR's protégé struggled into Ffestiniog from the south.

BALA & FESTINIOG RAILWAY

In November 1865 the Vale of Llangollen company promoted a 31-mile (49.8km) Bala Festiniog & Penrhyndeudraeth Railway, along a route similar to the later Bala & Festiniog but continuing from Ffestiniog to join the Cambrian west of Penrhyndeudraeth (Chapter X). The works would have been expensive and the Bill was withdrawn. By the 1870s, with an improved financial climate, the GWR backed a new company, the Bala & Festiniog, whose Act of 28 July 1873 empowered Henry Robertson, Samuel Holland and others to make a railway from Llangower (Bala Junction) (p 144) to the Festiniog & Blaenau station at Ffestiniog. The GWR and the three Dee Valley companies east of Bala (Chapter IX) together put up £156,000 of the £190,000 capital. Colonel Rich reported on the line, from the Lion Hotel, Bala, on 19 August 1882. The 22-mile (35.4km) single-track standard gauge railway, with provision for doubling, had 42 under- and 15 overbridges, and no fewer than 16 viaducts. Again, mortar work was poor : 'In some places it is like wet clay and in others like dry mud'. The stations were incomplete and permission to open was refused. The company was also converting the Festiniog & Blaenau to standard gauge, the F&B having reached agreement for purchase by the Bala & Festiniog in 1876, confirmed by the GWR Act of 1880.

Opened on 1 November 1882, the Bala & Festiniog climbed north from its new Bala town station up the wooded Treweryn Valley through Frongoch station, before following the river westwards between the twin peaks of Arenig Fach, 2,259ft (689m), to the north and Arenig Fawr, 2,800ft (854m), to the south. In the valley, amidst gaunt and rugged scenery, Arenig station, with loop and two platforms, and sidings to nearby slate quarries, was 1,135ft (346m) above sea level. The summit of the line, 1,278ft (390m), was reached at Cwm Prysor—station opened 1902 and loop shortly after—situated by Llyn Treweryn. The descent to the south-west was by a valley cut by the Afon Prysor which flows into Trawsfynydd Lake, some eight miles (12.8km) distant. Here a great viaduct of nine 36ft oin (11m) span brick arches on stone piers took the line 105ft oin (32m) above the diminutive Afon Prysor to a route of ledges and cuttings on sharp curves along the north side of the valley, through Llafar to Trawsfynydd station, after which it curved to the north towards the next station, Maentwrog Road 2½ miles (4km) distant from Maentwrog village. There followed a horse-shoe curve around the head of the Cynfal Valley, and a mile further on a gradient of 1 in 50 and a small viaduct landed the railway at its end-on junction with the Festiniog & Blaenau.

Colonel Rich inspected the F&B, with altered gauge, in July 1883. The large viaduct now consisted of eleven brick arches of 25ft oin (7.6m) span. The stations at Manod and Blaenau were not ready, however, and the opening was postponed. Re-inspection on 3 August found the works completed, and 'the narrow gauge rail is to be taken up next week and applied to all curves of ten chains radius and under as a check rail'. The converted line was re-opened on 10 September 1883, bringing the GWR face to face with the LNWR in the fastness of the Welsh mountains. Actual contact was avoided by an intervening length of 'no-man's land' Festiniog narrow gauge which ran from the FR Diphwys terminus at the east end of the town to the back of the GWR station where there was an island platform for passenger interchange, thence to the LNWR/FR interchange station. Between the two an FR mineral branch left to run into the LNWR interchange yard.

Built to take slate 'direct' to Birmingham, the Bala & Festiniog did little to shorten overall route mileage. Serving only local scattered communities, passenger traffic was meagre, but for nearly 80 years three trains ran daily each way, and latterly five or six. An extended loop and second platform were inspected at Trawsfynydd in November 1911, together with a siding and two special platforms 'for the detraining and entraining of troops and horses, which are sent to this place for artillery practice'. In 1925 a new siding for reservoir construction work was laid between Maentwrog Road and Trawsfynydd. Halts were erected at Tyddyn Bridge and Capel Celyn, north of Frongoch; at Bryncelynog and Llafar, between Cwm Prysor and Trawsfynydd; at Trawsfynydd Lake for anglers; and at Teigl, south of Manod. After nationalisation the LNWR and GWR stations at Blaenau became respectively North and Central.

In 1957 a new reservoir in the Treweryn Valley was authorised for Liverpool Waterworks. This would have flooded the line, and instead of deviating, it was decided to close it. Steam traction remained until the last regular passenger train ran on 2 January 1960, freight ceasing on 27 January 1961. Meanwhile, the BTC Act of 1959 authorised a standard gauge connection—opened 20 April 1964—between Blaenau North and Central so that the new Trawsfynydd nuclear power station could be rail served via the Conwy Valley.

WORKING THE LNWR BLAENAU BRANCH

The 1863 Llanrwst passenger service was of three weekday trains each way, increased to five by June 1864. That month guard Williams was demoted: his crime—leaving the Llanrwst train staff at Llandudno Junction (on reaching Tal-y-Cafn he had sent a man on horseback to retrieve it). A year later the LNWR ruled that drivers should carry the staff. Betws-y-Coed first appeared with timings in *Bradshaw* in May 1868, five weekday trains running each way. For some years Lord Newborough could stop trains between Tal-y-Cafn and Llanrwst. By 1879, after introduction of block working, two trains left Blaenau and Llandudno Junction respectively at 8.05 am and 8.35 am, passed at Llanrwst, and arriving at the junction at 9.40 am and Blaenau at 10.10 am. A second pair passed at Dolwyddelen at 11.35 am. A mid-morning Llandudno Junction– Betws return trip was followed by another pair, Dolwyddelen pass 3.27 pm, then a single tea-time trip from the junction to Betws, followed by another pair, Tal-y-Cafn pass 7.07 pm. The daily working ended with a Llandudno Junction–Betws pair, Llanrwst pass 8.45 pm, Betws arrive 8.55 pm and Llandudno Junction 9.25 pm. Apparently mails were first carried to Blaenau on 1 May 1880. Rashly, a passenger coach was attached to a Sunday mail train, drawing the wrath of a landowner who cited the LNWR 1872 Act which forbade Sunday passenger trains. The company apologised, and received permission to continue Sunday passenger services. An LNWR hotel opened at Blaenau in 1881, but whereas the tourist trade at Betws flourished, that at Blaenau did not, and the LNWR soon let the hotel. In the early 1900s, after complaints of drunkeness, the hotel portion was isolated from the public house business and sold in 1906. The 'North Western Hotel' was still there in 1990, though no longer bearing that name.

From 1894 the Llandudno–Blaenau line was worked with the electric staff; at the same time Dolwyddelen signal box was replaced by a station ground frame. At Betws in July 1898 the goods loop became a down passenger line, with a new platform and footbridge. The signalling permitted use of the up line by down trains, these using the down platform only when the up was occupied, contravening Board of Trade requirements. Colonel Yorke insisted that approaching trains should normally take the left-hand road. 'As, however, certain trains from Llandudno Junction end their journey at and turn back from Bettws-y-Coed, it might be permitted for those trains to start back to Llandudno Junction from the down platform . . .'. A 10¼-mile (16.5km) standard gauge Conway Valley Light Railway, on the west side of the Conwy, was approved in 1912 but did not proceed. In 1908 the Abbey Dolgarrog & Trefriw Light Railway was approved, confirmed by the Dolgarrog Light Railway Order of 1910, and eventually built as a government work during World War I from the Blaenau branch across the river to aluminium works at Dolgarrog village. The light railway also served the North Wales Power Company's hydroelectric works at Dolgarrog, scene of a disastrous flood in 1926 when a mountain dam burst, taking many lives and destroying much of the village, including the church. Near the junction with the light railway, sidings came into use, and a new halt, 'Dolgarrog', on 18 December 1916. In 1917 a government-authorised loop was laid between Dolgarrog and Llanrwst to serve the Cae Coch sulphur mine.

From the mid-1870s the LNWR experimented with 'open' excursion coaches specially for the Blaenau branch. On 30 August 1911 a third-class bogie observation 'car' was introduced between Llandudno and Blaenau with an extra charge of 6d (2½p) for a morning journey to Blaenau and afternoon return. By 1913 two more cars had been built. They operated in the Conwy Valley, and occasionally to Llanberis (Chapter VII) until the coming of the dmus in March 1956. One escaped scrapping, to run on the Bluebell Railway in Sussex.

Dolgarrog and Glan Conway stations closed in 1964, reopening on 14 June 1965 and 4 May 1970 respectively. Most freight closures took place during 1964. The 1960s saw the branch loops removed except at Llanrwst. By the end of 1968 local freight traffic had ceased. Undoubtedly the Trawsfynydd power station gave the branch a fortuitous stay of execution. With unstaffed halts it remained open to passengers, freight reduced to a twice-weekly trip from Llandudno Junction bringing coal to Blaenau and removing atomic waste in special containers from Trawsfynydd. Of slate traffic there was none; Blaenau's population had dropped by 25 per cent between 1931 and 1951. In 1975 the Conwy Valley Railway Museum opened in Betws goods yard, the collection including a 1910 Pullman car (a camping coach on the site for some years) and other rolling stock, a museum housing two narrow gauge 0–4–0 steam locomotives, signalling equipment and other exhibits, and an outside 7¼in (18.5cm) gauge miniature steam railway. At Blaenau the Llechwedd Slate Caverns and Miners' Tramway opened to visitors in 1972, giving a railtour exploring the redundant slate mine workings, 'enlivened' by tableaux of Victorian working conditions: in 1979 a cable incline opened, descending to deeper caverns. Also at Blaenau, the Gloddfa Ganol Slate Mine and Narrow Gauge Centre opened in 1978, and from 1987 an associated ¼ mile (.4km) 2ft (61cm) gauge passenger line worked by a Simplex diesel. Though British Rail Sunday services ceased on the Blaenau branch in 1976, so popular were the attractions that for peak summer Sundays in 1977 Gwynedd County Council chartered a special train for tourists—an investment which has continued seasonally, giving much pleasure to patrons.

LATTER DAYS ON THE FESTINIOG RAILWAY

Closure of the Welsh Highland left the Festiniog as the only remaining narrow gauge line to Porthmadog. Winter passenger services ceased from October 1930, and the summer tourist and workmen's trains from mid-September 1939. Declining demand for slate and the moving away of key workers led inevitably to complete closure of quarries and railway; all working ceased after 1 August 1946. Happily, demolition did not occur and with the Talyllyn's success to spur it on, a preservation society interested Mr Alan Pegler in a scheme to re-open the line to tourists. On 23 July 1955 a public passenger train ran once more from Porthmadog to Boston Lodge. Minffordd was reached in 1956, Penrhyn in 1957 (with new intermediate Pen-y-Bryn Halt, closed 1967), Tan-y-Bwlch in 1958 (with new intermediate, but private, Plas Halt, opened 1963), and Dduallt in 1968. There progress was delayed, for in the 1950s a new hydro-electric pumped storage scheme had flooded part of the remaining original route north of Moelwyn tunnel. Undaunted, the society sought and received compensation from the CEGB, and with powers granted by Light Railway Orders of 1968 and 1975, and grants from the Wales Tourist Board and the government's 'Job Creation Scheme', a $2\frac{3}{4}$-mile (4.4km) deviation line was built. A new 311yd (284m) Moelwyn tunnel, reached by a spiral from Dduallt, was opened on 25 June 1977, public service trains reaching a temporary terminus at Llyn Ystradau from 8 July, and extending over the remainder of the deviation to Tan-y-Grisiau, on the outskirts of Blaenau, from 24 June 1978. A £340,000 project was launched by Gwynedd County Council and Merioneth District Council for a new terminal station to be shared by BR and the Festiniog on the site of the old GWR central station, $1\frac{3}{4}$ miles (2.8km) further on from Tan-y-Grisiau. This public commitment towards the future of the tourist industry at Blaenau Ffestiniog was inevitably to revitalise the British Rail branch too. (See Chapter XV.)

CHAPTER IX

Ruabon—Barmouth

For almost a century the 54½-mile (87.7km) Ruabon–Barmouth railway through the Dee Valley via Llangollen and Corwen to Bala, and then by the Wnion Valley through Dolgellau, gave visitors an incomparable introduction to Wales. After the long journey from Paddington, and a change of trains at Ruabon, suddenly it was all there, a moving panorama from the carriage window : narrow, forested gorges; rushing rivers; neat, historic towns and villages; a lake of quiet beauty; and the final approach, with quickening wheel rhythm, beside a wide estuary towards the sea; and all dominated by the mountains. It was a magical ride. One remembers the bustle of Bala Junction, the clatter of churns at little stations, greetings and parochial banter between station staff, passengers and enginemen in unhurried Welsh tongue, and the enveloping beauty of the country, glimpsed through dissolving wisps of steam. This could have been a busy main line had one of the 1845–6 mania schemes (p 21) come to pass; it remained a delightfully unspoilt route, served by an attenuated branch, the impetus for which came with the need to link Llangollen with the nearby Shrewsbury–Chester line.

INTO THE VALE OF LLANGOLLEN

Historic Llangollen, picturesquely placed in the Dee Valley, surrounded by the Berwyn, Llantysilio, and Ruabon mountains, was by the 1840s already much favoured by tourists. From 1848 visitors travelled by train to the nearest station, Llangollen Road on the S&C, whence numerous coaches plied to points on and near the Holyhead Road. The locality produced slate, coal at Acrefair, and lime from the spectacular, high cliff-like rocks at Trevor, north-east of the town—an impressive backdrop when coloured by the sun. To their south a ruined fortress crowns a conical hill. South again are the Berwyn foothills, and squeezed between, in a narrow gorge, are the river, the Holyhead and Ruabon–Llangollen roads, and the Llangollen branch of the Shropshire Union Canal. A tramway ran from the lime rocks to the canal, on which barges carried large quantities of slates and limestone. The roads took wheat, barley and malt to, and produce from, mills and breweries in Llangollen, and dairy produce and livestock out of Merionethshire. During construction of the Shrewsbury–Chester line there were Bills in 1847 for a Birkenhead and Llangollen Railway, and an S&C Llangollen branch, both withdrawn. That year the LNWR leased the canal.

Financial depression followed the mania. It was not until November 1853 that a Denbighshire Railway scheme briefly appeared, for a Ruabon–Rhyl line, via Llangollen, Corwen and Ruthin, followed in 1854 by a Llangollen Railway from Cefn on the S&C. A Ruabon–Denbigh line, planned by George Hammond Whalley who had colliery interests near Ruabon, and backed by Euston, was rejected in favour of a Vale of Llangollen Railway, engineered by Henry Robertson, supported by Paddington and the New British Iron Company. The LNWR and SU sought rejection of the V of L Bill in return for a promise to convert the canal into a railway. The V of L, however, received Royal Assent on 1 August 1859.

The first sod was cut by the wife of Colonel Tottenham, the V of L chairman, on 1 September 1859. Construction was carried out by Thomas Brassey as a single line on double formation, and similarly by him on later extensions through to Dolgellau. The 5¼-mile (8.4km) V of L, leaving the S&C ⅝ mile (1km) south of Ruabon, with intermediate stations at Acrefair – where it passed over the Pontcysyllte Tramway, and at Trevor – where the tramway reached the canal basin (p 47), opened to freight on 1 December 1861 and to passengers on 2 June 1862, worked by the Great Western. From the beginning Paddington saw the V of L as the first stage in an advance towards Cardigan Bay and even North Wales, and in 1859 plans were already prepared for extension to the market town of Corwen.

FROM LLANGOLLEN TO CORWEN

The Llangollen & Corwen Railway was incorporated by Act of 6 August 1860, with Colonel Tottenham as chairman. The line followed the ravine of the Dee, ledged into the hillside with the river far below. By October 1863 men were toiling around the clock on the short tunnel through a shoulder of the Berwyns, but eastwards to Llangollen the railway was already carrying goods traffic.

Meanwhile, the Corwen & Bala Railway (see below) had been authorised. Denbigh Ruthin & Corwen trains reached Corwen temporary terminus in the autumn of 1864 (p 73). In April 1865 Captain Rich inspected and sanctioned the $9\frac{5}{8}$-mile (15.5km) Llangollen & Corwen, which commenced 'at the old Llangollen station which is to be done away with, a new station having been built further on', and ended east of the Corwen & Bala's Corwen station. Intermediate stations were at Berwyn, Glyndyfrdwy and Carrog. There were two viaducts, one of six stone-and-brick arches, and the other of three wrought-iron girder spans on stone piers. The tunnel length was 686yd (627.7m). The captain also inspected a portion of the Corwen & Bala, 'about 68 chains [1.36km] long . . . single with sidings', which ran westwards from the L&C's termination to permit that company's trains to enter the C&B Corwen station. The L&C opened throughout on 8 May 1865. Finally, on 11 October 1865 Captain Tyler reported on a second line of rails alongside the C&B, extending for less than $\frac{1}{4}$-mile (0.4km) in continuation of the DR&C from its temporary station to the new C&B station :

> These two lines, each being single, now run, therefore, independently into the Corwen station of which one side is devoted to the traffic to and from the direction of Bala and the other to the traffic to and from Denbigh.

Thus by late 1865 both GWR and LNWR were at Corwen. Before coming to the Corwen & Bala, we must return to 1860, commencement of a struggle between the two major companies and their hangers-on for the route west of Corwen.

SCHEME AND COUNTER SCHEME

In October 1860 public meetings were held in Corwen and Bala to discuss a number of projects. A Corwen Bala & Barmouth Railway proposed to link Savin's Denbigh Ruthin & Corwen with his projected Aberystwith & Welch Coast Railway

Page 139 (*Top*) Manor class 4-6-0 No 7828 on down Cambrian Coast Express entering Welshpool, August 1963; (*centre*) Welshpool & Llanfair 0-6-2T *Joan* with train at Castle Caereinion, August 1977; (*bottom*) Class 2MT 2-6-0 No 46512 running round train at Llanfyllin terminus, September 1963. (*Author*)

Page 140 (*Top*) Train from Llanfyllin approaching Oswestry, September 1963; (*centre*) Llanidloes, looking south; (*bottom*) Tylwch, Mid Wales Railway, looking north, August 1935. (*Author; L&GRP, centre and bottom*)

(*sic*) (Chapter X). The GWR, intent on a take-over of the DR&C and Vale of Clwyd lines which would land it triumphantly in Rhyl, had no scheme west of Corwen. In opposition to the CB&B, the West Midland Company—angling for amalgamation with the GWR and thus not averse to the grandiose gesture—brought forth the West Midland Shrewsbury & Coast of Wales. This ran from Shrewsbury along a line similar to that of the later Shropshire & Montgomeryshire (Chapter XII) to Llanymynech, where junctions were planned to the Oswestry & Newtown main line and Porthywaen branch (Chapter X), thence via Llangynog and a $1\frac{1}{2}$ mile (2.4km) tunnel under the Berwyns to Llandrillo from where a branch went to Corwen. From Llandrillo the line ran via Bala, Dolgellau, and north along the coast through Barmouth and Harlech to Portmadoc, some 90 miles (144km), including branches. The prospectus emphasised the "urgent demand' of West Midland manufacturers for access to the sea. Slate would travel eastwards; coal and limestone would come west into Mid Wales. Passenger traffic was promising: 'The coast between Barmouth and Portmadoc . . . will become one large watering place', which was precisely what Savin had in mind for his schemes. Considering that the WM would have to make some 44 miles (70.8km) just to reach Corwen, the meeting there backed the CB&B. Perhaps because Colonel Tottenham supported the CB&B, and Paddington supported the colonel, Savin lodged a Bill for a straightforward DR&C extension to Bala, whence an allied Merionethshire Railway would link with a proposed A&WC Dolgellau branch. Though the WMS&CW failed early in Parliament, rejoicing in the Savin camp was shortlived : only his A&WC main line got through; the Dolgellau branch and DR&C extension were refused. Isolated, the Merionethshire scheme was withdrawn.

They returned in 1862 : Savin's Bala Railway, and the Merionethshire; in opposition a Corwen Bala & Portmadoc, via Trawsfynydd and Ffestiniog, promoted by GWR forces, and a Bala & Dolgelly (*sic*)—the West Midland scheme now drastically reduced and backed by the GWR, for amalgamation had been agreed upon. In April a Parliamentary committee examined the schemes. Benjamin Piercy was Savin's undoing, for his tortuous evidence revealed that if Savin got possession of the Barmouth–Corwen line, he would then control a vast area, even routing traffic circuitously north via Rhyl rather than relinquish it to the Great Western. Despite strenuous efforts by that formidable counsel, Edmund Denison, Savin's Bills were rejected. The CB&P (reduced to a Corwen–Bala line, and thus re-named), along with the Bala & Dolgelly, received Royal Assent on 30 June 1862. On 29 July the A&WC was authorised to make the Barmouth–Dolgellau link, Savin's companies receiving running powers between Dolgellau and Corwen, but framed to exclude the 'clandestine entrance' of the LNWR for, said the *Railway Times*, 'there is a certain character who climbs over the wall instead of making entrance by the door'.

The way was clear for completion of the line in favour of the Great Western. But to regain some perspective, what of Corwen and Bala at this time, to whose inhabitants extravagant claims and promises had been made by rival promoters? *Black's Guide*, 1866, said Corwen '. . . need not long detain the tourist . . . a small, quiet market-town. Any measure of prosperity it enjoys is derived from its situation . . . on the great Holyhead Road'. Population of the parish in 1861 was 2,042. And Bala: 'A small market-town, clean and neat . . . chiefly employed in weaving coarse woollens, and knitting worsted stockings, gloves, caps and neck wrappers . . . the women and children may be seen pursuing this work, when sitting in the open air, and walking along the road . . . a market on Saturday, and five annual fairs, chiefly for the sale of livestock . . . Population of the town of Bala, 1,341'. Stopped short of the coast, with only such rural goals immediately in view, Paddington lost its drive to complete the line; seven years were to pass before trains from Ruabon reached Barmouth.

OPENING CORWEN TO BARMOUTH

By Act of 21 July 1863 the Bala & Dolgelly agreed with the A&WC on the junction and joint station at Dolgellau, and obtained powers for a branch to the Bwlch Coch iron mines some two miles (3.2km) south of Dolgellau (not made). Throughout 1864 the Llangollen & Corwen and Corwen & Bala were still purchasing land, though by August Corwen station was nearly ready, and surveys were in hand for a line from Bala to Ffestiniog. A November 1865 Bill for amalgamation of the companies between Ruabon and Bala—the 'Dee Valley Railway'—was withdrawn. A portion of the Corwen & Bala, 4¾ miles (7.6km) from Corwen to Llandrillo, with intermediate Cynwyd station, opened on 16 July 1866. Paddington now consolidated its position by taking powers in 1867 for eventual amalgamation with the four small companies.

The remaining $7\frac{3}{4}$ miles (12.4km) of the C&B, with five small viaducts, a 76yd (69.5m) tunnel at Llanderfel, and stations at Llanderfel and Bala, opened on 1 April 1868. On 2 July 1868 Lt Col Hutchinson reported on the Bala & Dolgelly Railway, $17\frac{1}{4}$ miles (27.7km) in length. It ran for some $3\frac{1}{2}$ miles (5.6km) along the east shore of Lake Bala, at the south end of which was the first stopping place mentioned in the report, a private halt, Glanllyn 'Flag' station, linked by ferry with a residence on the far shore. Beyond the lake the line climbed past Pandy station (soon renamed Llanuwchllyn) to the head of the short Afon Dyfrdwy Valley, crossed the watershed at Garneddwen— summit of the line at 760ft (232m)—into the narrow valley of the Wnion which rises from and is watered by 2,970ft (906m) Aran Mawddwy, two miles to the south. The line continued down the steep-sided valley, with 2,408ft (734m) Rhobell Fawr to the north, through Drws-y-Nant station, and with the valley opening out, down the steepest gradient between Ruabon and Barmouth Junction—1 in 50—to Bontnewydd station before easing-off to reach Dolgelley station (renamed Dolgellau in 1960), dominated to the immediate south by Cader Idris. Except for a small booking hut, none of the intermediate stations had accommodation; Glanllyn had nothing. The colonel gave grudging approval to the railway and it opened on 4 August 1868. That month the B&D directors' report noted that Dolgelley station building, then in progress, had been delayed 'in consequence of negotiations with the Cambrian', and that the GWR had organised a 'very efficient service' between Ruabon and Dolgelley.

The town of Dolgellau, with just over 2,000 inhabitants in the 1860s, lies in a fertile valley formed by the confluence of the Wnion with the Mawddach flowing down from the Merioneth Mountains to the north. The main industry was the manufacturing of webs, a coarse woollen fabric, and the town was the principal market for the area, through which stage and mail coaches had operated to Llangollen since 1862. The Cambrian's Dolgellau branch opened to Penmaenpool on 3 July 1865, but financial troubles delayed completion. The Cambrian was prodded into action by the GWR and B&D; anxious to reach the coast, they obtained powers to construct the Penmaenpool–

Dolgellau length if not opened by the Cambrian by August 1869. The railways into Dolgellau did not meet head-on. The B&D station was some distance from that line's termination, while the Cambrian branch, planned to terminate at a separate station, required a deviation to effect a junction. Lt Col Rich inspected the final 1¾ miles (2.8km) of Cambrian, and ¼ mile (0.4km) of B&D beyond Dolgelley station, on 11 June 1869. Cambrian trains commenced running into Dolgellau on 21 June. Though the GWR absorbed the B&D in 1877, it did not amalgamate with the other three companies until 1896.

IMPROVEMENTS AND SERVICES

There was now an alternative route to the coast. As traffic built up, improvements were made. East of Barmouth Junction, Arthog opened in 1870, and a passing loop and second platform at Glyndyfrdwy in 1877. In 1880 a junction went in at Bala for works trains on the Bala–Ffestiniog branch (Chapter VIII), opened on 1 November 1882 to its own Bala station in the town. The original C&B building became Bala Old station (later Bala Lake Halt), and a new down loop and platform, and an island platform for the up line and the Ffestiniog branch single line, as a passenger interchange with no outside public access, were established at the new junction ½ mile (0.8km) eastward. Colonel Rich, inspecting the junction station in May 1884, thought it inadequate for the large summer passenger traffic; it remained unaltered. In 1895 a passing loop and down platform were opened at Drws-y-Nant; Llanuwchllyn down platform was rebuilt and the loop extended.

Stations were crowded in summertime, notably that on the river bank at Llangollen. According to 'Reminiscences of a Retired Great Western Railway Superintendent' (*Railway Magazine*, June 1930), the town was:

> the favourite inland resort of Welsh people in North Wales and Liverpool . . . The biggest crowd the place ever had was in 1889 when Queen Victoria came here on a visit . . . I was one of eighteen people in a compartment that day. On Bank Holidays, if wet, people wanted to leave early, if fine the last trains were packed. At Llangollen for some years there was but one line of rails for up and down trains, which added to the difficulties. The jovial humour and good natured fun of the crowds were an abiding feature.

In September 1900 Major General Hutchinson inspected the doubling of the line between Ruabon Junction and Llangollen, and the improved arrangements at Pentrefelin carriage and wagon storage sidings—where Llangollen excursion trains awaited return—situated $\frac{3}{4}$ mile (1.2km) west of the station and $\frac{1}{4}$ mile (0.4km) beyond Llangollen goods yard where the doubling ended. Acrefair, Trevor and Llangollen stations were remodelled. Rail motors appeared in 1905, Garth & Sun Bank Halt (Sun Bank Halt from 1906) opening midway between Trevor and Llangollen. Before World War I new passing loops went in at Deeside, between Berwyn and Glyndyfrdwy, and at Garneddwen, to which heavy trains were banked from Llanuwchllyn, some three miles (4.8km) to the east. In the early 1920s Bontnewydd station was reconstructed with a new loop and up and down platforms slightly west of the first station. During the first three decades of the 20th century more halts opened: Bonwm, Llangower, Llys, Garneddwen, Wnion, and Dolserau, all except Bonwm (Carrog–Corwen) being between Bala and Dolgelley. Sun Bank closed in June 1950 and Dolserau in October 1951, but most of the others remained until passenger services ceased.

As for services, in the mid-1870s the 10.00 am out of Paddington, with a change at Ruabon, gave a Barmouth arrival at 6.41 pm. There were two down and three up Ruabon–Barmouth trains on weekdays with, additional each way, one Corwen–Barmouth and three Ruabon–Corwen, where connections were made with DR&C trains. Sundays saw one Ruabon–Barmouth and one Ruabon–Corwen train each way. For years Corwen boasted a shed for two tender or six tank engines (closed 1927), and goods, exchange and carriage sidings west of the station. West of Dolgelley, until the Grouping, Cambrian locomotives took over from the GWR. At the turn of the century passengers could leave Paddington at 9.50 am and arrive at Barmouth at 5.50 pm.

The most intensive service operated between the wars. Taking just the down trains, on Mondays to Fridays the 9.10 am from Paddington, with restaurant car to Ruabon, had through coaches to Pwllheli, reaching Barmouth at 3.21 pm—some $2\frac{1}{2}$ hours' improvement over the 1870s timings. There were over 20 different down journeys, six making the complete run, of which two conveyed through Paddington and Birkenhead coaches for Pwllheli. On Saturdays three additional trains ran over the whole line, two having through coaches: Paddington, Birkenhead and

Manchester; and Reading, Birmingham and Birkenhead. Six weekday trips were made by the Ruabon–Llangollen shuttle, five Ruabon–Dolgelley, and two Ruabon–Corwen, one of which on Thursdays and Saturdays took passengers by road motor between Llangollen and Corwen. An afternoon road motor trip ran between Corwen and Dolgelley. Trips south of Bala included two between Drws-y-Nant and Barmouth, and four Dolgelley–Barmouth. Sunday morning saw a through Birkenhead–Barmouth train, and through coaches arrived in mid-afternoon at Llangollen from Liverpool and Chester. There were three Sunday Ruabon–Llangollen shuttle trips, two continuing to Corwen by road motor. World War II saw a much reduced service, with Sunday trains taken off, not to return. Following withdrawal of the Ffestiniog and Denbigh line services, the timetable became progressively simplified, though the line west of Corwen was host in the 1950s to the land cruise trains (p 79).

CLOSURE AND NEW LIFE

The route narrowly missed being the one retained after the Beeching Report (p 168). All freight services, except Ruabon-Llangollen, ceased in 1964. On 12–13 December 1964 there was severe flooding, breaching the line east of Bala and near Dolgellau. Though Ruabon–Llangollen and Bala–Dolgellau passenger services were resumed, the rest of the line remained closed, since total closure was already fixed for 18 January 1965 when a new Wrexham–Barmouth bus service commenced. Trevor goods to the Monsanto Chemical Works at Pontcysyllte closed from 1 January 1968, and the Ruabon–Llangollen Goods Junction freight service ceased from 1 April 1968. Track lifting started soon afterwards. In 1977 Dolgellau station made way for a town bypass; 5½ miles (8.8km) of the westerly end of the line was opened as the 'Penmaenpool-Morfa Mawddach Walk' in 1979.

In 1970 there was a proposal for a 28-mile (45km) Bala–Morfa Mawddach narrow gauge railway. Nothing came of this, but on 13 August 1972 the Bala Lake Railway, a 1ft 11⅝in (60cm) gauge tourist line, opened from Llanuwchllyn station 1¼ miles (2km) to Pentrepiod Platform, worked by a small Ruston diesel and two semi-open bogie coaches. A further ¼ mile (1.2km) to Llangower—slightly west of the old halt—opened from 15 September 1972. The terminus (formerly Bala Lake Halt), 4½ miles (7.2km) from Llanuwchllyn, was reached on 28 March 1976. Another Ruston and a Bo-Bo diesel-hydraulic

Meirionnydd arrived in 1973, followed by Henschel 0–4–0 tank *Helen Kathryn* (p 106). This and another steam locomotive proving to be unsuitable, ex-Dinorwic Hunslet 0–4–0 saddle tank *Maid Marian* (see p. 106 and Chapter XVI) arrived to join *Meirionnydd* on passenger services. The two Rustons were exchanged in 1976 for a larger one (named *Chilmark* in 1979 in memory of its time at RAF Chilmark) for use on works trains. Two-train operation became possible in May 1977 when Llangower received a passing loop. In 1978 restoration was completed on another Dinorwic Hunslet, *Holy War*, built in 1902. (See Chapter XVI.)

Llangollen station and three miles (4.8km) of trackbed became home to the Flint & Deeside Railway Preservation Society in 1975; with just 60ft (18m) of standard gauge track relaid, the station 'reopened' to visitors on 13 September. In 1977 Shell Oil UK donated a mile (1.6km) of track which was laid towards the site of Pentre Felin sidings where there would be a loop; that year the members decided to adopt the name of the Llangollen Railway Society. Items of passenger and goods rolling stock were acquired, with some locomotives: 1932-built Kitson 0–6–0ST *Austin 1* (later renamed *Burtonwood Brewer* after its owners), 1917 Hudswell Clarke 0–6–0T *Richborough*, 1948 Peckett 0–4–0ST, 1939 Fowler 0–4–0 diesel *Elisig*, 1955 Sentinel 4-wheeled vertical-boilered tank, and 1920 Peckett 0–6–0ST *Ackton Hall*. The 1980s were to see transformation into a restored railway to Berwyn, with the intention of reaching Corwen. (See Chapter XVI.)

CHAPTER X

The Cambrian Main Line

WREXHAM AND WHITCHURCH TO ABERYSTWYTH AND PWLLHELI

The history of the Cambrian Railways Company has been told comprehensively by Christiansen and Miller. Here, the frequently stormy financial and political background is largely omitted. Little will be said about locomotives, except for mentioning some used on construction and opening services, and those whose re-appearance in other chapters may be of interest. The main line consisted of several small railways which joined to form the sole Welsh company of any size in the region—hence its plural title. Though often land was bought and works made for eventual double track, the finished line was mostly single.

EARLY SCHEMES, OSWESTRY TO MACHYNLLETH

In the late 1830s an Irish mail route planned by Brunel through Ludlow, Newtown, and Barmouth to Porth Dinllaen came to naught; not until 1845–6 did schemes appear along the route of the later Cambrian. A premature appearance was made by the Manchester & Milford Haven Railway, from Crewe via Oswestry, Welshpool, Newtown, Llanidloes, Tregaron, Lampeter, and Haverfordwest, with a Cardigan branch. Boasting 86 provisional directors, the M&M failed to deposit plans by November 1845 and amalgamated with the Manchester & Birmingham Continuation & Welsh Junction, with the same route to Llanidloes and then to Aberystwyth, whence a steamer service to Wexford was planned. Renamed as the Manchester & Aberystwyth, its eastern end was discarded in favour of a proposed Shropshire Union Crewe–Newtown line, in turn shelved after the SU lease to the LNWR. The M&A Bill was withdrawn.

Concurrently, the Great North & South Wales & Worcester proposed two lines : from Carmarthen via Cardigan, Aberystwyth, Machynlleth, and Dolgellau to Porth Dinllaen; and Machynlleth to Newtown, Ludlow and Worcester. When the GWR's Worcester and Porth Dinllaen project appeared (p 92), the GN&SW put forward a Newtown–Machynlleth–Aberystwyth line with a branch to Cardigan, but its Bill was withdrawn. By 1851 Newtown, at the southerly end of the Montgomeryshire Canal, had a population of 3,784. Fourteen miles to the south-west, at the head of the Vale of Severn, lay Llanidloes, with a population of 4,604. Both towns, thriving centres of the flannel industry and Welshpool, 4,391 souls, with flannel, malting and tanning sought connection to the nearest railhead at Oswestry.

Late 1852 saw two schemes : the Shrewsbury & Aberystwith (sic), via Criggion, Welshpool, Newtown, Machynlleth and the Dovey Estuary; and the Montgomeryshire Railways, via Minsterley, Newtown, Llanidloes and Llangurig to Aberystwyth, with an Oswestry branch. Euston, attracted by Welsh ventures, intended subscribing to the S&A, but for safety's sake deposited Bills for a Shrewsbury–Newtown line and Oswestry branch, and a Crewe–Shrewsbury line. This threat to the Montgomeryshire Bill, cut back anyway to Newtown, caused the town of Llanidloes to promote its own railway along the Severn Valley to Newtown, there to join whatever Parliament passed. The Llanidloes & Newtown received Royal Assent on 4 August 1853, the other schemes failing. The L&N's isolation triggered plans to link and extend, and by Act of 26 June 1855 the Oswestry & Newtown Railway was incorporated, joining the L&N and GWR. A clause protected LNWR aspirations towards a Shrewsbury–Welshpool line (Chapter XII). The L&N and O&N chairman was George Hammond Whalley.

OPENING LLANIDLOES TO NEWTOWN

For the L&N sod-cutting the directors decided to invite an important shareholder, Mrs Ann Warburton Owen, to do the honours. Unaccountably they neglected to inform her. On learning of her star billing through a local newspaper, she took umbrage and refused the invitation. The ceremony, in heavy rain, was conducted by Whalley at Llanidloes on 3 October 1855. Construction was let to David Davies, whose home village of Llandinam was on the route (his statue now stands by the riverside there). It was at this time that he took into partnership Thomas Savin. In late 1857, when virtually complete, the works ceased for lack of money, following which Davies and Savin moved to the Vale of Clwyd Railway. Their methods of financing and constructing that line (Chapter V), were applied to the L&N which they leased by Act of 21 July 1859, having already recommenced work. A goods service started on 30 April that year, and in June Colonel Yolland inspected the 11½-mile (18.5km) line, with intermediate Llandinam station. Meanwhile, the Manchester & Milford returned to the scene, using part of the L&N. The colonel thought L&N construction unsuitable for the heavy projected M&M traffic, and the Newtown turntable and platforms, and station buildings, termed 'wooden boxes', at Llandinam and Llanidloes, were incomplete. Rain on inspection day hastened his requirement for a second visit. He noted the line was to be worked by the contractors who had two loco-motives available, only one of which was fitted for passenger traffic. As the gradients were against the greater part of the goods traffic a second locomotive was 'absolutely indispensable'. The locomotives arrived by road from Oswestry, stores coming by canal. The first used by Davies on construction of the L&N is thought to have been an 1839 Sharp, Roberts ex-Birmingham & Derby Junction 2–2–2 tender locomotive *Dove*; others were two by Manning Wardle, o–6–o saddle tank *Llandinam*, and *Enterprise* (probably an o–6–o side tank, used later during con-struction of the Llanfyllin branch and the Carnarvonshire Railway, which became Cambrian Railways' No 1); *Milford* (sister to the three V of C locomotives, and which went to con-structing Savin's A&WCR (p 157), becoming Cambrian No 3); and three known merely by their names, *Squirrel*, *Llanidloes* and *Llewelyn*.

On 6 August Captain Ross passed the line, and an extra station at Dolwen. The official opening took place on 31 August 1859, presided over by a presumably happier Mrs Owen, when *Milford* and *Llewelyn* hauled 48 carriages and trucks, carrying 3,000 persons. Three passenger trains commenced running each way on weekdays from 2 September.

COMPLETION OF THE OSWESTRY & NEWTOWN

Under direction from Joseph Cubitt, O&N engineer, the con-tractors, Davidson and Oughterson, started work from the lime-producing area around Llanymynech on the Welsh border, northwards along the Berwyn foothills towards Oswestry. Again money troubles plagued construction; again Davies and Savin stepped in.

The LNWR Crewe–Shrewsbury line opened on 1 September 1858. With the Shrewsbury–Welshpool line under construction the O&N agreed to allow LNWR trains to run from Cefn (Buttington Junction), where the S&W joined the O&N, into Welshpool, and for doubling between those points (p 190). A joint station was planned with the L&N at Newtown, and an O&N Act of 3 July 1860 authorised a 1¾-mile (2.8km) branch from Llynclys, north of Llanymynech, to Porthywaen lime quarries (p 180).

In April 1860 Colonel Yolland inspected 11¼ miles (18.1km) of the O&N (single line on double formation) between Oswestry and 'Tyn-y-Celyn or Bank Pool Quay' station, parallelling the Oswestry–Welshpool–Newtown road and carried by iron viaducts over the canal and the River Vyrnwy. 'In no instance', he reported, 'were the underbridges or viaducts completed for a double line'. 'Completed' is significant: it seems that the Vyrnwy viaduct at least had sets of triple caisson piers allowing for an additional deck. There were stations and sidings at Llynclys, Llanymynech, 'Llandysilio' (Four Crosses), and Pool Quay. Oswestry to Pool Quay opened on 1 May 1860. The 4¾-mile (7.6km) Pool Quay–Welshpool line, with two iron girder bridges over the Severn which inadequately—a common central girder being unsuitable for half the load of each line—provided for future doubling, opened on 14 August 1860 with an Oswestry–Welshpool service of six trains each way and two on Sundays. On the same day Llandloes & Newtown company trains reached Abermule, seemingly prematurely, for the 14½-mile (23.3km) Welshpool–Newtown single line with stations and sidings at Forden, Montgomery, and Abermule, was not inspected until 4 June 1861. As well as several timber viaducts, this length included a five-span iron skew viaduct over the Severn at Cil-Cewydd and a climb to Forden, being on a deviation made necessary solely by the refusal of an O&N shareholder, the doughty Mrs Ann Owen, to have the railway near her home, Glansevern, near Berriew.

The O&N was open throughout on 10 June 1861, all but one of the six trains continuing on to Llanidloes. The fine 'French Renaissance' style Welshpool station housed the O&N headquarters between its move from Oswestry in February 1860 and transfer to a London address in January 1862, from which time a joint committee worked the O&N and L&N. According to Christiansen and Miller, Llynclys, Llanymynech, Welshpool, Montgomery and Abermule had passing loops. Doubling Buttington–Welshpool was passed by the Board of Trade in January 1862, and Oswestry–Llanymynech in February 1864, when Oswestry station still had only one platform. At Llany- mynech, a new second platform was shortly to serve the West Shropshire Mineral Railway, then building (Chapter XII). Buttington Junction station opened concurrently with the S&W in 1862, Pant and Ardleen by 1864.

NEWTOWN–MACHYNLLETH LINE

During construction of the Oswestry–Llanidloes lines, surveys were made towards Aberystwyth, goal of the 1852 promoters. Barring the way lay mighty Plynlimon, 2,469ft (753m). An avoiding route was found, leaving the L&N south-east of Caersws and ascending the Carno Valley to Talerddig summit, to cross the Severn–Dovey watershed, thence down the Iaen and Twymyn valleys to Cemmes Road and the Dovey and on to the market town of Machynlleth, population 1,673 in 1861, some five miles from the estuary.

The Newtown & Machynlleth incorporation Act of 27 July 1857 sanctioned traffic agreement with the L&N, O&N, S&W, GWR, and LNWR. Earl Vane was chairman, the countess cutting the first sod in November 1858. David Davies was the main shareholder; he and Savin were the contractors. Progress was hindered by bad weather, land acquisition, and difficult construction, including river diversion and heavy earthworks. The 120ft 0in (36.6m) deep excavation through a gritstone ridge at Talerddig was for some years the world's deepest railway cutting. Meanwhile, Davies cautiously backed extension of the N&M to Aberystwyth, in conjunction with the Corris Railway (Chapter XI). Savin, heading the N&Ms eastern neighbours, aiming for tourist traffic, was for plunging ahead with a coastal Aberystwyth–Pwllheli line, some 50 miles (80km) of difficult construction. To Davies and the N&M, Savin's project appeared rash; a slow and sure approach was preferred. The difference led in 1860 to dissolution of the partnership, Davies continuing with the N&M works. The first contractor's train reached

Machynlleth on May Day 1862; in December Captain Tyler sanctioned the 22¾-mile (36.6km) single line. Negotiations for the GWR to work the N&M failed, the line being leased to the O&N. The joint committee's trains extended to Machynlleth from 3 January 1863, calling at the intermediate stations of Caersws Junction (renamed Moat Lane), Pontdolgoch, Carno, Llanbrynmair, and Cemmes Road, the last three having passing loops.

Locomotives working the joint committee services were *Milford* (but see p 150), and three types of tender engine: six Sharp, Stewart 0–4–2 mixed-traffic, built 1859–60, Nos 4 *Wynnstay*, 5 *Montgomery*, 6 *Glansevern*, 7 *Llanerchydol*, 8 *Leighton*, and 9 *Volunteer*; and a number of the firm's 0–6–0 small goods and 2–4–0 small passenger classes, delivered in batches respectively from 1861 and 1863. Their history does not concern us here, save to say that under Savin's rule some strayed to his other ventures, but nearly all came to form the Cambrian's working stock for three decades. Two of the goods worked the N&M opening service, Nos 34 *Talerddig* and 35 *Countess Vane*. These two were eventually renamed, the name *Talerddig* going in 1875 to a new Sharp, Stewart 0–6–0 side tank, No 13, which was shedded at Machynlleth for banking trains up the 14-mile (22.5km), 1 in 52 ruling gradient, climb to Talerddig summit.

OSWESTRY TO WHITCHURCH

With the opening of the LNWR Crewe–Shrewsbury line the Welsh companies grasped the opportunity to reach Crewe. October 1860 saw a projected Oswestry Ellesmere & Whitchurch Railway, with a branch to Ffrith (p 52). Euston welcomed the scheme. Paddington backed rival Bills: the Shrewsbury Oswestry & Ellesmere, and the Ellesmere & Whitchurch. These failed, the OE&W receiving Royal Assent on 1 August 1861, though the Act postponed construction west of Ellesmere until September 1862 pending possible LNWR and GWR agreement on a more suitable link between Ellesmere, Ruabon, Oswestry and Shrewsbury. While Savin started work at the easterly end, a scramble developed between the competing parties. For 1862 the OE&W promoted a Ruabon–Ellesmere–Wem line, to divert Mold–Wrexham traffic south via the Crewe–Shrewsbury line, leaving the GWR out of the picture. An Ellesmere Oswestry Ruabon & Shrewsbury Bill, offering something similar, was rejected. The GWR lodged an Oswestry Shrewsbury & Ellesmere Lines Bill, including Ellesmere to Whittington on the S&C, with running powers to Whitchurch and Llanidloes, and undertook to complete the OE&W if that company took sufficient fright at this onslaught as to give up the ghost altogether; the Bill failed in the Lords. Out of this turmoil, only the OE&W's Ellesmere–Wem branch received Royal Assent, and even that was not made. Proposals in 1863 and 1864 for extensions to Ruabon and the Vale of Llangollen were rejected.

The first $10\frac{3}{4}$ miles (17.3km) of the OE&W, Whitchurch to Ellesmere, included the crossing of Fenn's Moss by a timber-framed brushwood raft. The line was single, with land and bridges for double track. Captain Tyler reported in May 1863 that 'it will be worked as a branch by the London & North Western Railway Company', which was enlarging Whitchurch station. Goods services started from 20 April, and passenger trains from 4 May, with intermediate stations at Welshampton, Bettisfield, and Fenn's Bank. The largest station was at Ellesmere, a two-storey brick building suitable for the company's head-quarters. The $7\frac{1}{4}$-mile (11.6km) single line on to Oswestry, which crossed another peat bog, opened on 27 July 1864 with Whittington as the only intermediate station; Frankton, on the Welsh border, opened in 1866.

FORMATION OF THE CAMBRIAN

In 1862 the O&N sought amalgamation with the L&N and Shrewsbury & Welshpool, and to subscribe to the little Bishops Castle Railway which, commencing at Craven Arms on the Shrewsbury & Hereford, doubled back on itself but had pretensions, via Montgomery, to become a cut-off to South Wales (BC powers in 1884 to this end were abandoned in 1887). A similar amalgamation Bill involved the LNWR, while the GWR attempted to lease the Newtown & Machynlleth. All three Bills were withdrawn. While the Machynlleth company flirted with Paddington, the L&N, O&N, and OE&W made agreements with Euston. Bills to confirm these, and to unite the three into a Cambrian Railways Company, were lodged for 1863. The powers sought affected a dozen Welsh companies in one way or another, as well as the GWR and LNWR, and could have resulted in a vast undertaking, covering a large area of Wales: they were rejected by Parliament. An O&N Bill, however, for a branch to Tregynon (not made) and a siding at Porthywaen, received Royal Assent on 29 June 1863. Finally, by Act of 25 July 1864, the four Whitchurch–Machynlleth lines amalgamated as the Cambrian Railways Company, with agreements with the Mid Wales and Manchester & Milford companies (Chapter XIII) and mutual traffic facilities with the GWR. A separate Act confirmed LNWR agreements. The Aberystwith & Welch Coast Railway was to seek powers in 1865 to unite with the new company.

ENTER THE ABERYSTWITH & WELCH COAST RAILWAY

So far, emphasis for major Welsh railway development had been on the Chester & Holyhead in the north, and the South Wales Railway; the country along Cardigan Bay was still unprovided for. The slow advance westwards by the Cambrian constituents, and the belief that Porth Dinllaen might yet develop for Irish traffic, revived interest in a railway to serve that port and the coastline south to Aberystwyth. Here was an area of growing tourist potential. Hotels were springing up, at Aberystwyth, Borth, Towyn and Barmouth. With a population of 5,561 in 1861 Aberystwyth was the terminus logically claimed by the Newtown & Machynlleth. That year saw failure of Bills from the West Midland Shrewsbury & Coast of Wales Railway (p 141), via Llangynog and Bala to Portmadoc, and a Portmadoc & Porth Dinllaen project. By Act of 22 July 1861, however the Aberystwith & Welch Coast Company (*sic*) was incorporated for a line from Aberystwyth, through Towyn, Barmouth and Portmadoc to Pwllheli, with a connection south of the Dovey to the N&M at Machynlleth. Whalley was the chairman, Piercy the engineer, and Savin the contractor. While the L&N and O&N subscribed a quarter of the share capital, the hostile N&M insisted on a clause that failing prompt construction between Machynlleth and Aberystwyth, it might take over and complete that length itself.

At the northerly end of the A&WC was the newly authorised Carnarvonshire Railway, sharing the Afon Wen–Portmadoc length, for which the A&WC exercised the duplicated powers. By Act of 29 July 1862 the A&WC was authorised to extend to Porth Dinllaen (not exercised, but see p 162); and from Barmouth up the Mawddach Estuary to Dolgellau (spelt Dolgelley or Dolgelly for many years), there to block extension towards the coast by pro-Great Western companies advancing down the Dee and Wnion valleys. An A&WC Bill in 1863 for a branch to Blaenau Ffestiniog met combined opposition from the Festiniog Railway and the Blaenau quarry owners and was thrown out by Parliament.

OPENING MACHYNLLETH TO ABERYSTWYTH

The Machynlleth–Aberystwyth line was built first, to secure quick returns, as a railhead for extension northwards, and to scotch N&M acquisitiveness. In June 1863 Captain Rich reported on the 12¼-mile (19.7km) single line (land for double) Machynlleth–Borth section along the Dovey's flood plain, with intermediate stations and passing loops at Glan Dovey and Ynys Las (*sic*), and including eleven wooden viaducts. The opening to Borth on 1 July, worked by the contractor, attracted many visitors to the coast from the hitherto virtually inaccessible hinterland. The remaining 8¾ miles (14km) single line through the hills to Aberystwyth was inspected in May 1864, when it was in use for freight. It opened to passengers on 23 June (*Bradshaw's Shareholders' Guide* gives 1 August), with stations and passing loops at Llanfihangel and Bow Street. Completion of the OE&W in 1864 saw the first through service, including two up and three down Whitchurch–Aberystwyth trains, and a through coach between Euston and the resort. Trains passed each other at Oswestry, Llanymynech, Buttington Junction–Welshpool, Montgomery, Newtown, and Moat Lane, with locomotive changes at Oswestry and Welshpool.

PIECEMEAL NORTH OF THE DOVEY

Postponing crossing of the Dovey Estuary, construction had been proceeding on the 10¾ miles (17.3km) of single line (again, land for double) between Aberdovey and Llwyngwril, with an intermediate station at Towyn. Apart from a narrow stretch near Llangelynin, where the foothills of Cader Idris, 2,927ft (892m), reach the coast, this length crossed the flood plain of the rivers Dyffryn, Dysynni and Fathew. There were three wooden viaducts. For construction, Savin had locomotives ferried across from a temporary siding at Ynyslas on the Machynlleth–Aberystwyth line (shown on contemporary Ordnance Survey maps) to Aberdovey harbour. These included

Milford (p 150), and Manning Wardle 0–6–0 saddle tanks *Cardigan* and *Merion* (p 179), all three of which went into Cambrian stock. After coaching stock had likewise arrived, Aberdovey harbour to Llwyngwril opened to the public on 24 October 1863 (*Bradshaw's Shareholders' Guide* gives November, and other sources 1 November), with three trains daily each way.

North of Llwyngwril the flanks of Cader Idris fall steeply to the sea, and the railway climbs as high as possible before running for about ½ mile (0.8km), some 100ft (30.5m) above the shore, ledged into the cliffs at Friog, with the road 100ft higher still. In June 1865 Captain Tyler inspected the 3¾ miles (6km) from Llwyngwril to the Mawddach Estuary where a junction was to be made with the uncompleted continuation to the north, and 5½ completed miles (8.8km) on to a temporary terminus at Penmaenpool on the branch to Dolgellau (Chapter IX). The branch junction was only single-line, 'but a triangle is to be formed in connection with it, with a double line on all sides'. Llwyngwril to Penmaenpool opened on 3 July 1865.

COMPLETING THE COAST LINE

Attempts to cross the Dovey proved too difficult and the railway was diverted around the estuary, avoiding Aberdovey harbour by taking a sinuous route behind the town, with heavy earth-works, sea walls, and four tunnels totalling 1,139yd (1,042m). The necessary Bill sought purchase of the Dovey and Mawddach ferries, and running powers over the Wnion and Dee valley lines (Dolgellau–Llangollen) which were to be reciprocated so that users of those lines could reach Aberystwyth. The Dovey deviation, with eastbound trailing junction to the Machynlleth–Aberystwyth line at Morben, denied through running to the resort from the north, and Paddington insisted on the right within ten years to construct the original cut-off, bridging the estuary. The A&WC Bill received Royal Assent on 5 July 1865, the same day as the Cambrian and Coast Railways (Amalgamation) Bill, incorporating the A&WC into the Cambrian system, and a separate Cambrian Act which abandoned the OE&W's Wem branch and authorised a lease of the entire Cambrian undertaking to Savin who, for works done, had acquired a considerable shareholding. An attempt by Whalley in 1864 to remove Savin had backfired, Whalley and other directors resigning. David Williams of Castle Deudraeth had become chairman, and Henry Conybeare had replaced Benjamin Piercy as Cambrian engineer.

After Savin's bankruptcy the company continued the works, and an Act of 6 August 1866 authorised a deviation in Abererch, improvements at Oswestry, Welshpool and Newtown. In September 1866 Captain Tyler inspected the 6-mile (9.6km) single line Dovey deviation between Morben Junction and Aberdovey. The Dovey was crossed just west of Morben Junction by a 140yd (128m) viaduct with 17 timber and three iron spans, and a 37ft 0in (11.28m) rolling section to let vessels through. The captain found deflection in the viaduct, and required the telegraph to be installed to protect trains in the tunnels. Sea walls, earthworks and tunnels required completion. Morben Junction '. . . will necessarily be a staff station, but it is not, I understand, to be used at present for the interchange of passengers, and no platforms or other accommodation has been provided . . .'. In November the works were still unfinished and clearance was insufficient in the tunnels. That month Conybeare was replaced by George Owen.

Meanwhile, construction proceeded north of the Mawddach Estuary. *Black's Picturesque Guide to North Wales* (1866) described conditions at Barmouth Ferry, the only intermediate station between Llwyngwril and Penmaenpool, and later superseded by Fairbourne station :

> We are requested to mention, that until the railway-bridge over the estuary of the Mawr is opened, passengers per rail from the south or east should go on to Dolgelly, and drive the ten miles to Barmouth, especially if they have much luggage or the weather be unfavourable, instead of getting out at Barmouth Ferry station.
>
> In the latter case there are two miles to drive in an open car, followed by a walk from 50 to 300 or 400 yards, according to the state of the tide, over the rough pebbly beach, to reach the small boat, which has only one man to manage it. The sail is often very rough, and nearly half-a-mile in length. If it is low water, there is a bar of rough gravel (perhaps 300 yards long) in the centre of the estuary, over which it is necessary to walk, and then another boat has to be taken to reach Barmouth – a mode of proceeding not very convenient for ladies and children.

The 33¼ miles (53.5km) between the junction south of the estuary and Pwllheli (including Portmadoc–Afon Wen, for which the Carnarvonshire Railway had given notice of opening) were inspected by Captain Tyler in March 1867. He was not impressed :

> I have been placed in considerable difficulty during my inspection from the want of any plans or details of the line, except on the Carnarvonshire portion. . . . I find on my return to London that the plans &c which were borrowed from the Board of Trade by Mr Conybeare in November 1866 have now been returned. But no drawings have been furnished of the Barmouth Viaduct which is the most important work on the line . . .

There was inadequate fencing and the permanent way needed attention. Accommodation was lacking 'for the signalmen at the level crossings at the Croesor Railway and Gorsedda Railway' (Chapter VIII). Pwllheli required a road approach and goods accommodation; at Afon Wen 'the branch line from Pwllheli should run into a siding at the back of the north platform and a second siding should be provided for the engine to run round its train'. Goods facilities were lacking at other stations, and the passenger accommodation was 'of limited description'.

At Portmadoc the railway ran on the landward side of the cob (Chapter VIII), and required only a small viaduct over the Glaslyn. On the long Mawddach Estuary viaduct, of 113 wooden and eight iron spans, with rolling section, the captain found it took two men 37 minutes to open and close the bridge, which he thought excessive. The cross-girders on the opening portion actually hung on the main-girder rivet heads, while the cast-iron tripod columns beneath, unless protected from shipping, could cause collapse of the structure. Also tested were girder deflection and column stability. At Barmouth Junction (for the Dolgellau branch) 'shelter is much required and a second platform should be provided . . .'.

At the Dovey deviation, though tunnel linings had been rebuilt, they were still too narrow. The captain's suggestion of barring the carriage windows was endorsed by Major Hutchinson in May 1867 when, north of Barmouth Junction, he found that 'no works whatever have been executed . . . since Captain Tyler's inspection'. Trains called at Barmouth Junction from 3 June, when Barmouth Ferry station closed. Passengers were conveyed by horse-drawn carriage over the viaduct; it was officially passed for passenger traffic that September. Apparently the ferry was not completely superseded until the opening of the viaduct footpath, authorised in 1868.

The Aberdovey line, known to locals as the 'Doveyation' (H. M. Pearson, *Railway Magazine*, July 1937), opened on 14 August 1867 with a small branch to Aberdovey harbour, and an isolated island platform interchange between the Aberystwyth and Pwllheli lines amidst windswept marshland at Glandovey (late Morben, later Dovey) Junction. In the north, Carnarvonshire Railway trains started running to Afon Wen from 2 September 1867 (but see p 98), continuing on the Cambrian to Penrhyndeudraeth. With the Merioneth mountains as a backdrop and the sweep of sea and sky to the west, the remaining coast line opened on 10 October 1867. The first and main intermediate station was Barmouth, serving the small town (in Llanaber parish, population 1,672 in 1861), where houses were terraced up the slopes of the mountain, whose people traded in flannel and hosiery and boasted 'a hundred small sloops' belonging to the 'port'. The next station was Dyffryn (later Ardudwy was added), followed by Llanbedr & Pensarn, and Harlech, at the foot of the cliffs beneath the castle. A straight level stretch across Morfa Harlech followed to Talsarnau, then a sharp westerly curve across the mouth of the Vale of Ffestiniog, through Penrhyndeudraeth, and a climb to Minffordd (where an exchange passenger and goods station with the Festiniog opened in 1872). A descent followed to Traeth Mawr —reclaimed marshland (Chapter VIII)—crossed on the level for 1½ miles (2.4km) with a marvellous panoramic view to the north of the Glaslyn Estuary, half circled by mountains and with Snowdon majestically beyond. After the next station, Portmadoc (Chapter VIII), the railway climbed through woodland, and then descended south-westwards to Criccieth, with another castle. The isolated Afon Wen Junction station was followed by Abererch, and the railway ended at the first Pwllheli terminus. Intermediate stations had passing loops, save Llanbedr, Talsarnau and Abererch. The first service was of four weekday trains each way, traversing the 125 miles (201km) between Whitchurch and Pwllheli.

The opening day ended appropriately: the first passenger train left Portmadoc at 7.00 a.m.; at Barmouth Junction the officials were embarrassed to be served (or perhaps they were used to such things) with a Chancery injunction for landowners between Pensarn and Barmouth. 'It is not true, as stated by some of our contemporaries', said the *Oswestry Advertiser,* 'that trains have ceased running between Barmouth and Portmadoc'. The opening throughout coincided with an attempt to amalgamate the Cambrian, the Potteries Shrewsbury & North Wales (Chapter XII), the Mid Wales (Chapter XIII) and the Brecon & Merthyr Tydvil Junction, into one undertaking, to be known as the Welsh Railways Company. A similar grandiose idea led to construction of the last portion of the main line.

WREXHAM & ELLESMERE RAILWAY

After failure of the Wrexham Mold & Connah's Quay Railway to construct its 1862 Wrexham–Bettisfield and 1864 Wrexham–Whitchurch lines, nothing further was attempted until the company came under the influence of the MS&L, at the time when the latter's chairman and the Cambrian authorities—themselves negotiating towards a working agreement with the Mid Wales Railway—conceived the possibility of furthering their Welsh Railways Union scheme with an independent route between the South Wales coalfield and Birkenhead. Two links were wanting : Connah's Quay to Bidston, and Wrexham to Ellesmere on the Cambrian. Schemes in the 1870s for such a route have been mentioned (p 57), while in 1884 the Denbighshire & Shropshire Junction intended a Wrexham–Bettisfield line. Success went respectively to the Wirral and Wrexham & Ellesmere Railways, both backed by the MS&L and incorporated by Acts of 31 July 1885. The $12\frac{1}{2}$-mile (20km) W&E was to run through the North Shropshire Plain, crossing the River Dee and passing through the isolated 'Part of Flint'.

There were delays and extensions of time, the first sod of the W&E not being turned until 11 July 1892. Lt Col Yorke, inspecting the railway in October 1895, thought the bridge over the Dee, a single 190ft 0in (58m) span of two steel lattice girders, 'a very fine work'. The three intermediate stations, Bangor-on-Dee, Marchwiel, and Overton-on-Dee, had passing loops and two platforms. A footbridge was required at Ellesmere for passengers changing trains, and certain works needed completion 'before 2nd November which is the date on which the Company wish to open the line for passenger traffic' (and so opened). Wrexham station consisted of the old WM&CQ

terminal platform, with new platforms and a footbridge. Trains were worked by new 4–4–0 side tanks, probably Nos 3, 5 or 7. September 1896 saw sanction of the ½-mile (0.8km) double-tracked Ellesmere loop, authorised in 1895 to give through running to Oswestry. The loop became disused but was re-opened in 1905. Halts opened at Sesswick and Trench in 1914.

The Cambrian worked the W&E, which remained inde-pendent until 1923, passing to the GWR, who opened more halts: Hightown in 1923, Cloy 1932, Elson 1937, and Pickhill 1938. Through trains between the Great Central system and Wales, including an express between Manchester and Aberyst-wyth, and South Wales–Birkenhead coal trains, did not compensate for poor local receipts. Much through traffic was diverted via Crewe during World War I, never to return. World War II saw the Royal Ordnance Factory established at Marchwiel; priority for munitions traffic required suspension of passenger services between 10 June 1940 and 6 May 1946.

PORTH DINLLAEN AND EXTENSION AT PWLLHELI

In 1871 the North Wales Narrow Gauge promoters (Chapter VII) contemplated a Pwllheli–Porth Dinllaen line. Six years later the Cambrian unsuccessfully sought to revive the A&WC 1862 Porth Dinllaen powers. The Porthdinlleyn Railway Company was incorporated in 1884 for a line from Pwllheli, but abandoned it in 1892. An electric railway was discussed in 1901, but rejected in favour of motor buses, introduced by the Cambrian between Pwllheli and Nevin in 1906. In 1913 the company obtained powers for a rail extension to Porth Dinllaen, but World War I intervened and thereafter the line could not be justified.

On 26 June 1909 Lt Col Druitt reported on a ½-mile (0.8km) extension at Pwllheli, authorised by Cambrian Act of 2 July 1901. From the first station the extension ran on an embank-ment, constructed by Pwllheli Corporation for harbour works, to a new two-platform terminus. Though connection between the old and new lines was not quite completed, the Colonel sanctioned the extension, which opened to traffic on 19 July 1909, final alterations at Pwllheli East box being inspected in 1910. Between 1896 and 1927 the privately owned 3ft 6in (107cm) gauge horse-worked Pwllheli Tramway took passengers a further four miles (6.4km) westwards to Llanbedrog.

A SHORTLIVED IRISH SERVICE

Proposals for a Cambrian steamer service foundered in the wake of Savin's bankruptcy; a small steamer, *Elizabeth*, chartered by the railway, worked the Dovey Estuary prior to completion of the coast line, being disposed of in 1869. In 1883 powers were obtained to improve Aberdovey harbour, used for shipping slate, and the Aberdovey & Waterford Steam Shipping Company put on two passengers steamers, *Cambria* and *Liverpool*. In 1889 the Cambrian was authorised to operate steamers between Aberdovey, Aberystwyth, Portmadoc, and Pwllheli, and Irish ports. The Aberdovey service was acquired. All to no avail: Euston protecting its Holyhead steamers, and backed by Paddington, operating from South Wales, threatened a rate war. The Cambrian capitulated, selling the two steamers.

TROUBLES WITH THE WORKS

In 1868 floods damaged several bridges. Captain Tyler, reporting that construction was not all it should have been, admitted his concern at some of the structures when first inspected in the early 1860s. Timber viaducts were decayed and required renewal. He suggested the appointment of a bridge inspector. 'The Cambrian system now comprises a length of 178 miles and the Engineer has no competent person to assist him in this important duty.' Two years later the line at Friog cliffs between Llwyngwril and Barmouth Junction was threatened when the rock, already suffering from erosion, was disturbed by a mine heading. Colonel Rich suggested a tunnelled deviation, an enormously expensive work which the Cambrian could not contemplate. On 1 January 1883 on the incline to Llwyngwril the evening train from Machynlleth ran into a landslide. The locomotive fell to the rocks below, killing the crew. Following a repeat of the tragedy on 4 March 1933, to the morning mail from Machynlleth, a reinforced-concrete avalanche shelter was built and the cliff face strengthened; additional reinforcement was completed in 1975.

THE MIDDLE YEARS

Broadly speaking, the Cambrian's slow development resulted

from its geographical situation. The town of Oswestry, where in 1866 a large red brick two-storey headquarters and station block had been built on the west or up side of the single line, and where concurrently an O&N-initiated plan for locomotive and carriage and wagon works came into operation, together with the Oswestry–Whitchurch line and connections with the GWR and LNWR—all this, in more highly-developed and populated England, was in contrast to the quiet Welsh countryside traversed by the greater part of the railway. While the 1861 Oswestry population of 5,414 grew to 7,306 in ten years, swollen by railway and associated development, and to 9,479 by 1901, to south and west the mountains restricted operation of the long, sinuous, heavily-graded, single line to a confined rural catchment area through the valleys where there was no dramatic growth, and frequently a decrease: compare the 1901 populations of Welshpool 4,328, Newtown 3,920, and Llanidloes 3,875, with those of 1851 (p 149). Generally, the coastal towns remained small: Towyn's 2,859 population of 1861 rose to 3,307 in 1871, levelling-off until 1901 when it reached 3,765 (1971 figure 3,818); Barmouth (p 160) was 1,733 in 1871 and 2,155 in 1881 (1971, 2,103); Criccieth went from 769 in 1861 to 901 in 1871, and reached 1,410 a decade later (1971, 1,509); while Pwllheli, 2,420 in 1861, reached 3,232 by 1901 (3,832 in 1971). Cardigan Bay competed with the North Wales resorts, reached more expeditiously by the LNWR, and the Cambrian coast was also served by the LNWR via Afon Wen, and Great Western via Dolgellau. The exception, untainted by 'foreign' competition —the Manchester & Milford (Chapter XIV) brought tourists from South Wales who otherwise might not have reached the resort at all—was fast-growing Aberystwyth (5,561 in 1861, 6,720 in 1871, over 8,000 by 1901 and 10,000 by 1971), whose rail approach the Cambrian treated as 'main', the coast line being seen as a 'branch'. In early and middle years the services were sparse and slow. Trains, frequently mixed passenger and goods, hauled by old locomotives, more often than not ran late. On coast line journeys, complicated by manoeuverings of con-necting trains and notoriously long delays at Dovey Junction, no expresses were run and up to $2\frac{3}{4}$ hours could be spent reaching Pwllheli. It was no accident that refreshment rooms proliferated by the 1870s at no fewer than ten stations on the main and coast lines. For an idea of just what conditions were like in those years, see Alan Godfrey's delightful cameo 'Winter on the

Cambrian' (*Railway World*, March 1976).

Beside the geographical constraint there was another—finance. Heavy expenditure and borrowing, low receipts, and quarrelling between shareholders and directors, led *Bradshaw's Shareholders' Guide* to state flatly in 1870: 'The affairs of this company are in a complicated condition'. By the end of the decade there was internal order and arrangements had been made with the company's creditors. The late 1880s saw revitalised management, and growing tourist traffic from the Midlands, Lancashire, and London. The fastest trains, hauled by new 4-4-0 passenger locomotives, did the 75-mile (120km) Machynlleth–Whitchurch stretch at an average 28mph, including four intermediate stops. Gross unpunctuality became nearly a thing of the past, helped by technical improvements required by the Regulations of Railways Act of 1889.

IMPROVEMENTS TO THE LINE

During the 1890s many stations received passing loops and second platforms, existing platforms were lengthened, and there was extensive interlocking and re-signalling. At Glandovey Junction in 1890 the single island platform was lengthened and the actual junction moved towards Machynlleth, the intention being to make the station the 'terminus' for the coast line. In 1891 many of the Whitchurch–Aberystwyth stations were re-signalled; Dyffryn received a new loop and up platform. The platforms were lengthened and tracks doubled at Barmouth Junction in 1892. At Oswestry in 1893 a down line platform with footbridge was constructed, and a new goods yard formed with a goods line at the back of the down platform. Nevertheless, in March 1893 Major Yorke found that 'at Oswestry and at certain other stations where the line is double, block working is not in force . . . telephonic communication between the signalmen being the mode of working adopted'. That year an additional platform at Aberystwyth made three in use, plus that used by the Manchester & Milford trains, and 'a commodious refreshment room' was under construction, while Buttington Junction received a double connection between the parallel and single Cambrian and LNWR lines, the two tracks continuing to Welshpool as a double line; the abandoned Llanbrynmair passenger train passing place was restored to that purpose, and Pant got a new double platform station. In 1894 a down platform, footbridge, and rearranged goods yard went in at Portmadoc; and the down platform was lengthened at Barmouth, where a locomotive turntable had lately been installed. While inspecting re-arrangement of Afon Wen in 1895 Colonel Yorke complained of the position of the refreshment room, north of the sidings at the east end of the station, and only reached by crossing on foot over two tracks. At Newtown the platforms were extended, new road and footbridges built.

In January 1896 Colonel Yorke inspected a small single platform at Tonfanau, near Towyn, 'provided solely for the use of one or two local residents . . . not to be advertised . . . and only one train a day is I understand to be stopped at it'. That year a passing loop and down platform were put in at Pool Quay. In 1898 a two-platform station at Whittington superseded the single platform a short distance to the south-west. 1899 saw a loop and second platform at Four Crosses, and in 1900 the passing place at Talerddig summit received a second platform. Reconstruction of Barmouth viaduct started in 1899, providing a centrally pivoted swing bridge and four steel spans in place of the eight-span iron rolling section; the remaining structure was renewed in timber between 1906–9. Five years later the timber Dovey viaduct was renewed, but as a fixed structure, and the timber Traethmawr viaduct was partly replaced by embankment and the remainder renewed. Improvements were also made to accommodate heavy troop traffic to and from Territorial Army camps around Aberystwyth: in 1911 new passing loops and down platforms were inspected at Llanfihangel (Llandre after 1916) and Borth; 1912 saw completion of the Newtown–Moat Lane doubling (curiously no down platform was provided at Scafell); and in 1914 a passing place went in at Clatter Crossing between Carno and Caersws.

Cambrian trains remained relatively leisurely; for Barmouth or Pwllheli, knowing passengers took the GWR 'Birmingham, Birkenhead and North Wales Express', with a Pwllheli portion via Dolgellau. An elderly relative has recalled interminable waits in the early 1900s at Dovey Junction, particularly bad in winter, and the slow rumble to Oswestry—a journey she 'absolutely hated'. Mr A. S. Wilson-Jones (*Railway Magazine*, November 1974), recollecting a holiday at Harlech in 1911, noted the inability to be positive which train was which:

One busy evening at about six o'clock a train was seen approaching from the south, I remember, and as the portly grey-haired station-master came out on the platform he was asked by an imposing-looking lady if this was the 5.40. His reply, in a strong Welsh accent, was 'I don't know, I think it is the four twenty-eight'. (It was!)

Of interest was a minor accident which suggested indifferent signalling procedure, and that 'the same sort of laxity in working which led to the disaster at Abermule was not unknown on the Cambrian years before'. That awful event, on 26 January 1921, was the second fatal accident on the single-track railway (the first, a derailment at Welshampton on 11 June 1897, tragically killed eleven children). It was caused by the carelessness of Abermule station staff (the regular stationmaster was on leave) and the driver of a down local who went to his death believing he had the tablet for the Abermule–Newtown section, in which an express was approaching, whereas unwittingly he had had returned to him that which he had surrendered for Montgomery–Abermule. The drama is inimitably conveyed in the late L. T. C. Rolt's *Red for Danger*. The collision killed 15 passengers, including Lord Herbert Vane-Tempest, a Cambrian director.

During World War I there was considerable South Wales coal traffic through Llanidloes, thence to the LNWR, destined for the fleet at Scapa Flow; timber traffic increased more than five-fold. North of Oswestry the railway served a military camp at Park Hall. After the war outward appearances were of good receipts and credit balance, but operating costs were not met from revenue, a situation confronting many railways and which led to the government-sponsored uniting of companies into four major undertakings. The Cambrian amalgamated with the GWR in 1922, the year before the nation-wide Grouping.

IN GREAT WESTERN TIMES

Paddington made improvements. At Oswestry the north end down ticket platform was replaced by extension of the down platform; the up platform was extended and an up bay made, used by Gobowen trains from 7 July 1924. Welshpool–Forden was doubled in 1925; Barmouth received an up bay on the south side of the level-crossing; Harlech an up platform; Afon

Wen was remodelled; Pwllheli and Aberystwyth had their single approach lines doubled, Aberystwyth getting new station buildings. Halts were opened: in the 1920s at Black Rock, Gogarth, Talwrn Bach, Tygwyn, and Llandanwg; and in the 1930s Llangelynin, Commins Coch, Penhelig, Penychain (a full station since provision of a second platform and doubling the line from Afon Wen in 1947 to serve a Butlin holiday camp), Abertafol, Llandecwyn, and Tinker's Green (in 1939 for Park Hall military camp).

In July 1921 a new summer weekdays restaurant car service started: the 9.50 am Paddington to Aberystwyth, Barmouth and Pwllheli, with a noon up train from Aberystwyth. Officially titled 'Cambrian Coast Express' in 1927, in early years it took the Shrewsbury curve, avoiding the station; Castle class locomotives were exchanged at Wolverhampton for the lighter Duke 4-4-0s which worked the Cambrian line. Stops were at Welshpool, Machynlleth, Dovey Junction, and Borth, arrival at Aberystwyth being just before 4.00 pm. The express, by then Saturdays only, was withdrawn during World War II but returned for summer Saturdays in 1946, the name being reinstated in 1951. Three years later it became again a daily service, through Barmouth and Pwllheli coaches working from Machynlleth instead of Dovey Junction as before. The express now reversed at Shrewsbury, where an immaculate Manor class 4-6-0 backed-on for the run to the coast. The Birmingham and north through services ceased when the new electric trains from Euston came into operation; adorned with headboard and wreath, the last steam-hauled Cambrian Coast Express ran on 4 March 1967.

ON THE EDGE OF OBLIVION

Wrexham–Ellesmere passenger trains ceased after 8 September 1962, freight also being withdrawn, though private siding traffic continued. Abenbury (excl)–Pickhill (Cadburys) and the Maelor Gas Works siding at Marchwiel were taken out of use from 22 May 1973 (see also Chapter XV). During 1963-4 many Cambrian main line stations closed to freight; one, Whittington, had closed to passengers on 4 January 1960. The Beeching Report proposed retaining only one of the four railways which reached to the Mid Wales coast. The choice narrowed to two: Ruabon–Barmouth

(Morfa Mawddach since 1960), and Shrewsbury–Aberystwyth, which served a larger population and linked more directly with the basic main line network. From May 1964 freight became concentrated on the Cambrian, though for a time Pwllheli traffic continued via Caernarvon. Track-singling commenced. Augmented traffic required maximum line occupation: freight loadings were increased and banked over Talerddig and other heavy gradients, and holiday passenger trains were double-headed between Shrewsbury and Machynlleth. From 23 November 1964 diesel multiple-units ousted steam trains, only the Cambrian Coast Express and two night mail trains remaining steam-hauled. After closure of the Mid Wales line (p 213), Moat Lane–Llanidloes remained open until 2 October 1967 for cement traffic from Aberthaw to the vast new Clywedog dam, some three miles from Llanidloes.

From 18 January 1965 the Whitchurch–Oswestry–Welshpool passenger service ceased and Ellesmere (*excl*) – Oswestry (*excl*) closed to all traffic, Ellesmere closing to freight on 29 March 1965 (the station building survives). On the Shrewsbury–Aberystwyth line, longer signalled sections became possible when 14 intermediate passenger stations were closed from 14 June 1965, leaving just Welshpool, Newtown, Caersws, Machynlleth, Dovey Junction, and Borth, and reducing overall journey time by some 40 minutes.

Five years later a Ministry of Transport cost-benefit study showed that even with economies, the Machynlleth–Pwllheli line was difficult to justify. Declining population and rail holiday traffic, increased car ownership, poor freight outlook, soaring costs, and higher grants required from the Ministry, led in March 1971 to closure notice for the line north of Dovey Junction.

Public reaction was vigorous. After an inquiry in June, when the bus service alternatives—especially for schoolchildren—were seen to be a very poor substitute for the trains, notably the relative road and rail distances between Barmouth and Llwyngwril being very obvious, it was reported that closure would bring widespread hardship, and weaken chances for retention of the Aberystwyth line. In July 1974 the coast line was 'unconditionally reprieved'.

Gogarth Halt was washed away (replaced afterwards) during a storm in January 1976 which flooded the line in the Dovey estuary and stopped services for over a week. In 1976 Criccieth–Pwllheli was singled, with only a run-round loop and a refuge siding remaining at Pwllheli. Black Rock Halt closed 'officially' from 27 June 1977. The

following year saw the loop at Borth—disused for some time—
dismantled, making one section of Dovey Junction–Aberystwyth.
Bi-lingual nameboards appeared at many stations in 1978. From the
start of the 1978–9 timetable Dovey Junction began once more to
rival Machynlleth as the interchange between the two coast lines,
and Talwrn Bach and Llanbedr & Pensarn were renamed
respectively 'Llanbedr' and 'Pensarn', a geographical correction.
Such were the minor events of the late 1970s, with the railway,
particularly the 'north' coast line, existing on a knife edge. During the
autumn of 1980 the future of that line came under renewed threat
following the unavoidable closure of Barmouth viaduct; it was
questionable whether British Rail could justify the cost of expensive
repairs found to be necessary. (See Chapter XV.)

Gobowen–Oswestry was singled from 2 November 1971 with an
'on demand' freight working from Shrewsbury via Gobowen,
Oswestry and Llynclys to Llanddu quarry (some 600yds or 549m
short of Blodwel Junction) to obtain ballast for rail use. Latterly a
daily (SX) working to Bescot, the train ceased running after 28
October 1988. At Oswestry the up or west side station building
remains, part occupied, at the time of writing, by a retail business.
The adjacent yard is the headquarters of the Cambrian Railways
Society. Here could be found 1879–built Beyer Peacock works
shunter No 1872, 1916 Peckett No 1 *Adam* and 1951 Peckett No 6, all
0–4–0 saddle tanks; 1900 Andrew Barclay 0–6–0ST No 8, 1952
Planet four-wheel diesel No 322, 1954 Hudswell Clarke 0–4–0 diesel
No 1, 1954 Hunslet 0–6–0 diesel No 3, 1947 four-wheel Sentinel and
1946 Hibberd four-wheel diesel. There were various items of
passenger and freight rolling stock. The star of the show in August
1989 was 1952 Hunslet 0–6–0ST No 3770 *Norma* (ex-Coal Board),
recently brought into steam, shunting stock on the 400yds (366m) of
track available to the society. The immediate aim was to extend to
Middleton Road bridge in Oswestry, but the ultimate goal remained
of operating steam passenger trains between Gobowen and Blodwel
Junction—a distance of about 8½ miles (12.8km).

CHAPTER XI

Cambrian Branches and Minor Railways

Several small railways of various gauge, feeders to the main lines, are now a colourful and successful part of the Welsh tourist industry. The remainder have gone, their formations merged into the landscape. This chapter outlines most of those on the Cambrian network, but the Festiniog, Welsh Highland, Shropshire & Montgomeryshire, and Vale of Rheidol are discussed elsewhere.

TALYLLYN RAILWAY

But for the American Civil War there might have been no Talyllyn Railway, for it forced William McConnel, Lancashire cotton magnate, to diversify. He formed the Aberdovey Slate Company to work the Bryn Eglwys quarry, on the southern slopes of the narrow valley south of Cader Idris and below Lake Talyllyn, whence packhorses took the slate to Aberdovey. Following success of the nearby Corris Railway, and of steam traction on the Festiniog Railway (Chapter VIII), McConnel instructed James Swinton Spooner (son of James and brother of C. E., both of Festiniog fame) to plan a railway to Aberdovey, altered to Towyn after arrival of the A&WCR.

The Talyllyn Railway Company was incorporated by Act of 5 July 1865. Gauge might be standard, or a minimum of 2ft 3in (69cm), which latter was chosen. From an exchange wharf with the Cambrian at Towyn, the railway climbs at a ruling gradient of 1 in 60 through Rhydyronen and Brynglas, thence shelved into the valley side, through woods and rock cuttings, over a 52ft 0in (15.8m) high 3-arch stone viaduct at Dolgoch, near the famous falls, to a point above the village of Abergynolwyn and below the quarry. Captain Tyler reported in September 1866 on the 6⅝-miles (10.6km) line. Stations were Towyn Pendre,

½-mile (0.8km) from the wharf and about a mile (1.6km) from the Cambrian's passenger station, and Abergynolwyn, beyond which the rails extended ¾-mile (1.2km) to Nant Gwernol where a three-incline tramway served the quarry, two miles (3.2km) to the south-east and 500ft (152m) above. The single passenger carriage was too wide to pass safely between bridge abutments, a problem solved by fastening doors and barring windows on one side, and slewing the rails to allow sufficient space on the other. McConnel told the captain that he expected only three or four passengers on each train, except Saturdays when 30 or 40 might travel. There were two 0–4–0 Fletcher, Jennings locomotives: a short-wheelbase saddle tank No 1 *Talyllyn*, which was the first large piece of freight to arrive by the newly-opened A&WC at Towyn; and a well tank No 2 *Dolgoch*, with a relatively long wheelbase for an 0–4–0. 1867 saw *Talyllyn* altered to an 0–4–2, and the arrival of two more carriages and a guard's brake van.

Regular passenger traffic started on 1 October 1866 with two trains each way daily; February 1867 saw a locomotive shed ready at Towyn Pendre and the services became based on that end. By then Rhydyronen intermediate station had opened, to serve a small slate quarry and manganese mine; Brynglas and Dolgoch opened in 1873. About then a cable incline was constructed from Nant Gwernol down to Abergynolwyn village. Five halts came into use: Hendy, Fach Goch, Cynfal, Tynyllwyn, and Quarry Siding. From the 1880s, in conjunction with the Corris Railway, tourists could make a tour via Talyllyn Lake (p 176). In 1911 the railway was sold to Henry Haydn Jones (MP for Merioneth, and later knighted) who undertook to run it during his lifetime. Slate traffic tailed off, but there was considerable local and tourist passenger traffic. World War II increased the demand for slate to repair bomb damage, but the quarry closed in the late 1940s. All services ceased from 6 October 1950, shortly after Sir Haydn's death. The railway had become very run down, but with herculean effort a preservation society successfully re-opened it to Rhydyronen on Whit Monday 14 May and to Abergynolwyn on 4 June 1951—a saga told by the late L. T. C. Rolt, one of the society's pioneers and its first general manager, in his classic *Railway Adventure*.

New passing loops have gone in at Brynglas and Rhydyronen; an island platform, run-round loop and extended buildings with

Page *173* Mid Wales Railway: (*Top*) Builth Road, looking north towards Central Wales line overbridge, August 1935; (*centre*) Builth Wells, looking west, August 1935; (*bottom*) Three Cocks Junction, looking north, date uncertain. (*L&GRP*)

Page 174 Central Wales Railway: (*Top*) Down train entering Bucknell station, c.1900; (*centre*) Builth Road, looking north, c.1900; (*bottom*) Down Swansea train at Llandrindod Wells, August 1977. (*Ludlow Museum; National Library of Wales; Author*)

a narrow gauge museum at Towyn Wharf, and a new station building, crossover, colour-light signalling and other improvements at Abergynolwyn, whence a ¾-mile (1.2km) extension opened to Nant Gwernol in May 1976. Remarkably, the two locomotives worked the traffic for 86 years. *Dolgoch* was patriotically renamed *Pretoria* in 1900 but later reverted to its more homely appellation. Both have been rebuilt. In 1951 two ex-Corris saddle tanks joined them: No 3 *Sir Haydn* and No 4 *Edward Thomas*. Other steam locomotives are No 6 *Douglas* a 1918 Barclay 0–4–0 well tank, and No 7 *Irish Pete* a 1949 Barclay 0–4–2 tank. (See Chapter XVI).

CORRIS RAILWAY

In the early 1850s owners of slate quarries at Aberllefenni and Corris in the narrow, well-wooded Dulas Valley in the eastern foothills of Cader Idris made surveys for rail connection at Machynlleth with the abortive Montgomeryshire and Shrewsbury & Aberystwith (*sic*) projects (p 149). In the latter case a standard gauge branch from the S&A was planned by the quarry owners to Aberdovey and Towyn. These schemes did not proceed, but encouraged by the successful Newtown & Machynlleth Railway, an 11-mile (17.7km) narrow gauge line was promoted from Corris to Machynlleth, thence westwards to a wharf at Quay Ward on the Dovey at Derwenlas, which had been used for decades for shipping lead brought down from mines on Plynlimon. The Corris Machynlleth & River Dovey Tramroad Act was passed on 12 July 1858; the twisting 2ft 3in (69cm) gauge line, worked by horses and gravity, with ruling gradient of 1 in 32, opened on 30 April 1859. The largest work was a timber viaduct over the Dovey.

Following the opening of the main line through to the coast at Borth in 1863, slate traffic was exchanged at Machynlleth. A CM&RD Bill lodged in November 1862 for extension northwards to near Dolgellau in the Wnion Valley and conversion to standard gauge, possibly offering the GWR a short-cut to Aberystwyth, failed, but on 25 July 1864 Royal Assent was received for the Dolgellau line (not built), abandonment of the Machynlleth–Derwenlas length, use of locomotives, and change of name to Corris Railway. In 1878 Imperial Tramways Company of Bristol acquired the Corris, relaying with steel rails and easing some curves. Though three 0–4–0 saddle tanks arrived from the Falcon Engine Company in 1879, a Bill seeking to

carry passengers failed after the slate proprietors protested
against disruption of their traffic. With local support the Corris
successfully carried passengers by horse bus between August and
October 1879. By Act of 1880, authority was received, Major
Marindin inspecting the 5¼-mile (8.4km) length for passenger
use that October. There were four first-class and six second-
class 4-wheel carriages; intermediate 'stations' and passing places
existed at Pandy (Llwyngwern) and Esgairgeiliog. Corris had the
only platform, and Machynlleth a 'bare shed'. Due to sharp
curves, use for passengers was refused, and again in 1882. A
further Act in 1883 sanctioned passenger working, and with
improved curves, and intermediate stations removed, passenger
services started on 4 July 1883. The two intermediates, reinstated, were passed for passenger use in March 1884. The 1½
miles (2.4km) on to Aberllefenni opened to passengers on 25
August 1887. Later there were halts at Ffridd Gate, Dolydderwen
Crossing, Lliwdy, and Garneddwen.

The horse buses were used for a new tourist service via
Talyllyn Lake to Abergynolwyn on the Talyllyn Railway, as
part of a circular 'Grand Tour' using the Cambrian and the two
small lines. The Corris management energetically sought
revenue: annual journeys by workmen, schoolchildren, market-
goers and tourists reached nearly 150,000 by the turn of the
century. In 1907 Machynlleth received a superior station for
such a little line. There were two mineral branches: from
Maespoeth Junction—south of Corris and where the locomotives
were shedded—worked by horses to quarries at Abercwmmeiddaw
(the Upper Corris branch, springboard of the 1860s Dolgellau
plans, and in 1907 for an unsuccessful projected electrified
extension to the Talyllyn); and from north of Aberllefenni to
Ratgoed quarry. After World War I the slate industry declined
and the company started local bus services. The three locomotives were rebuilt as o–4–2s (1895–1900), and an o–4–2 Kerr
Stuart saddle tank arrived in 1921. The Corris was purchased
by the GWR in 1930, passenger services ceasing from 1 January
1931. Nos 1 and 2 being cut up. Freight continued, together
with occasional and possibly hair-raising private passenger
journeys: Dr H. E. Vickers (*Railway Magazine*, 1942) told of
observing two persons at Corris in a wagon which, sharply
nudged by a locomotive, swiftly disappeared solo downhill
towards Machynlleth. In 1942 the Upper Corris branch was
lifted. In 1946 the main Corris line carried up to 40 tons of

slate during a thrice-weekly service. Following floods the line
closed after 20 August 1948 and was dismantled by 1950. Locomotives Nos 3 and 4 went to the Talyllyn. By 1979 the Corris Railway
Society had opened a museum at Corris and were hoping to buy the
engine shed and works at Maespoeth, towards which track was
relaid. (See Chapter XVI).

MAWDDWY RAILWAY

At the head of the beautiful Dovey Valley lies the village of
Dinas Mawddwy, centre of local agriculture, and with nearby
quarries from which in early years slate went by packhorse down
the valley. By the 1860s the farmers and slate owners were
losing-out to competitors already enjoying rail communication.
About this time the ancient lordship of the manor passed to the
young Edmund, later Sir Edmund, Buckley, who immediately
set about putting Dinas Mawddwy on the railway map.
Authorised by the Mowddwy (sic) Railway Act of 5 July 1865,
a standard gauge 6¾-mile (10.8km) single line was made entirely
at his expense from a station ½ mile (0.8km) south of Mawddwy
to a station and siding junction with the Cambrian at Cemmes
Road, whence farming produce would be taken on to the towns
and slate forwarded to Aberdovey harbour. The railway, contractor Richard France, opened on 1 October 1867, worked by
Mawddwy (p 198). A similar locomotive, *Disraeli*, arrived in
1868. Shortly after the opening, the Hendre Ddu Tramway was
built to bring slate down the Afon Angell Valley to a wharf on
the Mawddwy at Aberangell, four miles (6.4km) from Cemmes
Road. Aberangell station opened in the early 1870s, there then
being five passenger trains daily each way. In 1896 a station
opened at Mallwyd. It lacked buildings, but Colonel Yorke
permitted its use as 'it is a convenience to the residents in the
neighbourhood and has been opened in accordance with their
wishes'. Tickets were issued from the guard's van.

Freight traffic was disappointing; despite extensive tourist
publicity, particularly aimed at anglers for the Dovey's salmon
and trout, passenger receipts fared no better. The timber bridges
became unsafe and from 17 April 1901 passenger services
ceased, *Bradshaw* noting them until 1905 as 'discontinued pending repairs'. The Buckley family was unable to help financially,
however, and further deterioration of the railway forced withdrawal of freight trains from 8 April 1908. Loss of the railway

was keenly felt, the local authority facing rising expenditure on the parallel valley road. The line was rescued by Lt Col David Davies (grandson of *the* David Davies) chairman of the Cambrian in 1909, who was to hold that office from 1911 to 1922. He bought out the private interests in the Mawddwy Railway and promoted a Light Railway Order, confirmed 2 March 1910, the Cambrian undertaking reconstruction and working. The re-opening, with the single platform stations at Cemmes Road, Cemmaes, Aberangell, Mallwyd and Dinas Mawddwy bedecked with bunting, took place on 29 July 1911, public services starting two days later with four trains each way, soon supplemented by summer coach tours from Dinas into the 'Switzerland of Wales'. *Mawddwy*, reconditioned for the re-opening, became Cambrian No 30 in 1913, but *Disraeli* was scrapped in 1912. Shortly after, No 30 went to other duties, 'Small Passenger' class 2–4–0s Nos 28 and 43 taking over on the Mawddwy until replaced in 1916 by Nos 44 and 56, sister engines rebuilt as tanks, and these eventually by No 24 (p 180). During World War I slate and tourist traffic fell away but timber increased. Parts of the Hendre Ddu system, which had several branches, remained variously in use for slate, timber and even occasional tourist specials, until lifted early in World War II. The Mawddwy passed to the GWR at the Grouping; it never prospered and, like the Corris, passenger services ceased from 1 January 1931. The last freight ran on 5 September 1950; after floods the line closed entirely from 1 July 1951.

Since closure, Dinas Mawddwy station has become the home of Meirion Mill Ltd, which has done much to promote a fresh and creative approach to woollen manufacture in Wales. Along with other enterprises, including a pottery and mill shop for the public, the company laid a 600yd (549m) length of 2ft 0in (61cm) gauge track from the mill to a picnic area at Maescanlan. With two open coaches worked by a Simplex diesel the line opened on 19 July 1975. Not in service was a new 0–4–0 saddle tank *Trixie*, one of the two previously tried on the Bala Lake Railway. Sadly, this latest Mawddwy line closed in 1977.

VAN RAILWAY

In the hills some 2½ miles (4km) north of Llanidloes there was much lead mining near Van, to which Lord Vane and David Davies, respectively N&M chairman and contractor, planned a branch. A difficult line from Llanidloes was discarded in favour of one 6½ miles (10.4km) long via the Cerist Valley, leaving the Cambrian at Caersws. The Van Railway Company was registered in June 1870, the works being constructed under powers of the Railways Construction Facilities Act of 1864. In August 1871 Lt Col Rich inspected the line, noting it had 'been worked for mineral traffic for some time'. There were wooden viaducts over the Rivers Carno, Trannon and Cerist, and platform stations at Caersws, Trefeglwys (later Pwll-glas), and Garth & Van Road (at 6¼ miles); only Caersws had a building— separate from the Cambrian station to which there was a goods siding connection. The Colonel remarked on the lack of buildings :

It appears very desirable to encourage the construction of Light Railways, which can be made at very moderate expense, and I therefore recommend that station buildings should be dispensed with and that the passenger fares should be collected by the Guard of the Train, as is proposed to be done on the Van Railway. The short platforms will be sufficient for present purposes.

Certain works required completion, and sanction for passenger traffic was refused. The line opened for freight on 14 August 1871, though there were some earlier leadminers' specials.

It seems trains were worked at first by *Merion* (p 157), on hire 1870–71, until a new Manning Wardle 0–6–0 saddle tank arrived, followed by another in 1877, one of them being named *Caersws*. A service of mixed trains—two or three each way taking passengers—operated from 1 December 1873 until 1879. There were short-lived halts at Trewythen Siding, at Red House, and a station at Cerist. The first manager was John Hughes, 'the finest Welsh poet of the last century'.

The mines, highly productive over a 12-year period when hundreds of men were employed, ceased output in the early 1890s, though the crushed stone inimical to weed growth remained useful for ballasting the Cambrian's permanent way. The railway closed in 1893, but the Cambrian wanted the ballast and undertook to work the line with Van locomotives. It re-opened from 1 August 1896 (some authorities give 29 July and others 1 October). The mines recommenced operations, continuing until 1920. The Van locomotives became Cambrian

Nos 22 and 25. There is some dispute over which became what. No 22 was withdrawn in 1899, and an explanation may lie in 'cannibalisation' at Oswestry works whereby the surviving No 25 was attributed to the 1877 delivery. The vacant No 22 was filled in 1901 by a new Manning Wardle 0–4–0 saddle tank which went to working the Elan Valley traffic (p 212), joined there, sometime, by No 25. Nos 22 and 25 were sold in 1916 and 1917 respectively. Locomotives later working the Van Railway in Cambrian times included 0–6–0 side tanks Nos 24, 26 and 35 (ex-Lambourn Valley Railway, purchased 1904) and No 30 formerly *Mawddwy*. The branch locomotive was shedded at Caersws and took water by its own fitted pump while standing on the Carno bridge. Sometimes it worked the Kerry branch (see p 182). During the early 20th century the Van service was of one train each way thrice weekly. The line remained independent until passing to the GWR in 1923. Occasional freight and ballast trains ran during the inter-war years, but final closure came on 4 November 1940.

PORTHYWAEN AND NANTMAWR BRANCHES

By the 1820s a 1½-mile (2.4km) horse tramway was operating between Porthywaen lime quarries, some two miles (3.2km) north of Llanymynech, and Crickheath Wharf on the Ellesmere & Chester Canal. On the other side of Sweeney Mountain, the 3¼-mile (5.2km) Morda Tramway ran from a coal pit at Coed-y-go to a wharf near Morton, a mile north of Crickheath Wharf. When the Oswestry & Newtown Railway arrived nearby, the Savin brothers built a branch, opened 1 May 1861, along the north side of the Crickheath Tramway to the quarries, bringing mineral traffic on to the O&N north of Llynclys station. They also made a steeply graded private branch of a little over two miles (3.2km), from the Porthywaen line to their Coed-y-go pit. This branch opened in March 1863. Six years later the pit closed and by the late 1870s both the old Morda Tramway and the Coed-y-go branch had been abandoned. In contrast the 2ft 6in gauge (76cm) Crickheath Tramway closed in 1913.

The Nantmawr branch belongs in Chapter XII, but is mentioned here for its part in transforming the layout at Llanymynech. The branch—a portion of the Potteries Shrewsbury & North Wales Railway, with powers to extend to Llanyblodwel (spelt thus by the Cambrian) and the Nantmawr quarries—

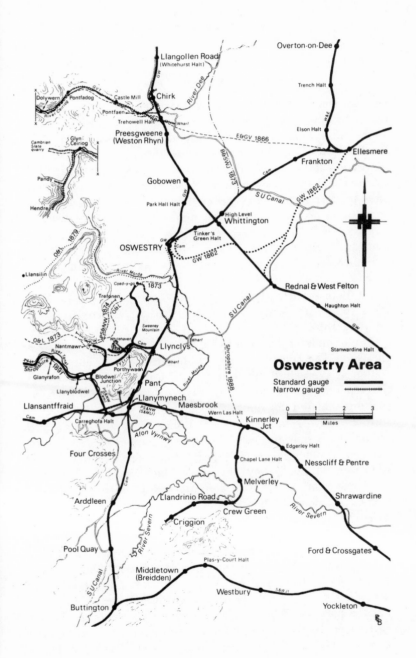

Oswestry Area

Standard gauge
Narrow gauge

0   1   2   3
Miles

opened in 1866, being used for minerals until 1870 when passenger workings reached Llanyblodwel. It closed in 1880, but from 11 February 1881 the Cambrian worked it for minerals, taking a lease in 1898.

LLANFYLLIN AND KERRY BRANCHES

On completion of the Oswestry & Newtown the market town of Llanfyllin, population 1,880, at the head of the farming valley of the Afon Cain in the Berwyn foothills and some eight miles (12.8km) west of Llanymynech, saw the opportunity for rail connection to Oswestry. Thus the town opposed the West Midland scheme (p 141), which went through Llangynog. A WM offer to deviate the route through Llanfyllin was answered by the town lodging instead a Bill for an independent branch to join the O&N at Llanymynech. Meanwhile, 18 miles (28.9km) south of Llanfyllin, John Wilkes Poundley, then building up the famous breed of Kerry sheep on the slopes below Clun Forest, sought a rail link to Kerry village. The private Llanfyllin Bill failed, both branches being authorised by the Oswestry & Newtown Act of 17 May 1861; Captain Rich inspected them on 27 June 1863.

The 8¾-mile (14km) Llanfyllin branch followed the course of the Cain. The first three miles (4.8km) to the only intermediate station at Llansaintffraid were formed for eventual double line; the remainder was single. At Llanymynech a north-end bay platform catered for the Llanfyllin trains which, in order to surmount the Montgomeryshire Canal, used the long 'Rock Siding' to a shunting neck, reversing on or off the branch. Services commenced on 10 April 1863, trains running through to Oswestry from 17 July. Stations at Llanfechain and Bryngwyn (a 'flag station', where passengers worked a signal to stop trains) opened in 1866. In the 1880s there was heavy traffic of construction material for the Vyrnwy reservoir, and an increased number of passenger trains. On 27 January 1896 a ½-mile (0.8km) curve was opened to the Nantmawr branch at Carreghofa, south of where the two lines crossed. It gave access to Llanymynech from the south via the Nantmawr line which, according to Lt Col Yorke, 'has been disused for several years, but the portion referred to (as to running powers over which an agreement [with the Shropshire Railways] has been entered into) has been relaid'. Carreghofa Halt opened in 1938. Part of the redundant Rock Siding remained until 1939. Freight on the Llanfyllin branch ceased in 1964, and all traffic from 18 January 1965 concurrently with the Whitchurch–Welshpool passenger services.

The single-track 3⅝-mile (5.8km) Kerry branch climbed 'through a very narrow glen' at a ruling gradient of 1 in 42 and with sharp curves, which 'should be worked with great care and at low speed . . . with one engine in steam'. At Abermule a small separate passenger station served the branch, which opened to passengers on 2 March, and freight on 1 July 1863. It was worked by the veriest of Victorian branch trains, known with ironic affection as the 'Kerry Express', consisting of one of the 1863 vintage Sharp, Stewart 0–4–0 saddle tanks Nos 36 *Plasfynnon*, 37 *Mountaineer*, and 38 *Prometheus*, shedded at Kerry, a 1st/3rd coach with 'Kerry Branch' blazoned on its flanks, and usually several wagons. This cavalcade took some 25 minutes to ascend the narrow, wooded gorge, with watermills powered by the tumbling River Mule, and the open hillside beyond, before wheezing into the terminus a mile from Kerry village. Following withdrawal of the three sisters (1905–7) the branch got one or other of Nos 24, 26 and 35 (p 180), occasionally assisted by No 22 (p 180). At Kerry, privately from 1888 to 1895, and as a government timber area between 1917 and 1922, the goods sidings interchanged with the steam-worked Kerry Tramway, some 5 miles (8km) of 1ft 11½in (60cm) gauge). As with others, the branch passed to the GWR, which opened halts at Fronfraith and Goitre in 1923, and worked traffic with Cambrian 0–6–0 and 2–4–0 tanks. The passenger service—at its peak seven weekday trains each way—ceased from 9 February 1931. Freight—bricks from Goitre brickworks (until World War II), timber, coal, fertilizer, and sheep in September during the Kerry sales—gradually declined, and the branch closed from 1 May 1956, being dismantled by 1959.

TANAT VALLEY LIGHT RAILWAY

North of Llanfyllin lies the Tanat Valley, scene of projected railways to or through the town of Llangynog. Nearby were granite and slate quarries, copper and lead mines, and on three sides the Berwyns, over which a road runs to Bala. Several proposals of 1845–6 passed through the valley, but none was successful.

In the 1860s a narrow gauge line was unsuccessfully planned from Welshpool via Llanfair Caereinion (p 185). There was another from Llanfyllin in 1873, and a standard gauge Oswestry & Llangynog Railway in 1882 both receiving Royal Assent, only to be abandoned.

The Light Railways Act of 1896 provided the opportunity for a less costly project. The O&L promoters, and in opposition the Llanfyllin people who knew that a direct Tanat Valley line would kill-off their through trade, each went to the Light Railway Commissioners in 1897. Local mineral production had dwindled to nothing; a direct rail link could start a revival. There was much outward agricultural traffic, with lime, coal and other goods coming into the valley. Thus the 10½-mile (16.9km) 2ft 6in (76cm) gauge Llanfyllin & Llangynog Light Railway was rejected in favour of the 15-mile (24.1km) standard gauge Tanat Valley Light Railway, the Order being confirmed on 4 January 1899.

The first sod was cut at Porthywaen on 12 September 1899. After a further Order, to raise money, construction started in July 1901. In November 1902 Major Druitt travelled on the contractor's locomotive over 13¼ miles (21.3km) of line. In December 1903 he re-inspected the TVLR, 'which has a certain amount of goods traffic already on it'. The line extended from Llangynog to a trailing junction with the Nantmawr branch at Blodwel, ¼-mile (0.4km) beyond which it recommenced to run for 1¼ miles (2km) to join the Porthywaen branch, by which trains would reach the Cambrian main line to Oswestry. There were stations at Porthywaen, Blodwel Junction, Llanyblodwel, Llansilin Road, Llangedwyn, Pentrefelin, Llanrhaiadr Mochnant, Pedairffordd, Penybontfawr, and Llangynog. Llangedwyn and Llanrhaiadr had passing loops and two platforms. TVLR directors and guests opened the line with a special train from Oswestry on 5 January 1904. Public services started on the following day with four weekdays-only trains each way, worked by the Cambrian. Glanyrafon Halt opened shortly afterwards. Regular goods services started in July 1904. Locomotives working the line were either Nos 24, 26 or 35 (ex-Lambourne Valley), or 30 (ex-Mawddwy), Seaham 2–4–0 tanks and sometimes 0–6–0 tanks. TVLR trains were also intended to run over the Nantmawr branch so as to reach Llanymynech and allay the Shropshire Company's fears that Tanat Valley traffic would otherwise be denied to its Llanymynech–Shrewsbury line. In fact the Shropshire remained moribund until 1910, and a TVLR west curve at Blodwel Junction, for through running, was not built. From 1904 carriages were shuttled in with the mineral trains to Llanymynech, but these forays ceased from 1 January 1917.

Minerals were the TVLR mainstay, bringing in by the early 1920s some 20 times the passenger revenue. Nevertheless, the company remained in debt until passing to the Cambrian in 1921 and GWR in 1922, after which there was increasing competition from local and GWR bus services and carriers. The passenger service ceased from 15 January 1951. Mineral and livestock traffic, eroded by a decline in quarrying and increasing use of farm lorries, ceased west of Llanrhaiadr from 1 July 1952, and thence to Blodwel Junction from 6 January 1964.

WELSHPOOL & LLANFAIR LIGHT RAILWAY

A narrow gauge railway runs westwards from Welshpool through rolling farmlands to the market town of Llanfair Caereinioñ in the Banwy Valley. It has an ancient pedigree: from about 1818 to the mid-1850s, over part of the route now closed, the $\frac{3}{4}$-mile (1.2km) Welshpool Railroad connected the Standard Quarry, off Brook Street, with the Montgomeryshire Canal.

Welshpool is the market for the area, and after arrival of the Cambrian there were schemes for a railway to serve the country to the west. A narrow gauge project in 1865 fell foul of the Earl of Powis, whose castle and lands lie to the south and west. In the following year the Shrewsbury & North Wales planned a line via the Meifod Valley to Llanfair (p 196). A standard gauge scheme received Royal Assent in 1877 but was abandoned in 1882; ten years later a similar fate befell another narrow gauge line, authorised in 1887. As with the Tanat, a light railway was the apparent answer. As with that line, there was disagreement, Llanfair wanting a $13\frac{1}{2}$-mile (21.7km) standard gauge railway via the Meifod Valley to the Cambrian at Ardleen, whereas Welshpool wished it to start there and be to 2ft 6in (76cm) gauge. On 8 September 1899 the Welshpool & Llanfair Light Railway Order incorporated a company to make a $9\frac{1}{8}$-mile (14.7km) 2ft 6in gauge railway, including provision for electric traction. The first sod was cut at Welshpool on 30 May 1901, the Cambrian having agreed to construct the line, maintain it, and work it with stock provided by the W&L, to which would go a percentage of gross receipts.

The single-track line started in the Cambrian's Welshpool yard, ran alongside Smithfield Street and crossed the canal before approaching the town, through which it ran along streets and through passages between houses. From Welshpool it climbed at 1 in 29 for nearly a mile (1.6km) up Golfa Bank and then switchbacked with severe gradients and curves through country of considerable beauty, following the Sylfaen Brook and the Welshpool–Llanfair Road until at Cyfronydd it encountered, followed, and crossed by a three-span steel girder bridge near Heniarth, the River Banwy. Stations were at Welshpool terminus, Seven Stars, Raven Square, Golfa, Castle Caereinion, Cyfronydd, Heniarth, and Llanfair Caereinion. Each had rail-level gravel 'platforms', both termini boasting booking offices and waiting rooms.

Two Beyer, Peacock 0–6–0 side tanks, No 1 *The Earl* and No 2 *The Countess* were delivered, with three bogie passenger carriages. All had central buffing gear, which Major Druitt—who inspected the line in February 1903—thought would cause derailments on sharp curves. The company altered the couplings and invited the major on a trip, the train consisting of locomotive, carriage, two covered trucks, three open trucks, and a brake van, 'which when loaded will comprise an ordinary mixed train on this line'. The W&L opened for freight on 9 March 1903, officially on 4 April, and for regular passenger services two days later. From 1904 passenger trains called at Sylfaen and Dolarddyn. Castle Caereinion received a passing loop in 1907.

The railway, though worked by the Cambrian, remained independent until taken-over by the GWR in 1923. From 1925 the GWR's Welshpool–Llanfair–Dinas Mawddwy bus spelt doom for the rail passenger service, withdrawn from 9 February 1931. Agricultural traffic continued, usually of two trains daily, reduced to one after World War II. The line closed in 1956; the last train, an enthusiasts' special, ran on 3 November. A preservation society was formed, rehabilitation starting in 1959. On 6 April 1963, sixty years after first carrying passengers, its two locomotives repaired and repainted, the W&L was re-opened by the Earl of Powis. At first trains left from Welshpool station yard, but passenger services were limited to west of Castle Caereinion: the Golfa incline required attention as well as the fitting of continuous brakes on passenger stock. The Raven Square to Welshpool station section, needed for road improvements, closed in August 1963. Castle Caereinion to Sylfaen re-opened from 6 June 1964. Floods in December 1964 weakened the Banwy bridge. This was rebuilt with the help of Royal Engineers, and a temporary Llanfair–Heniarth shuttle replaced by full services from 14 August 1965, though only to Castle Caereinion, re-opening to Sylfaen being on 15 July 1972. Sylfaen loop came into use in 1976. During the W&L's new existence additional locomotives and rolling stock arrived, with some unusual backgrounds for their new surroundings: No 6 *Monarch*, a 1935 Bagnall 0–4–4–0 articulated tank; No 10, a Franco–Belge ex-German Wermacht 0–8–0 tank, later named *Sir Drefaldwyn*, and five Zillertalbahn coaches; No 12 *Joan*, a 1927 Kerr Stuart 0–6–2 tank from Antigua; and No 14, from Sierra Leone, a 1954 Hunslet 2–6–2 tank, and four SL coaches. In 1978–9 work started on restoring down to Raven Square, Welshpool. (See Chapter XVI).

FAIRBOURNE RAILWAY

This tourist line started as a 2-mile (3.2km) 2ft 0in (61cm) gauge horse tramway, opened about 1890 by Arthur McDougall (of the flour empire) to carry building materials for speculative boarding houses from a brickyard near the site of the early Barmouth Ferry station along the shore to Penrhyn Point, where the ferry plied across the estuary. The tramway was soon opened to the public, passengers increasing after Fairbourne main line station opened in 1899. In 1916 Narrow Gauge Railways Ltd (associated with the model engineering firm of Bassett-Lowke) bought the tramway, altered the gauge to 15in (38cm), and re-opened it, worked by a new Bassett-Lowke steam locomotive, Little Giant class No 22 *Prince Edward of Wales*. The line was taken over in 1924 by the Fairbourne Estate & Development Company. The railway closed completely during World War II, and was extensively damaged during military exercises. Reconstruction during 1946 resulted in partial re-opening for Easter 1947. After this most of the line came back into use, with improved layout and signalling. The later steam locomotives included a 1949 4–6–2 *Edward W. Twining*; and the elegant 2–4–2s *Sian* (built 1963) and *Katie* (arrived 1965), with trains of open and closed passenger coaches, some in articulated sets. The service boasted a steam-hauled 'boat train', connecting with Barmouth ferry motor boats. The 1980s were to see dramatic changes to the railway. (See Chapter XVI).

PLYNLIMON & HAFAN TRAMWAY

From the Cambrian's Llanfihangel (later Llandre) station, the
7¼-mile (11.6km) 2ft 3in (69cm) gauge Plynlimon & Hafan
Tramway ran east via Talybont and the Afon Leri Valley into
the foothills of Plynlimon to get lead and granite from the
Hafan mine and quarry. Its promoters, who had no statutory
powers, originally sought access to the sea but the Cambrian
blocked their way and Llanfihangel became the exchange point.
On 12 May 1897 a squat, vertical-boilered locomotive, rather
unkindly named Victoria but referring to the diamond jubilee,
was put on the rails at Llanfihangel. Built to the company's
order by John Slee of Earlestown, a P&H director, Victoria
was a poor runner and in August 1897 a conventional Bagnall
2–4–0 tank Talybont arrived, followed in September by a little
Bagnall 0–4–0 saddle tank Hafan, to work the quarry end. A
rather superior bogie carriage, with end balconies, arrived with
Talybont, and without any apparent official approval a
Mondays-only passenger service started from 28 March 1898,
connecting with the Cambrian's market train. There was little
demand and the service ceased in mid-August 1898. Though
mineral and quarry traffic continued, financial troubles
terminated the Hafan Tram's existence in 1899. Talybont, however, went on to greater things (p 235).

CHAPTER XII

West of Shrewsbury

The present Cambrian line connects with the main railway network via the link from Buttington Junction to just south of Shrewsbury where it joins the Shrewsbury & Hereford, which was authorised 1846, opened 1852, leased to the GWR and LNWR a decade later, and vested in them in 1870. Shrewsbury, an important railway junction, is outside the scope of this volume. From the 1850s it was dominated by the GWR and LNWR, both of jealous disposition, though in this case the latter proved the more ambitious. Having arrived at the town, what promise did the country hold to the west?

For some 20 miles lay flat open farmlands watered by the Severn which, fed by the Tanat and the Vyrnwy, drains from the Berwyns into the Shropshire Plain. Two spurs—Long Mountain and Breidden Hill to the west, and the Stiperstones to the south-west—intruded into the plain. Both contained lead and granite, while at Llanymynech were considerable limestone quarries. The plain itself, for centuries the scene of recurring border strife between the Marcher lords and the Welsh princes, was undeveloped, pastoral, prone to flooding, and sparsely inhabited. There appeared little to tempt the railway entrepreneur. But across the plain there was at the least a possible direct access to the mountain passes to the Cambrian Coast and, at most—a dream sustained for nearly 50 years—a potential short-cut from the Midlands to Ireland via Porth Dinllaen. Euston's early interest in reaching Aberystwyth from Shrewsbury, and its *carte blanche* from the Oswestry & Newtown company to promote or support instead a link between Shrewsbury and the nascent Cambrian at Welshpool, has already been mentioned.

OPENING SHREWSBURY TO MINSTERLEY

The Shrewsbury & Welshpool Railway Company was incorporated by Act of 29 July 1856, for the main line and a branch south-west from Hanwood along the Rea Valley to the market town of Minsterley. The LNWR was to use and maintain the line. In 1858, when the O&N's acute financial troubles threatened its own completion, Euston's determination to reach Newtown by converting its Shropshire Union Canal to a railway fell through when the resuscitated O&N agreed to an S&W request to double its line between Buttington Junction and Welshpool, the LNWR to have running powers and to contribute to maintaining Welshpool station. By August 1859 the S&W directors reported that construction was let to Alexander Thomas Gordon, and that navvies were engaged on heavy cuttings at the Welshpool end, where the line surmounted the saddle between Long Mountain and Breidden Hill. Alterations of levels and extensions of time were sanctioned in 1858 and 1860, in which latter year a Bill for an extension to Bishops Castle was rejected.

In November 1860 Col Yolland inspected the S&W line from Coleham Junction, where it left the single-track Shrewsbury & Hereford about $\frac{3}{4}$-mile (1.2km) south of Shrewsbury station, to Minsterley—a length of $9\frac{1}{4}$ miles (14.8km), of which $4\frac{5}{8}$ miles (7.4km) would form part of the main line to Welshpool. The railway was single throughout, though on the main line portion the land and some of the bridges allowed for eventual doubling. Powers were being sought to double the Minsterley branch proper. There were sidings at all three stations: Hanwood, Pontesbury, and Minsterley. The S&H, crowded with traffic, was being doubled between Shrewsbury and Coleham Junction. As works were incomplete, opening of the Minsterley line was refused, as was the S&H doubling in December. The colonel found the latter virtually unchanged in February 1861, but to his surprise was informed by the S&H engineer that their lordships in Whitehall had already given permission to open the second line. The Minsterley branch was now in order, and a 'small roadside station has been established . . . at a Level Crossing at Plealey Road'. The S&W, Shrewsbury to Minsterley, opened to the public on 14 February 1861.

Page 191 (Top) New Quay Road (later Bryn Teify), looking south, c.1890s; (centre) Opening the Aberayron branch, 12 May 1911; (bottom) Llanrhystyd Road, early 1900s. (National Library of Wales)

Page 192 (Top) Manchester and Milford line train with GWR locomotive, departing from Aberystwyth, September 1919; (centre) Cambrian 61 class No 66 on passenger train and ex Metropolitan Railway No 15 (Cambrian No 36, converted to tender engine in 1916) at Aberystwyth, c.1910; (bottom) Devil's Bridge, Vale of Rheidol Light Railway, August 1977. (National Library of Wales, top and centre; Author)

COMPLETING THE SHREWSBURY & WELSHPOOL

The main line works were interrupted by an accident near
Hanwood in October 1861, when derailment of the contractor's
daily navvy train to Middletown killed two men and injured
several more. By now the contractor was Richard France, whom
we met earlier and will come across again. In January 1862
Col Yolland inspected the remaining 11⅝ miles (18.7km) from
Cruckmeole Junction (Hanwood), single throughout, with sidings
at the stations at Yockleton, Westbury, a temporary station at
Middletown, and at Buttington Junction (then known as Cefn
Junction). Again, there was provision for eventual doubling. A
short tunnel near the 13-mile post (21km) had been abandoned
and the line deviated instead with steep gradients and heavy
earthworks. The S&W, worked by the LNWR, and the O&N's
Buttington–Welshpool second line, opened on 27 January 1862,
gave a more direct link between the incomplete Cambrian main
line and the Midlands, and served the agricultural community
west of Shrewsbury. Doubling for four miles (6.4km) between
Coleham and Cruckmeole Junctions was authorised by Act of
29 June 1863, which with Acts of 1864 and 1865 provided for
sale or lease to the LNWR and GWR jointly. Opening of this
second line was approved in March 1866.

MINSTERLEY BRANCH DEVELOPMENTS AND THE SNAILBEACH
DISTRICT RAILWAYS

Despite improved communication, Minsterley's population
remained fairly steady: the 890 persons in 1861 increased to
930 in 1871, fell to 798 by 1891, was 788 in 1921, and just over
900 in 1961, a decade after closure of the railway to passengers.
The branch nevertheless proved useful as an outlet for lead and
granite in the Stiperstone Hills.

Most productive was the Snailbeach lead mine which in turn
created a demand for coal, and Pontesbury station became the
exchange point. Between 2,000 and 3,000 tons of lead were
mined annually until the 1880s, after which output dropped to
nearly nothing by World War I, eclipsed by the growing extrac-
tion of barytes, a total of 42,327 tons being taken out between
1865 and 1913, while during World War I output climbed to
5,000 tons annually. The minerals came down from the Stiperstones on the Snailbeach District Railways; the plural form

remained a mere hope, for after the SDR Act of 5 August 1873 all that matured was a 3¾-mile (6km) 2ft 3¾in (71cm) gauge single line from Pontesbury up to Crows Nest, with a branch to Snailbeach. Extensions authorised by the Shropshire Mineral (Light) Railway Act of 5 August 1891 came to nothing. Some 40 wagons and two saddle tanks worked the traffic: 0-4-2 *Belmont* (delivered 1877), and 0-6-0 *Fernhill* (1881). In 1898 the Ceiriog Granite Company opened a new quarry near Habberley, to which a branch was opened in 1905, boosting SDR mineral traffic to a peak of 38,000 tons in 1909. Sir Henry Dennis was on the boards of the SDR and the Glyn Valley (p 46), which served the main Ceiriog quarries, and for a short time one of the GVT's locomotives, *Sir Theodore*, was loaned to the SDR to work the new traffic. Constant derailments led to its return, and in 1906 a new 0-6-0 side tank, *Dennis*, was delivered to the SDR. Despite the promising new traffic the SDR did not prosper, and in 1923 ownership passed to Colonel Stephens, a staunch believer in light railways and to whom many ailing lines were to owe a new lease of life. Three further locomotives were purchased, and under revitalised management over 26,352 tons of granite were carried in 1938 from Callow Hill, this having been the sole source of revenue since 1932. In 1947 the Shropshire County Council, lessees of the Callow Hill quarries, leased the line, traffic having been worked since the previous summer, when the last locomotive failed, by a diesel farm tractor which straddled one of the rails. Granite traffic by rail continued thus until 1959 when road haulage took over.

Despite the doubling powers, the Minsterley branch remained a single line. Passenger services consisted of four trains daily each way, with none on Sundays. From 5 April 1919 a private bus service started to Shrewsbury, and though market tickets and other inducements staved off immediate decline, the branch closed to passengers from 5 February 1951, freight remaining until 1965.

The S&W train service connected with main line trains at each end. It was operated by the LNWR between Stafford, Shrewsbury and Welshpool, with through GWR and LNWR carriages to Aberystwyth and Barmouth. To avoid confusion with Middleton in Lancashire, Middletown became Middletown Hills in 1919 and Breidden in 1928. In 1935 Plas-y-Court Halt was opened between Breidden and Westbury. In 1960 work started on a rail holding and flash-butt welding depot at

Hookagate near Shrewsbury to supply long-welded rails for
the Western Region. On 12 September 1960 the intermediate
S&W stations and halt were closed. Nevertheless, the strategic
cut-off role of the S&W has kept it in business (see also p 169).

(see also p 169)

THE 'POTTS' LINE

Starting with high aspirations, the Shropshire & Montgomeryshire Railway had a chequered life with a confused history out
of all proportion to its usefulness. The railway dated back to
1862 when, following failure of the West Midland scheme
(p 141), the West Shropshire Mineral Railway was incorporated
by Act of 29 July to make a line from the Cambrian at Llanymynech via Kinnerley to Westbury on the S&W. Chief promoter
was Richard France, proprietor of quarries near Llanymynech
and contractor to the S&W and the Mold & Denbigh Junction
(p 76).

In the following November the projected Potteries Junction
Railway unsuccessfully lodged plans for lines connecting
Newcastle-under-Lyme with Market Drayton and the LNWR
at Whitchurch and the GWR at Gresford, with running powers
into Shrewsbury. In the same session the West Shropshire
Mineral obtained powers by Act of 13 July 1863 for a branch
from Kinnerley south to Moat Hall, abandonment of the
Westbury junction, and connection instead with the S&W at
Redhill, much nearer to Shrewsbury. Behind this alteration, and
linked with the failed Potteries scheme, lay the germ of a hope
of an eventual direct route to Ireland, following on the demise
of the West Midland scheme over just such a course in 1861.
On this Irish connection as it concerned the WSM in the 1860s,
Charles F. Klapper (*Railway Magazine*, September 1934) mentioned that Colonel Stephens—under whom the Shropshire &
Mongomeryshire was to enjoy its only successful period—once
stated that the Great Northern Railway had an interest. Whatever the truth of this, by two Acts of 30 June 1864 the WSM
renamed itself as the more grand Shrewsbury & North Wales
Railway and obtained powers for branches from Kinnerley to
Abberbury and Great Ness, and south to the Breidden quarries
at Criggion, and from Llanymynech westwards to Llanyblodwel
and the Nantmawr lime quarries with running powers over the
intervening length of the Oswestry & Newtown.

Following another unsuccessful attempt by the Shrewsbury

& Potteries Junction in 1864 for a line linking the Potteries with Shrewsbury, that company was authorised by Act of 5 July 1865 to make several lines via Market Drayton : to the Crewe–Shrewsbury line, the S&W, Severn Valley, and S&H. In August the S&PJ directors reported on their success, gained despite much opposition from Euston and Paddington. The new line 'on one hand would communicate with very productive mineral districts, and on the other, by means of running powers over a portion of the North Staffordshire, they would reach the populous district of the Potteries'. The contractor was to be Richard France.

In the country to the south of the Shrewsbury & North Wales, the S&PJ sought in 1866 to make branches, none being sanctioned, but including a 5¾-mile (9.2km) line from the authorised Moat Hall branch to join an 1865 extension of the Bishops Castle Railway from Chirbury to Minsterley, and an 11-mile (17.7km) line from the first near Pontesbury to the BCR at Lydham. These were intended to be owned jointly with the Bishops Castle—an impecunious company with a mission to link the Cambrian at Montgomery with the Shrewsbury & Hereford, affording a cut-off avoiding Shrewsbury—and running powers for both were intended to get them into Staffordshire by means of the Drayton Junction Railway. A BCR Bill in 1866 for running powers for itself and the S&PJ from Montgomery—to which a BCR extension had been authorised in 1861—over the Cambrian to Llanidloes, where the Mid Wales and the Manchester & Milford might be reached, also failed. Thus between 1862 and the end of the Mania of 1865–6 there were unceasing attempts to effect a separate main line linking the Potteries with Mid Wales. A start was made on the Market Drayton line but works were abandoned in 1866.

The S&NW and S&PJ amalgamated by Act of 16 July 1866 to form the Potteries Shrewsbury & North Wales Railway, known with a mixture of affection and exasperation simply as the 'Potts' in later years. Another concurrent Act confirmed a deviation of the S&PJ to join the S&NW at Redhill, running thence parallel with the Shrewsbury & Welshpool to Shrewsbury where, after passing over the River Rea, it terminated at a new station behind the Abbey, with a separate spur to the Shrewsbury–Birmingham line. In the same session the S&NW had also sought powers for a 14-mile (22.4km) line, the Meifod Valley Extension, from Llanymynech, following the Rivers Vyrnwy and

Banwy to Llanfair Caereinion in Montgomeryshire. This further step towards the distant goal of Irish traffic failed (Richard France ran out of funds); only a ¼-mile (0.4km) branch to Bryn Tanat, and substituted curves at Llanymynech, were authorised in the company's Act of 1866.

Captain Rich inspected the 'Potts' line early in July 1866. The S&NW section was just over 14¼ miles (23km), from a junction with the Cambrian at Llanymynech to an end-on junction at Redhill with the S&PJ which continued for just over 3¼ miles (5.2km) into Shrewsbury. The entire line was optimistically double-tracked. From Llanymynech to Shrewsbury, intermediate stations, with small platforms and wooden booking offices, were at Maesbrook, Kinnerley, Nesscliff, Shrawardine, Ford (*later* & Cross Gates), Hanwood Road, and Red Hill (*sic*). There was a locomotive shed and turntable at Llanymynech, also at Shrewsbury, where a branch of just under ½-mile (0.8km) ran down into the 'Shrewsbury Abbey Yard' station. Commented Captain Rich :

> The gradient of this branch is 1 in 47. All trains should be brought to a stand at the place where the junction with this branch and the branch to the LNWR to Birmingham is now being formed at the top of the incline and the trains should be worked at very low speed into the Abbey station.

Earthworks, mainly between Redhill and Shrawardine, were fairly extensive; west of Shrawardine the line was practically level, with many road crossings. There were eight viaducts, mostly small, but including that at Shrawardine over the Severn, which had six wrought-iron spans on cast-iron columns with masonry piers and abutments, and a five-span timber viaduct on the S&PJ section.

The line opened quietly for passengers and freight on 13 August 1866 with five passenger trains (four in winter) each way on weekdays, and two each way on Sundays. Shrewsbury–Aberystwyth excursions started from 26 August. Two single-track branches opened for freight : from Kinnerley through Melverley, over the Severn by a timber viaduct, to Criggion and nearby granite quarries—the line level and with many road crossings—and from Llanymynech to the Nantmawr quarries. The services were short-lived. Creditors pressed for repayments, and bailiffs took possession of the line; the trains ceased running

on 21 December 1866. There followed the sale of some locomotives and wagons, and singling of the main line except through
some of the stations. Services restarted in December 1868 with
three weekday trains each way, four on Saturdays, and one on
Sundays.

Richard France supplied the locomotives. Early ones included
four bought by him from Manning Wardle in 1865 : 0–6–0
saddle tank *Alyn* (which soon went to the Mawddwy Railway,
being renamed *Mawddwy*, and later becoming Cambrian No
30), and 0–6–0 tanks *Powis*, *Sir Watkin*, and *Viscount*. Others
were 0–4–0 saddle tank *Nantmawr* built in 1864 by Hughes of
Loughborough; an 1865 0–4–0 well tank *Breidden* from
Hawthorns; an 1847 ex-LNWR 0–4–2 tender locomotive; and
an 0–4–2 tank *Tanat*, builder and date unknown. A 2–4–0 tank,
Hope, built by the Yorkshire Engine Company, arrived in 1872,
about which time *Sir Watkin*, *Nantmawr*, and *Breidden* were
sold. There were twenty-one 4-wheeled carriages at the opening
and over 200 wagons, which nearly doubled by the mid-1870s.

In March and April 1870 Lt Col Rich inspected the Llanyblodwel (Nantmawr) line prior to opening for passenger traffic.
The single track was just under $2\frac{1}{2}$ miles (4km) in length to
Llanyblodwel and crossed the Tanat by two timber viaducts
of seven and five openings. An aqueduct carried the Montgomeryshire Canal over the railway. At Llanyblodwel station
the line, on a gradient of 1 in 88, was double-tracked and there
was a small platform, beyond which the railway extended to
the Nantmawr quarries. Passenger traffic commenced on 18
April. A $2\frac{1}{2}$-mile (4km) extension northwards from Llanyblodwel
to Trefonen, authorised by the PS&NW Act of 1874 was not
made.

October 1870 saw the colonel inspecting the Breidden
(Criggion) branch, $5\frac{1}{8}$ miles (8.2km) in length, with stations at
Melverley, Crew (*sic*) Green, Llandrinio Road, and Criggion :

The line has been covered with water very lately. It is probable
that if the Railway had been required to be made above the
level of the floods, that the traffic would not have warranted
such an outlay and that it would not have been made at all,
added to which, I understand that the landowners required it
to be made at its present level. It will be very necessary for
the company to examine it carefully when flooding takes
place . . .

The line has been made and worked to a small extent for mineral traffic during the last five years . . . There are no turntables. It is proposed to work the line with one tank engine in steam.

Various works required alteration and completion. The branch opened to passengers on 2 June 1871.

Peak PS&NW receipts were reached in 1872 when 68,259 passengers and some 90,000 tons of minerals and goods were carried. Even so, profits were negligible. The sparse population and closure of some of the quarries upon which the railway depended to remain solvent hastened its decline, evidenced by an increasingly unkempt and ramshackle appearance, reduced staff and services, and lack of essential maintenance. Hopes of extension to the Potteries and attraction of traffic competing with the GWR and LNWR had gone. Increasingly, passengers deserted the line, preferring a safer though slower road journey. A Receiver was appointed in 1877.

In 1879 there appeared a ray of hope: the Great Northern Railway, thrusting westwards through Burton and Derby to the North Staffordshire Railway, gained running powers into Stafford. The authorities at King's Cross saw the opportunity, by obtaining running powers over the LNWR to Wellington, and thence to Shrewsbury, to gain access via the 'Potts' to the Cambrian system. But no GNR express ever ran through Kinnerley; deterioration of the 'Potts' had gone too far. The death blow was dealt by Col Rich in 1880 following an inspection of the entire line, when he found timber bridges rotting and unsafe, sleepers decayed, fences missing, signals and crossing gates in need of repair, and rails out of line and level. 'This Railway', he pronounced, 'requires to be thoroughly overhauled and repaired. . . ' But the Receiver had no funds, and the 'Potts' directors ordered closure of the whole railway to public traffic from 22 June 1880. The company was wound-up by Act of 18 July 1881. Only the Nantmawr line remained in use, worked by the Cambrian (p 182).

The 'Potts' was to remain derelict for 30 years during which, by Act of 7 August 1888, the Shropshire Railways Company was incorporated to take over the moribund concern and to construct extensions. These included one from Shrewsbury to Hodnet on the GWR Wellington–Market Drayton line, whence a link was to be built to the North Staffordshire company's

Stoke, Silverdale and Market Drayton branch, over which the Shropshire was to enjoy running powers, with reciprocal NSR rights into Shrewsbury Abbey station. As a house-clearing prelude, any saleable 'Potts' rolling stock was disposed of, and in August 1888 the four remaining locomotives, *Viscount* (renamed as *Bradford*), *Powis*, *Tanat*, and *Hope* were taken away.

Though some reconstruction started in 1890, including relaying, and an Act of 1891 extended the time for completion of works, the expense of resurrecting the 'Potts' proved prohibitive. The Shropshire company became the frustrated freeholder of a railway rapidly disappearing beneath the undergrowth. For an excellent description of the line at the turn of the century, see T. R. Perkins, 'A Derelict British Railway' (*Railway Magazine*, May/June 1903).

SHROPSHIRE & MONTGOMERYSHIRE SUCCESS . . .

Mr Perkins' article may well have contributed to local moves to re-open the line, taking advantage of the Light Railways Act of 1896. Backed by the Earls of Bradford and Powis, and the local authorities, Holman F. Stephens, civil engineer of Tonbridge, already well-known for successful promotion of light railways, took charge of events. On 11 February 1909 a Light Railway Order was confirmed whereby the line would be taken over and worked by the Shropshire & Montgomeryshire Light Railway Company. Reconstruction started immediately from the Llanymynech end. Fortuitously, the largest work, the Shrawardine viaduct, was in good order. A full account of the works is given in a further article by a plainly delighted Mr Perkins (*Railway Magazine*, September 1911). The line was soon transformed.

On 7 April 1911 Lt Col Druitt reported favourably on the single-track main line, with passing places and double platforms at Kinnerley, and Ford & Crossgates. New halts at Shrewsbury West and Meole Brace supplemented the earlier stations, followed later by halts at Cruckton, Edgebold (replacing Hanwood Road), Shoot Hill, Edgerley, and Wern Las. Hookagate & Redhill replaced the old Red Hill station; Nesscliff and Crossgates became Nesscliff & Pentre, and Ford & Crossgates. The railway re-opened formally on 13 April 1911, a special train hauled by *Hesperus* taking guests from the Abbey station to Llanymynech and back, punctuated by speeches, exploding fog signals, and cheers from crowds along the route—a very different welcome from that far-off day in 1866. The first 1911 service was of four mixed passenger and goods trains each way daily, with two on Sundays. Kinnerley was now the working hub of the line, with locomotive shed, repair shop and stores.

The S&ML locomotives were a very mixed lot: No 1 *Gazelle*, a diminutive 2–2–2 of toy-like outline, built in 1893 and used for inspection during reconstruction (later converted to an 0–4–2); No 2, an ex-LNWR 0–4–2 saddle tank, first named *Hecate* by the S&ML, and later *Severn*; No 3 *Hesperus* (a name favoured by Col Stephens) an ex-London & South Western 0–6–0 Ilfracombe class goods; No 4 *Morous*, an 0–6–0 Manning Wardle tank from the Stratford & Midland Junction Railway (later transferred to Col Stephens' West Sussex Railway); Nos 5 *Pyramus* and 6 *Thisbe*, new 0–6–2 side tanks, under construction by Hawthorns at the time of re-opening. According to Eric Tonks, in World War I they went to the Kinmel Camp line (p 78), being replaced—respectively 1914 and 1916—on the S&ML by two more Ilfracombe Goods which adopted the numbers and names. There were also three ex-London Brighton & South Coast Railway 0–6–0 Terriers which became No 7 *Hecate* (arrived 1921), No 8 *Dido* and No 9 *Daphne* (both 1923); and three ex-LNWR 0–6–0s LMS Nos 8108, 8182, and 8236 (1930–2). Carriage stock came second hand from various sources, including the Midland, North Staffordshire, and Plymouth Devonport & South Western Junction companies. Unique was the 1848 ex-LSWR royal saloon; other curiosities were a Wolseley railcar, a Ford 3-car set, and an ex-London County Council horse tramcar for use with *Gazelle*.

The Criggion branch needed much restoration before re-opening; in particular the Melverley viaduct had disintegrated over the years, requiring a new iron-and-timber structure. With prospects of improved transport, defunct quarries re-opened at Criggion. The line opened to goods on 22 February, and to passengers in August, 1912. Even so, Melverley viaduct foundations were suspect, and only *Gazelle* and its tram were allowed on passenger traffic. A new halt opened at Chapel Lane.

. . . AND DECLINE

By 1914 the S&ML was considering reviving the Market Drayton scheme, but war intervened. Thereafter traffic declined: the people in isolated villages, with stations some distance away, drifted to road transport where country carrier and bus services proved more convenient. The Ford railcar set, slow, noisy, smelly and boneshaking, was introducel by Col Stephens in an attempt at economy and a misplaced belief it would attract patrons. The Criggion branch service operated on Saturdays only from 1928, and because of increasing fears concerning the viaduct, passenger trains were cut back to Melverley in 1932. From February 1933 there was only one return trip daily on the main line, with two on Saturdays. Receipts plummetted. Two years after the death of Col Stephens, S&ML passenger services ceased from 6 November 1933, though excursions used the line for some years after. Only Criggion granite, and local coal and freight to intermediate stations kept the railway going. On the Nantmawr branch passenger services ceased from 1 January 1917 (p 185), and freight from 1925.

OHMS

Thus—again weed-covered and suffering encroaching decay—the S&ML struggled into World War II, when with bewildering rapidity everything changed. The War Department saw the sparsely inhabited countryside as ideal for a vast ordnance depot; the S&ML was requisitioned and the main line immediately put into good order. Marshalling yards went in at Llanymynech and Meole Brace; numerous War Department locomotives arrived. From 1 June 1941, when the WD started working the main line, traffic became the heaviest ever, especially during the lead-up to the Alamein campaign. W. J. Thorne penned a most illuminating account of his experiences on the military operating side (*Railway World*, October 1960). In 1946–7 Shrawardine viaduct was reconstructed by the Royal Engineers, using Bailey bridges.

The main line reverted to WD civilian status in 1947 and at nationalisation passed under joint WD and Western Region control. Normal rail facilities ceased from 29 February 1960, after which work started on laying-in a connection from Shrewsbury Abbey yard to the Severn Valley line. Throughout the war the Criggion branch remained under civilian control; it was closed and abandoned from 4 January 1960. On the main line WD traffic continued outwards via Llanymynech until, after final removal of WD equipment, it reverted to British Railways for dismantling.

CHAPTER XIII

Central Wales Area

The rival Mid and Central Wales lines through the hills and mountains of Radnorshire, Breconshire and Carmarthenshire, were built to bring South Wales coal to industry in the Midlands, Lancashire and Yorkshire. They were also to convey those areas' imports and exports from and to Swansea and Milford Haven, the two then most important potential ports for American trade. Impetus came with the opening of the Vale of Towy Railway.

MID AND CENTRAL WALES RIVALRY

The Llanelly Railway & Dock Company, incorporated in 1828, Llanelli Dock, and 1835, a broad gauge line from Llanelli northwards via Pontardulais to Llandeilo in the Vale of Tywi, opened throughout by 1857. An Act of 10 July 1854 incorported the Vale of Towy Railway for a mixed-gauge line from Llanelly at 'Llandilofawr', north-east to the agricultural town of Llandovery, situated on the River Bran near its confluence with the Tywi, flanked from north through east to south by mountains, and with less than 2,000 population. The $11\frac{1}{4}$-mile (18.1km) single line V of T, with five wooden viaducts over the Tywi, and stations at Lampeter Road (later Llanwrda), Llangadock (Llangadog) and Glanrhyd, opened on 1 April 1858, worked by the Llanelly company which leased the line by Act that year. Llandovery now became the goal of railway promoters aiming south from Montgomeryshire and Shropshire.

Almost any such line would pass through or near Builth Wells in the Wye Valley. There was some early skirmishing in that direction: the Shrewsbury & Hereford (p 189) proposed extension of the Leominster & Kington to Builth was countered by an Oswestry & Newtown scheme to extend the Llanidloes &

Newtown south via Rhayader and so shifted ground, supporting a more direct line south from its Craven Arms station, named after the solitary nearby inn, on the crossroads for Bishops Castle, Clun, Knighton and nearby villages. Thus after a false start in 1857 an Act of 21 May 1858 incorporated the Knighton Railway, from Craven Arms along the Clun and Teme Valleys to the border town of Knighton.

A year later, with Euston supporting extension of the Knighton towards Llandovery, Montgomeryshire promoters formed the provisional Manchester Liverpool Swansea & Milford Haven Railway, then took it to Parliament re-titled as the Mid Wales Railway, in two sections: from the L&N through the Dulas and Marteg Valleys to Newbridge-on-Wye, and from Newbridge to Llandovery. The northern section received Royal Assent on 1 August 1859, the Llandovery continuation being rejected in favour of the Central Wales Railway—an extension of the Knighton through the Radnorshire Hills to Llandrindod Wells and on to Llandovery, but authorised only as far as Llandrindod, by Act of 13 August 1859.

Having 'hiccupped' en route for Llandovery, both companies renewed their attempts in 1860. Concurrently, determined to scotch LNWR and Central Wales aspirations towards Milford Haven the old Manchester & Milford scheme (p 148) was re-surrected, from Llanidloes westwards through Llangurig, whence a costly route was planned through the mountains along the Wye and Mynach Valleys to Devil's Bridge, then south through Ysbyty Ystwyth to Pencader on the authorised Carmarthen & Cardigan Railway, over which M&M trains would run to Carmarthen and on to Milford Haven.

As well as trying for Llandovery, the Mid Wales proposed a line from Newbridge along the Wye valley via Builth to join the authorised Hereford Hay & Brecon at Aberllyfni (Three Cocks), thence south up the Llyfni Valley through Talgarth to terminate by a curve into the Hay Railway at the eastern end of Talyllyn tunnel (see later). The Central Wales Extension Bill, meanwhile, aimed south from Llandrindod to Builth, then south-west into Breconshire, through Llangammarch Wells and Llanwrtyd Wells, before surmounting the high land into Carmarthenshire to drop down to Llandovery.

Both Bills received Royal Assent on 3 July 1860, the CWE in its entirety, the Mid Wales restricted to its Wye Valley route; followed on 23 July by the Manchester & Milford. Duplicated

M&M and Mid Wales powers for a short distance south of Llanidloes to Penpontbren were resolved by the Llanidloes & Newtown Company undertaking by Act of 17 July 1862 to make that length itself, with running powers to both companies into Llanidloes where it planned a joint station for all three users. Mid Wales entry to Brecon was via the Hereford Hay & Brecon—a Savin line, authorised 8 August 1859—which by Act of 6 August 1860 had purchased the 3ft 6in (107cm) gauge Hay Railway, authorised 1811 and 1812 as a 24-mile (38.6km) horse tramway from the Brecknock & Abergavenny Canal at Brecon via Talyllyn to Aberllyfni and then beside the Wye through Hay to Eardisley. This purchase, originally designed to control access by the Mid Wales and Brecon & Merthyr Railways, the latter leased to Davies and Savin in 1860, to Brecon, was frustrated by clauses requiring that Three Cocks to Talyllyn should become Mid Wales property, Talyllyn to Brecon going to the Brecon & Merthyr, confirmed by MW and B&M Acts of 1861. By Act of 17 July 1862 the MW was authorised to make alterations between Penpontbren and Talyllyn, and a short junction curve to the Central Wales Extension near Builth. As to the Central Wales, by agreement the Llanelly promoted a Llandeilo–Carmarthen line, aiming towards Milford Haven, and one from Pontardulais to Swansea (see South Wales Regional History), powers being obtained in the Llanelly's Act of 1 August 1861.

SOME 'MIGHT-HAVE-BEENS'

A number of schemes following authorisation of the two main lines throw light on local railway politics. In 1861 an M&M branch was sanctioned from Devil's Bridge to Aberystwyth, immediately kindling Mid Wales enthusiasm to reach the resort, resulting in a Marteg Valley–Llangurig proposal. Dropped early in 1862, this was revived, tacked to a MW Bill seeking operating agreements with the M&M in the north and the HH&B and B&M in the south, which received Royal Assent on 22 June 1863. By Act of 5 July 1865, however, the M&M abandoned its mountain route west of Llangurig in favour of one north from Alltddu (p 227). The Mid Wales, therefore, by its concurrent 'Western Extensions' Act, jettisoned the Llangurig branch in favour of a line partly following the Wye and then the Rhayader–Aberystwyth mountain road through Cwmystwyth

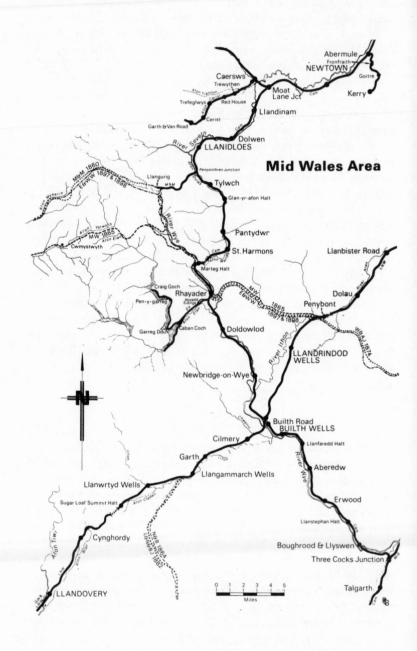

Mid Wales Area

Abermule
Fronfraith
NEWTOWN
Goitre
Kerry
Caersws
Trewythen
Moat
Lane Jct
Afon Trannon
Cerist
Trefeglwys
Red House
Cam
Llandinam
Garth & Van Road
Cerist
Cam
River Severn
Dolwen
LLANIDLOES
M&M 1860
E&WW 1891 & 1896
Afon Mytherin
Llangurig
M&M
Penpontbren Junction
Tylwch
Glan-yr-afon Halt
Afon Ystwyth
MW 1865
Afon Elan
Cwmystwyth
River Wye
Pantydwr
Cam
St. Harmons
Afon Marteg
Marteg Halt
Llanbister Road
River Lave
Craig Goch
Pen-y-garreg
Rhayader
Noyadd
Sidings
Afon Elan
MW 1865
E&WW 1891 & 1896
Dolau
Penybont
River Ithon
Garreg Ddu
Caban Coch
Afon Elan
Doldowlod
LLANDRINDOD
WELLS
K&E 1874
Newbridge-on-Wye
Afon Ithon
Chwefru
Builth Road
BUILTH WELLS
Cilmery
Llanfaredd Halt
Garth
Afon Irfon
Llangammarch Wells
River Wye
Aberedw
Llanwrtyd Wells
Afon Cledan
Erwood
Sugar Loaf Summit Halt
N&B 1864
(N&B) 1897 1882
Llanstephan Halt
Afon Tywi
Cynghordy
Afon Bran
Boughrood & Llyswen
Three Cocks Junction
GWR 1868
LLANDOVERY
Talgarth

0 1 2 3 4 5
Miles

and Pontrhydygroes to the new M&M Aberystwyth line at Trawscoed over which running powers were granted, with a connecting branch to Llangurig which, by running powers, offered reinstatement of direct M&M access to Llanidloes. An 'Eastern Extension', authorised 29 June 1865, linked Rhayader to the Central Wales at Penybont. But whereas this line, together with an 1864-authorisfied second loop near Builth, was abandoned by MW Act of 1869, time for completion of the Western Extensions was successively extended until the coastal dream was reluctantly abandoned by Act of 1876 for lack of money. Two schemes followed parts of the MW extension routes: the 1874-authorised Worcester & Aberystwyth Junction, from the Kington & Eardisley at New Radnor to the MW at Rhayader, potentially bringing traffic to the Western Extension; and the East & West Wales Bills of 1897 and 1898, linking New Radnor with Aberystwyth. After altering its proposed termination to Builth in 1877 the W&AJ was wound-up in 1880. The E&WW did not proceed.

In 1863 the Brecon & Merthyr promoted the Brecon & Llandovery Junction, from Brecon westwards via Defynnog to Llandovery, to foil the newly-formed Neath & Brecon's Bill for extension through Defynnog and Brecon to link up with the HH&B. The N&B, however, received powers in 1863, the B&LJ being authorised only west of Defynnog. An 1864 N&B Act authorised a line north from Defynnog to join the Central Wales Extension at Llangammarch, a blow at the Mid Wales but welcomed by the Central Wales. The B&LJ, offering a route for V of T traffic via the Mid Wales, was not built. Neither was the Llangammarch line; the contractor, John Dickson (p 84), became bankrupt. The Usk & Towy, incorporated in 1877, and similar in intent to the B&LJ, lingered unbuilt into the 1880s. In 1888 the Llangammarch & Neath & Brecon Junction appeared, again via Defynnog, but despite extensions of time until 1892, nothing was done.

Moving north, in 1865 a Radnorshire Railways Bill for a Presteign–Llangunllo (Central Wales)–Llandinam (Cambrian) line was withdrawn, while a Lugg Valley Railway Presteign–Llangunllo length received Royal Assent but was not made. In 1866 the Knighton Railway unsuccessfully promoted a Presteign branch. Proposals east from Craven Arms included the Welsh & Midland Counties in 1863, and Central Wales & Staffordshire Junction of 1864 and 1865. The Midland & Central Wales

Junction obtained powers in 1883 for a 37-mile (59.5km) line to Willenhall, only to abandon it in 1886.

MID WALES RAILWAY CONSTRUCTION AND OPENING

The first sod of the Mid Wales Railway was cut near Rhayader during torrential rain on 2 September 1859, followed by a luncheon notable for public outbursts of temper between Whalley, Savin and Davies as to who controlled the company. Parliamentary expenses and difficulty in raising money delayed commencement of the works until 1862. Nevertheless the contractors, Watson and Overend, had much of the most difficult and imposing section of the line between Llanidloes and Rhayader ready by March 1863. South from Penpontbren it crossed by viaduct the River Dulas which it followed up the constricted valley to the 947ft (288m) summit at Pantydwr, eventually the highest point on the Cambrian system. Thence it followed the Marteg Valley, through Marteg tunnel, over a viaduct, and on high embankment through a narrow gorge and a sharp southerly curve to emerge into the Wye Valley, spanning the river before running alongside it to the market town of Rhayader (population 846 in 1861). While work continued south of Rhayader, the Brecon & Merthyr opened through Talyllyn to Brecon on 1 May 1863.

Captain Tyler sanctioned the 1½-mile (2.4km) L&N line south of Llanidloes in January 1864, one track for M&M use, the other for the MW, but required a double junction and up-and-down working as soon as the M&M opened. In fact, though M&M rails reached Llangurig, only one freight appears to have run to the village before work was abandoned. The M&M's Penpontbren–Llanidloes track remained unused until Penpontbren Junction was put in, the double line to Llanidloes, where a new down platform was opened, becoming available for normal up and down working by MW trains from July 1872 (R. W. Kidner points out that the MW working timetable for 1879 kept *all* traffic on the down line). Penpontbren–Llangurig was lifted in 1882, though a short siding and the junction signalbox remained objects of curiosity until after the 1923 Grouping.

In August 1864 Colonel Yolland sanctioned the 46¾ miles (75.2km) of single line between 'Pen-y-Pont Bren' and the B&M at 'Bryn-y-derwen', together with a short length north from

Three Cocks to join the HH&B. There were 'sidings and portions of double line' at stations at Tylwch, Pantydwr, Rhayader, Doldowlod, Newbridge, Builth, Erwood, Boughrood, Three Cocks, Talgarth, Trefeinon, and 'Bryn-y-derwen', but land and bridges provided for doubling. There was a 191ft (58.2m) span lattice girder bridge over the Wye at Boughrood. The colonel required block working, and wanted a turntable at Bryn-y-derwen (later Talyllyn) Junction for locomotives not running through to Brecon or Methyr.

Formal opening, by special train from Brecon to Llanidloes and back, took place on 23 August 1864. Thomas Savin reported to B&M shareholders on 26 August that though Talyllyn Junction east curve was incomplete, Mid Wales mineral traffic had started; MW goods trains commenced from 1 September 1864. Three Cocks–Talyllyn was used by HH&B trains from 19 September; two days later MW Brecon–Llanidloes services started, three passenger and two mixed trains running each way, worked by Watson and Overend. Three Cambrian trains connected Llanidloes with main line services at Moat Lane. Mail was carried from 1 May 1865. The Mid Wales purchased twelve new Kitson tender locomotives, Nos 1–6 being 0-4-2 passenger (for some years No 1 carried the name *James Watt*), and Nos 7–12 0-6-0 goods locomotives. The locomotive and carriage and wagon shops were at Builth Wells until 1903.

MIDLAND TRAINS THROUGH BRECON TO SWANSEA

Meanwhile, the ubiquitous Midland Railway had appeared on the scene as a rival for Swansea traffic. By Act of 5 July 1865 the HH&B was empowered to agree on amalgamation with the Brecon & Merthyr. The subsequent agreement having been pronounced illegal, it was cancelled by Act of 1868 and the amalgamation did not proceed. From October 1868 the HH&B was worked by the Mid Wales, HH&B running powers between Three Cocks and Brecon being confirmed by Act of 1869. The Midland, which had recently reached Hereford, set its sights on the HH&B and offered to work its traffic. Despite physical opposition from the GWR at Hereford, and a lengthy legal wrangle, from 1 October 1869 Midland-worked trains commenced running to Brecon. In 1872 the Neath & Brecon, which had gained access to Swansea, obtained running powers to Hereford via the HH&B. The Midland leased both the HH&B and the Swansea Vale in 1874, acquiring the latter in 1876, and by running powers extended its service over the N&B from 2 July 1877, opening a new route between Swansea and the north.

LATER YEARS ON THE MID WALES LINE

To paraphrase Christiansen and Miller, in such a sparsely inhabited area the Mid Wales would probably never have been made but for promoters who gambled on it becoming a major trunk route, and contractors who accepted shares in payment. Almost from the outset the company faced the post-Mania depression of the late 1860s: these were lean years with poor traffic and low receipts. When the contractors failed in 1866 and the company took over the working, services were cut and some rolling stock sold, including locomotives Nos 2, 6 and 10 to the Manchester Sheffield & Lincolnshire Railway, and No 11 to the Denbigh Ruthin & Corwen (p 74). Though the B&M reached Merthyr in August 1868, anticipated coal traffic to Birkenhead was largely retained by existing carriers.

Nevertheless, the 1870s witnessed a slow increase in traffic; even slower were negotiations with the Cambrian from 1879, which lasted nearly a decade and resulted in a working agreement in 1888, starting from 2 April but gross receipts (with minor exceptions) being pooled from 1 January. In 1873, the eight Mid Wales engines were renumbered and supplemented by two new Sharp Stewarts, similar to one acquired by the DR&C (p 75), so ten MW locomotives went into Cambrian stock in 1888. From that April a Moat Lane–Brecon express service started, and three years later a similar Aberystwyth–South Wales train, reversing at Moat Lane, calling at Llanidloes, Rhayader and Three Cocks, and changing locomotives with the B&M at Talyllyn. Such ventures continued and expanded, broken by World War I during which, day and night, heavy coal trains with precedence over other traffic, rumbled northwards, the Cambrian locomotives frequently running through to Crewe, where the LNWR took on the next leg towards the Grand Fleet at Scapa Flow.

As to works, in March 1867 Major Hutchinson sanctioned a new station at Llechrydd (Builth Road from 1889) where the Central Wales crossed above the MW. The station, with just a waiting shed was, according to the major, built by the Central

Wales as a passenger interchange with its own Builth Road station. The 1862-authorised ¼-mile (0.4km) junction curve was then open only for goods traffic (since 1866). In March 1872 Lt Col Rich authorised use of St Harmons station in the Marteg Valley. In 1869 the B&M opened a station at Talyllyn west junction; the original MW north junction station closed in 1878.

Moat Lane to Talyllyn was re-signalled and interlocked in 1891–92. South of Llanidloes, there were passing loops at Pantydwr, Rhayader, Doldowlod, Newbridge, Builth Wells, Erwood, Boughrood, Talgarth and Trefeinon. St Harmons and Aberedw had none. By 1893 the line through Builth Road had been doubled and a new up platform built; a proper down station building had been erected. At Talyllyn a new double junction to the B&M allowed MW passenger trains to run direct to Merthyr without entering Talyllyn station; in 1895 Col Yorke found it too short to hold a train without fouling the Brecon Junction! About this time Llanidloes down platform was extended and widened, the yard re-arranged, and the whole re-signalled. Tylwch originally had up and down platforms, but from introduction of electric train tablet working in 1891 the down loop became merely a siding; re-use as a passing place was sanctioned in 1899.

The Mid Wales was vested in the Cambrian by Act of 24 June 1904. In 1907 Trefeinon received a passing loop and down platform, and in Great Western days halts opened at Llangorse Lake in 1923, Glan-yr-Afon 1928, Marteg 1931, Llanstephan 1933, Llanfaredd and Groesffordd, both 1934.

ELAN VALLEY LINE

West of Rhayader, at the head of the Elan Valley, lie the great reservoirs which were made by Birmingham Corporation to supply water to the city by aqueduct some 73 miles (117.4km) long. For construction the corporation built a railway, with branches, from a junction with the Mid Wales, for some nine miles (14.5km) to the uppermost dam. Sanctioned by Act of 27 June 1892, the four great dams were commenced in 1893, built by direct labour, housed, fed, educated, ministered to, and watered (though there was a corporation pub), in a specially built village at Caban Coch.

The substantial railway works were contracted to Lovatt of Wolverhampton. The Elan Valley Railway Junction signalbox, and the corporation railway's double junction to a new passing loop on the Mid Wales line ½-mile (0.8km) south of Rhayader, were inspected by Major Yorke in July 1894. The Elan Valley line, completed by 1896 and single throughout, dropped to the valley floor and then rose along its side to the top north end of the first dam—the stupendous 556ft (169.5m) long, 122ft (37.2m) high Caban Coch. A branch served the village, railway shops, and foundation works of the dam. The main line kept just above intended water level, with a road blasted out of the rock above, to reach a submerged dam and 12-arch road viaduct at Garreg Ddu, two miles (3.2km) beyond which after a further climb, it reached the Pen-y-garreg dam and second reservoir. A deep rock cutting followed, before the final climb to the terminus at the magnificent curved Craig Goch dam and third reservoir. At its busiest, the railway had some 33 miles (53km) of track. From 1895 the Cambrian worked freight up the line as far as the Noyadd exchange sidings, near the junction, but from 1906 up to Caban Coch as specified periods daily. At some time Nos 22 and 25 from the Van line worked these trains. From the exchange point the waterworks traffic generally was hauled by the corporation's own saddle tanks : Manning Wardle 0–6–0s *Rhiwnant, Calettwr, Elan*, and *Claerwen*, and 0–4–0 *Coel* (used on daily workmen's and schoolchildren's trains composed of ex-Cambrian and GWR coaches); and Hunslet 0–6–0s *Methan, Nant Gwyllt* and *Marchnant* – all named after feeder streams into the reservoirs, though *Nant Gwyllt* also perpetuated the name of the poet Shelley's home, now beneath the waters.

The morning of 21 July 1904 saw Rhayader station host to numerous excursions and specials. Notables, guests and excursionists were quickly hauled away in trains of open trucks with planked seats by the waterworks saddle tanks, through Rhayader tunnel, and on to the Elan Valley line, where most took up positions of vantage along the nearby road, and the select few hurried to official places, to await the arrival of King Edward VII and Queen Alexandra to open the works. The LNWR royal train, hauled by Cambrian No 83, arrived at Rhayader at 12.25 pm, having travelled from Swansea via the Builth curve. Their Majesties transferred to a special 'royal train' of three antiquated but newly-painted 4-wheeled Cambrian coaches and a van, and the little *Coel* scurried along the valley line as pilot to *Calettwr* which drew its exalted burden between lines of troops and police to the ceremonies and inspections which followed. *Rhiwnant* arrived back at Rhayader with the royal party at 3.30 pm. C. C. Green has recently described some amusing sidelights to the day's events, in his *Cambrian Railways Album*. Even though the festivities were over, it took a further two years to complete the works. The main line loop and double junction were removed and the box closed by June 1908, replaced by a siding connection and ground frame. The Elan Valley branches were mostly lifted by 1912, but the final 'main line' only came out in 1916, Noyadd sidings remaining in use until early 1917. Today many vestiges of the line remain, with the formation and some bridge works clearly visible, in an area renowned for its beauty which yearly lures thousands of visitors.

MID WALES CLOSURE

The Mid Wales remained steam-worked. It was a likely candidate for closure; de-population, changes in modes of living, of private and local public transport, were compounded by the duplication of the nearby Central Wales which served marginally busier communities. Christiansen and Miller have discussed the 1962 public inquiry on closure of all railways to Brecon, when the Mid Wales was condemned. On 30 December 1962 a last special train ran through a snowbound countryside. There was considerable local feeling of having suddenly lost something which had been taken for granted as a friendly, permanent part of life. Substitute buses proved unpopular. Local bodies called for retention of the track, but the rails were lifted south of Llanidloes in 1964–65.

Some of the redundant railwaymen went elsewhere on the system, some found local jobs, including quarrying, but for many it was the end of a family career. One, who claims his grandfather drove the first Mid Wales train, and whose father was a signalman at Builth, tells of John Jones of Doldowlod who travelled on that first train, was a special guest on the last, and lived to be 106. The same source states that even after he had received redundancy notice he witnessed the painting of Doldowlod station six weeks before closure. Such things were not uncommon.

Today the Mid Wales route is perhaps the most evocative of all the lost lines in Wales. In the lovely Dulas Valley and by the side of the Marteg, where the great embankment broods above, or down in the cutting approach to Marteg tunnel, with purple hills around, now silent but once re-echoing from the exhausts of long coal trains, something of the sadness for its loss lingers on; in the beautiful Wye Valley too, where the little stations—and most remain along the line—stand as mute reminders. Many have become dwellings. Though Builth Wells has vanished under a roundabout, Builth Road is now 'The Cambrian Arms'. Doldowlod is a caravan site, the land having reverted to a descendant of the famous James Watt of Doldowlod Hall by agreement made when the railway was constructed. At Rhayader the neat little station is a council depot, while at Llanidloes, though platforms have disappeared beneath a relief road, the fine station building stands proudly refurbished, in use as light industrial and craft units.

For a while two parts of the Mid Wales route lingered on after the main closure: Builth Road low level yard continued to be served by the curve from the Central Wales until 6 September 1965; and in the hills some three miles (4.8km) north-west of Llanidloes, works on the Clywedog reservoir kept the railway between Moat Lane Junction and Llanidloes open for cement traffic until 2 October 1967.

CENTRAL WALES RAILWAY

Sir Charles Henry Rouse Boughton, chairman of the Knighton, also the Central Wales, and a power on the Shrewsbury & Hereford, presiding over the Central Wales October 1859 meeting, emphasised that the Knighton and the Vale of Towy were parts of the Central Wales route. So fast had the Knighton construction been that contractors Brassey and Field had half the earthworks completed. Henry Robertson (p 52), the Knighton and Central Wales engineer, hoped that the line would reach Llandrindod Wells in two years; it was to take six, the first delays being occasioned that winter when 'the ground was so hard that it was impossible to get a spade into it'. The following summer was remarkably wet.

The Knighton opened for mineral traffic for nine miles (14.5km) between Craven Arms and Bucknell on 1 October 1860. The 12¼-mile (19.7km) single line, which like all the route to Llandovery, excepting tunnels and some bridges, allowed for eventual doubling, was in England, together with its terminus, though Knighton itself is just over the border in Radnorshire. The Knighton opened on 6 March 1861, leased and worked by the contractors (also S&H lessees), using one locomotive, an o–4–2 saddle tank *Knighton*, new from Beyer, Peacock. Intermediate stations were Broome, Hopton Heath, and Bucknell. From 1 July 1862 the LNWR took over the working, the same day as the LNWR, GWR, and West Midland jointly leased the S&H. Knighton's 1851 population was 1,566, an increase to 1,853 in 1861 being attributed in the census to railway labourers. Even so, it stood at 1,946 in 1871, dropped slightly over the next 20 years, reached 2,139 in 1901 and was 2,010 in 1971.

Financial difficulties delayed the Central Wales works; the contractor, Richard Hattersley, eventually resorted to arbitration to get his money. Knighton – Knucklas opened for minerals in 1862, and public goods were carried to Crossgates (Penybont) from October 1864. It was another year before Captain Tyler reported on the 20-mile (32.2km) single line. It left the Teme Valley at Knucklas, where a fine 190yd (174m) long, 75ft (23m) high, 13-arch stone castellated viaduct crossed the Heyop Valley, and then climbed through the Clun Hills to the summit of the whole route 980ft (299m) above sea level, boring through Beacon Hill with the 645yd (590m) curved Llwyncoch tunnel. A descent followed through Llangunllo station, then called 'Llyncoch' (*sic*), where there was a passing loop, to Pye Corner in the Lugg Valley, which it followed westwards, climbing over the watershed to reach ‚the Aran Valley, passing through Llanbister Road and Dolau stations. Penybont tunnel 440yd (402m) preceded Penybont station, whence the railway followed the Ithon Valley to Llandrindod. The captain required that Knucklas station, on a 1 in 60 gradient, should have a loop and second platform, and that Penybont loop should also have a platform.

Knighton – Llandrindod was formally opened on 10 October 1865 to great local excitement, regular passenger services starting on 17 October, though Llandrindod station was described by one railwayman at the time as 'a wooden structure, about the size of a sentry box'. Known by the Romans for its medicinal springs, and a minor Regency spa, Llandrindod welcomed the arrival of the London & North Western. The 243 resident population in 1861 was to increase ten-fold by World War I, reaching 3,379 in 1971.

The Central Wales Extension works concentrated on the Sugar Loaf summit tunnel. Nevertheless, the first section com-

pleted was the 5⅝ miles (9km) from Llandrindod to the Mid
Wales crossing at Builth Road, the CWE station for Builth
Wells, some two miles distant. Builth lies on the confluence of
the tributaries Chwefru and Irfon with the Wye. Though
chalybeate and sulphur springs had been patronised for centuries, the present town dates only since an all-consuming fire
in 1691. The line was single, with the one station at Builth
Road, named Cwmbach in the Board of Trade report, which
noted that there was no second platform. Llandrindod – Builth
Road opened on 1 November 1866.

Five days later Captain Tyler reported on the 5⅜-mile (8.6km)
single line on to Garth. At Builth Road, 'the exchange siding
for goods waggons between the Mid Wales and the Central
Wales . . . has been commenced but is not yet connected with
the latter'. A 42ft 0in (12.8m) turntable had been constructed at
Garth, 'and I observed in passing that one similar has now
been supplied at the Craven Arms station'. (That at Garth was
on a 'railway progress', being moved forward to successive rail-
heads). An 88ft 0in (27m) skew span iron girder viaduct with
central masonry pier carried the line over the Wye into Breconshire, followed by the 64yd (58.5m) Builth Road tunnel and
another viaduct over the Chwefru, then Cefn-y-bedd tunnel,
115yd (105m), before reaching Cefn-y-bedd station (soon
renamed Cilmery), where the railway emerged into the Irfon
Valley. Incomplete works delayed the Builth Road–Garth opening until 11 March 1867 in heavy snow, which did not deter
many people anxious to try their first train ride to Builth
market.

The next section, 4¾ miles (7.6km) to Llanwrtyd Wells,
increasingly dominated by mountains to north and west and the
high moorland of Mynydd Eppynt to the south, included two
viaducts over the Irfon near Garth, and the 55yd (50m)
Llangammarch tunnel. Garth–Llanwrtyd opened on 6 May
1867, bringing fresh patrons to intermediate Llangammarch
Wells, with its lake, barium chloride springs and two hotels with
fine grounds, and to Llanwrtyd, which in its sheltered valley
already enjoyed a reputation for its sulphur springs, and as
a centre for fishing, shooting and climbing.

The Irfon Valley turns north from Llanrwtyd into scenery of
marvellous beauty, leaving the railway to make a three-mile
(4.8km), 1 in 70/80 climb up the Cledan Valley to the summit,
820ft (250m), followed by a descent of 1 in 70/60, boring

through the shoulder of 1,098ft (335m) conical Sugar Loaf
Mountain by a 1,000yd (915m) curved tunnel into Carmarthenshire. Hugging the hillsides, the line now lost height, spanning
the Bran Valley with the fine 100ft 0in (30.5m) high curved
18-arch brick and sandstone Cynghordy viaduct and, still at 1 in
60, passing through Cynghordy station and loop, to reach the
valley floor and make end-on junction with the Vale of Towy
line. These last 13½ miles (21.7km) of the Central Wales – the
most heavily engineered section – were reported on by Lt Col
Rich on 1 June 1868. That day Central Wales and LNWR
directors and officers travelled by special train to greet their
Llanelly Railway counterparts at Llandovery station.

Public traffic began on 8 October 1868. G. P. Neele, LNWR
superintendent of the line, noted in his reminiscences:

> The opening to Llandovery was availed of to make some
> striking announcements of the saving of 55 miles between
> Manchester, Liverpool, Birmingham, &c, and Llanelly,
> Carmarthen and Swansea; which notices were probably not
> very acceptable to the Great Western authorities . . .

That year the LNWR moved a timber engine shed at Llandrindod to
Llandovery; it was rebuilt in 1901.

ON TO CARMARTHEN

The 13½-mile (21.3km) single-track Carmarthen line commenced at Carmarthen Valley Junction, ½-mile (0.8km) south
of the Llanelly's Llandilo station, and ran westwards along the
agricultural Tywi Valley to Abergwili Junction with the Carmarthen & Cardigan Railway. In 1862 powers were obtained to
lay an additional rail for narrow gauge on the C&C down to its
junction with the South Wales Railway. The new line, and the
C&C into Carmarthen, were inspected by Colonel Yolland in
May 1865. The Carmarthen line had six viaducts, an 83yd
(76m) tunnel, and lattice-girder bridges of 125ft (38m) and
168ft (51m) span across the Rivers Cothi and Tywi, Freight
traffic started on 14 November 1864 and passenger trains on
1 June 1865, worked by the Llanelly Railway. Stations were at
Llandilo Bridge, Golden Grove, Drysllwyn, Llanarthney, Nant-
garedig, and Abergwili. By Act of 12 July 1869 the Llanelly
was authorised to lay a second narrow gauge track on the east

side of the C&C to where that line joined a spur of the Pembroke & Tenby Railway, the rails to be part of the C&C but available to Llanelly trains.

This prompts mention of the Pembroke & Tenby. Authorised in 1859 as a standard gauge line, with an 1866 extension from Tenby to the broad gauge South Wales Railway at Whitland, it took powers to extend alongside the latter to gain access to the Llanelly's Carmarthen line, the V of T, and the Central Wales line. Instead, the GWR (which had leased and worked the South Wales from 1852 and amalgamated with it in 1863) obligingly converted its up Whitland–Carmarthen line to standard gauge, a short P&T spur at Carmarthen joining the mixed gauge C&C. In May 1872 broad gauge ceased in South Wales; the P&T drew back to Whitland, through Central Wales carriages being worked by the GWR.

In return for financial help, in 1867 the Llanelly company granted the LNWR running powers over its entire system. Next it hived off the Swansea and Carmarthen lines, these being incorporated by Act of 16 June 1871 as the separate Swansea & Carmarthen Railways, worked by the LNWR from 1 July that year. Having sold the Swansea lines to Euston, in 1873 the S&C took the title Central Wales & Carmarthen Junction; it was vested in the LNWR by Act of 21 July 1891. The Llanelly, meanwhile, swung to the Great Western camp, and GWR trains worked remaining Llanelly lines from 1 January 1873.

CENTRAL WALES CONSOLIDATION AND IMPROVEMENTS

Jointly with the Llanelly, the three Craven Arms–Llandovery companies leased the Vale of Towy from 1 April, 1868, confirmed by V of T Act of 25 June 1868, on which day an Act amalgamated them with the LNWR, their part of the lease passing to Euston. The V of T amalgamated with the LNWR by Act of 28 July 1884. The lease remained with the Llanelly which amalgamated with the GWR five years later, GWR trains henceforth dominating local V of T joint line workings.

On the Mid Wales' Builth curve, the LNWR constructed a small locomotive shed, about 1870. The curve vested in the LNWR by Act of 4 July 1870, which also conveyed the S&H jointly to the GWR and LNWR. This coincided with doublings opened in 1871 : Craven Arms–Knighton, and Llanbister Road–Penybont tunnel. At Llandovery in 1872 the timber Llwynjack viaduct over the Tywi was renewed with a 15-span timber structure; it was replaced by four steel girder spans in 1890. Penybont–Llandrindod doubling opened in 1876, Llandrindod station being enlarged; Llanbister Road received a second platform. Llandrindod and Llanwrtyd acquired the suffix 'Wells' in 1876, Llangammarch likewise in 1883. In 1889 a timber siding was put in at Rhos Ferig, south of Builth Road where a passenger bay and up line of platform came into use. Llandilo received up and down platforms, a bay, and new buildings in 1897–8. From 1868 there was a siding at Sugar Loaf summit for emergency crossing of passenger trains; the summit became a block section in 1871; a halt for railway workers opened in 1899; and about 1910 the siding became a passing loop where heavy trains halted to pin down brakes. Other loops opened at Llanwrda in 1894, and at Howey between Llandrindod and Builth Road in 1911. Wartime works in 1943 included a lie-bye siding at Garth and extension of the Sugar Loaf loop. The tunnel has closed at least four times: July 1926, November 1949–January 1950, May–July 1955, and May 1956; buses provided connections. (As to Carmarthen, see South Wales Regional History.)

CENTRAL WALES HEYDAY AND DECLINE

In its heyday the Central Wales lines was very busy; 1911, for instance, saw 18 up and 19 down passenger trains. There was a ticket inspection stop at Knighton, where the occupant of the 1870 engine shed, a DX 0–6–0, piloted heavy trains on the climb to the staff exchange at Llangunllo, a distance of some 6½ miles (10.4km).

Llandrindod, Builth, Llangammarch and Llanwrtyd did not scintillate with bright lights and noisy entertainment; rather were their attractions—aside from the waters—good climate, clean air, and beautiful surroundings, the latter being made more accessible with weekly 'runabout' rail tickets. Llandrindod was the busiest station, with some 100,000 visitors during the season, hotel porters meeting the trains which sometimes waited up to a quarter of an hour for luggage to be transferred. The town was but 5¼ hours from Euston. Via the LNWR the route was about 60 miles (96.5km) more than via the GWR and Swansea, yet the fare was the same. There were many through coaches, from Euston, the north of England and the Midlands, to Llandrindod, Swansea, Carmarthen, Tenby and Pembroke

Dock. Through coaches to Llandrindod, shunted by the Llandrindod station pilot (which was shedded at Builth Road) returned on the following day's up service. In the inter-war years the 10.25 from Swansea conveyed a refreshment coach as far as Craven Arms, where it was detached to be returned on the 2.40 pm down from Shrewsbury. Freight traffic was heavy, including some 6,000 tons of anthracite travelling northwards weekly. At Builth Road there was interchange of goods via the curve, and of passengers' luggage between the two stations by hydraulic lift. A summer shuttle connecting with Mid Wales services, operated to Llandrindod (sometimes down to Llandovery), and for some years a GWR summer Saturdays Barry–Llandrindod train worked over Builth curve.

The Central Wales remained busy during LMS days though in 1931 Glanrhyd closed (reopening as a halt in 1938); Llanarthney lost its loop in 1938; and Cilmery and Talley Road were respectively unstaffed from 1938 and 1941. The 1945 weekdays-only Craven Arms–Llandilo service, four up and five down trains, plus a down morning and up evening mail conveying through Swansea–York coaches was, with variations, continued into the 1960s. In 1955 Glanrhyd and Talley Road closed, and Llandrindod Wells lost its up platform line from 11 December when No 1 signal box closed, trains henceforth crossing north of the station on the remaining double track. Knucklas, unstaffed from 1956, closed to freight in 1957, followed by Llanarthney and Cilmery in 1959. Passenger censuses in 1961 showed good use of only the important intermediate stations. Closure of Knighton shed from 1 January 1962 heralded moves to withdraw all through passenger trains and to abandon Carmarthen line services; that year Howey and Llanwrda loops closed, and 31 December saw Builth Road shed closed.

The weekdays-only Llandilo–Carmarthen service of four trains each way was withdrawn from 9 September 1963. Though the Central Wales was reprieved it was to be a very different railway, as evidenced by trial workings of a diesel multiple-unit on 2 April, followed on 13 June 1964 by the running of the last steam-hauled passenger train, the 6.25 pm Swansea–York mail, hauled by Class 5 4–6–0 No 45406. That month Llanbister Road–Penybont Junction, and Penybont–Llandrindod were singled. From 10 August all through freight services north of Llandovery ceased, and Llandovery locomotive shed was closed, freight diverting via Hereford. In 1965 the Llangunllo, Cynghordy and Llangadog passing loops and the up track at Builth Road ceased to be used. Many stations became unstaffed halts during 1964–5. Freight closures were Llangunllo, Llanbister Road, Dolau, Llangammarch and Cynghordy in 1964; and in 1965 Broome, Hopton Heath, Bucknell, Knighton, Penybont, Builth Road, Llanwrtyd, Llanwrda, and Llangadog, the daily (SX) Central Wales pick-up freight being withdrawn from 22 May, when Craven Arms shed closed. Llandrindod and Craven Arms closed to freight in May 1968. That year saw some station buildings demolished, leaving spartan platforms and shelters, and in December Llandrindod descended to being an unstaffed halt.

Neither the Mid or Central Wales lines led to significant development within the area which they served. Taking the town common to both, Builth Wells, a static population between 1841 and 1861, of around 1,150, actually fell to 1,080 in 1871, but then rose slowly to a peak of 1,805 at the turn of the century. From 1951 there was an accelerating reduction to 1,481 by 1971. Thus, with no freight traffic and a falling local population, together with reasons mentioned in the Mid Wales case, argument for retaining the Central Wales looked thin. Claiming a yearly loss of over £100,000 on the line, British Rail re-submitted closure proposals in 1967. Government policy to attract industry to Wales, coupled with hardship to local people if the line closed, produced instead a grant; and an improved service of five weekday trains daily each way, timed, for a change, to connect at each end, started from May 1970, when Llandrindod resumed station status. In 1971 the diesel railcars were equipped with headlights for use when approaching open level crossings—a requirement of the Order applied for, and granted in 1972, to operate the 79-mile (126km) line between Craven Arms and Pantyffynon as a light railway. The headlights were extended to class 37 diesels based at Pantyffynon, but this restricted the motive power and in 1979 portable headlights became available for visiting locomotives on excursion trains. In 1978 British Rail appointed a 'Central Wales Line Development Officer', based at Llandrindod, with the task of exploiting the potential of the line. What success there was may be inferred from the railway's continued existence throughout the 'eighties. (See Chapter XV.)

CHAPTER XIV

South of Aberystwyth

Between Aberstwyth on the mouths of the Rivers Ystwyth and Rheidol and the port of Cardigan on the Teifi, the foothills of the mountains form a wide coastal plateau to Cardigan Bay. A connecting lowland route between Aberystwyth, Cardigan, and Carmarthen – some 20 miles (32km) south-east from Cardigan – exists via the river valleys. The Ystwyth in the north is divided by high ground at Ystrad Meurig from its neighbour the Teifi, flowing south-west, some 12 miles (19km) inland, parallel to the coast, through the market towns of Tregaron and Lampeter to Llandyssul, thence west through Newcastle Emlyn to Cardigan. South from Llandyssul, Carmarthen is reached via Pencader, following the River Tyweli to its watershed with the Gwili which flows through Llanpumsaint and Cynwyl to drain into the Tywi.

The Vale of Teifi and coastal plateau support rich arable farming and good grazing; from early times woollen mills were established beside the fast-flowing rivers. From the ports of Aberayron, New Quay, and Cardigan lead, timber and agricultural produce were exported in exchange for coal, fertilizer and manufactured goods. Inland, Newcastle Emlyn suffered a decline in population from a peak in 1841 of 2,044 to 1,530 by 1891, four years before a railway arrived at the town. Lampeter, focal town in the vale, population 1,417 in 1841, was on the railway by the mid-1860s; here a fall in population was reversed, reaching 1,697 by 1871 and 3,000 by 1921. In 1971 the populations of each town were respectively 654 and 2,189.

CARMARTHEN TO NOT QUITE CARDIGAN

Cardigan was affected by several railway schemes during the Mania of 1845–6 (p 148). Autumn of 1853 saw a prospectus for a broad gauge Carmarthen & Cardigan Railway, 'under the

sanction of the Great Western and South Wales Companies',
and supported by the boroughs of Carmarthen, Cardigan and
Kidwelly, the last lying south of Carmarthen. The object was
to connect London with the 'important seaport and town of
Cardigan' by a line from the South Wales Railway at
Carmarthen, following the route offered by the river valleys.
Lime and coal would go to the agricultural areas in return for
produce to industrial South Wales. The port of Cardigan was
to be improved and a refuge harbour made, Cardigan Corporation envisaging 'a line of packets . . . between the principal Irish
ports and Cardigan . . . which was several hours nearer London
than by way of Holyhead'. Some 23 miles (37km) of mineral
branches were planned, including south-east from Carmarthen
via Mensel's Arms and Cross Hands to the Llanelly Railway,
and from Mensel's Arms via the Van lime rocks to the South
Wales Railway at Kidwelly. As the entire cost was £1 million,
however, the promoters initially applied only for powers from
Carmarthen to Newcastle Emlyn, 'with a view of being here-
after extended' to Cardigan. The Carmarthen & Cardigan
Railway Act passed on 7 August 1854.

In conjunction with the S&A and Montgomeryshire schemes
of 1853 (Chapter X), there had been another attempt to complete a link between Manchester and Milford Haven : the North
& South Wales Railway, from Llanidloes westwards through
the mountains to Pencader, thence to Newcastle Emlyn and
across the Prescelly Mountains to Haverfordwest and Milford
Haven. This did not proceed, and in November 1854 a proposed
Direct Manchester & Milford Haven Junction scheme failed to
deposit plans. The continuing possibility of such a line permeated
the Carmarthen & Cardigan's meeting in February 1855 when
Cardigan's aspirations were further dimmed by the directors'
view of their railway being potentially part of 'a trunk line
northwards to Oswestry, and thence to Liverpool and Manchester'. A construction contract had been signed, but only as
far as Llandyssul, the contractor being not bound to start until
many more shares had been subscribed. To avoid making an
embankment across the Tywi's floodplain, which could have
led to flooding of the bishop's palace at Abergwili, the route was
deviated by Act of 30 June 1856 to west of the river, more
directly serving Carmarthen and incidentally saving on construction costs. Construction started in mid-1857, but by late
1858 C&C finances were in a bad way : a meeting to issue

preference shares ran into trouble when shareholders accused the secretary of drawing cheques for railway purposes whenever he chose, and of entering into contracts without consulting the engineer. A Bill in 1859 to change the gauge from broad to standard was withdrawn after pressure from the South Wales Railway.

OPENING CARMARTHEN TO CONWIL

One mile (1.6km) of broad gauge from the SWR main line to Carmarthen Town station was opened on 1 March 1860. (As to Carmarthen stations and works in the vicinity, see *South Wales* in this series.) The six miles (9.6km) of single line from Carmarthen to Conwil (spelt thus throughout the life of the railway), twisting and turning as it followed the Gwili through a wooden gorge, was inspected by Captain Tyler in August 1860. After noting the substantial permanent way, similar to that of the GWR, of bridge rails on longitudinal timbers, and the sharp curves which required slow speeds, he remarked on the motive power:

> It appears that the Carmarthen and Cardigan Company do not as yet possess any engines of their own, but that they will depend for the next few months on the Great Western Railway for working the line with tender engines, until two tank engines which are being constructed for them are . . . ready for use.

Carmarthen to Conwil, worked by the South Wales Railway with GWR locomotives, and with intermediate Bronwydd Arms station, opened on 3 September 1860. The service was short-lived: the C&C could not meet hire charges and the line closed from 31 December 1860. After scraping together enough for some coaches, the C&C recommenced services with two trains each way daily from 12 August 1861, with two new 4–4–0 side tanks, *Heron* and *Magpie*, hired from Sharp, Stewart. Through 1859–60 the company looked hopefully northwards to the coming of the Manchester & Milford, authorised between Llanidloes on the Llanidloes & Newtown, and Pencader on the C&C, by Act of 23 July 1860. But a doubt was sown of M&M intentions in 1861, when that company took powers to go to Aberystwyth (p 205); thus the C&C's Act of 29 July 1862 revived the 7¼-mile (11.6km) Newcastle Emlyn line, while that of 1 July 1863 authorised the final 12½ miles (20.1km) to Cardigan.

TROUBLE AT PENCADER – OPEN TO LLANDYSSUL

The eight-mile (12.8km) Conwil–Pencader length to the M&M junction, built single (land for double), was inspected by Captain Tyler in January and March 1864. Earthworks were heavy as the line climbed through Llanpumsaint (spelt Llanpumpsaint by the railway), with 1,030ft (314m) Caug Bach to the west and the Carmarthenshire–Cardiganshire range to the east. The Alltwallis tunnel, noted as 42 chains (845m) long, took the railway through to the narrow Tyweli Valley, followed by a downhill run to Pencader. The captain required a second platform at Llanpumpsaint, and took exception to both stations being on gradients of 1 in 60, especially Pencader where trains would stand for passenger exchange and junction clearance. On 15 April he reported that though some requirements had been met :

> It appears that this portion of line was opened for Passenger Traffic on the 28th March, and the Company have evidently no intention of altering the gradient at the Pencader Passenger Station – To do so now would no doubt occasion great expense and delay, but I am unable . . . to recommend their Lordships to sanction so serious a defect in construction.

Nevertheless, according to Parris (*Government and the Railways in Nineteenth Century Britain*), the Railway Department of the Board of Trade felt that it could not successfully prosecute. Thus the station was in use when on 25 May 1864 Captain Tyler inspected the 3½ miles (5.6km) from Pencader to Llandyssul (railway spelling Llandyssil). He refused sanction, but as his objections rested on Pencader, the line opened to Llandissil on 3 June 1864.

There the works stopped : the C&C, with liabilities of about £1 million, was put in the hands of a Receiver in November 1864. That year Abergwili Junction to Carmarthen was converted to mixed gauge (p 217); a twice-daily each way Llandyssil–Cardigan horse bus service started, calling at Newcastle Emlyn, Cenarth and Llechrydd. *Heron* and *Magpie*

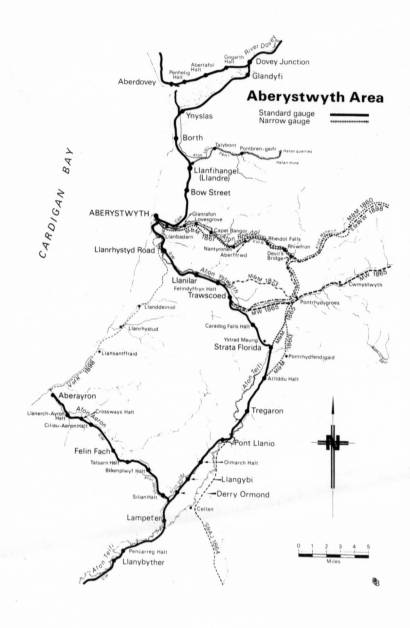

Aberystwyth Area

Standard gauge
Narrow gauge

CARDIGAN BAY

River Dovey
Gogarth Halt
Dovey Junction
Abertafol Halt
Penhelig Halt
Glandyfi
Aberdovey

Ynyslas

Borth
Talybont
Pontbren-geifr
Hafan quarries
Afon Llyfnant
Hafan mine
Llanfihangel (Llandre)

Bow Street

ABERYSTWYTH
Glanrafon
Lovesgrove
M&M 1860
GWW 1898
Capel Bangor
Rheidol Falls
Llanbadarn
Nantyronen
Rhiwfron
Llanrhystyd Road
Aberffrwd
Devil's Bridge

Afon Ystwyth
M&M 1873
MW 1865
Cwmystwyth
Llanilar
Felindyffryn Halt
Trawscoed
Pontrhydygroes
MW 1865
Llanddeiniol
Caradog Falls Halt
Llanrhystud
Ystrad Meurig
Strata Florida
Llansantffraid
Pontrhydfendigaid
Alltddu Halt
VofR 1898
Aberayron
Llanerch-Ayron Halt
Crossways Halt
Tregaron
Ciliau-Aeron Halt
Afon Aeron
Pont Llanio
Felin Fach
Olmarch Halt
Talsarn Halt
Blaenplwyf Halt
Llangybi
Derry Ormond
Silian Halt
Cellan
Lampeter
S&A 1864
Pencarreg Halt
Llanybyther

N

0 1 2 3 4 5
Miles

BB

returned to Sharp, Stewart when two new 4–4–0 saddle tanks, *Etna* and *Hecla* were acquired from Rothwell & Co, being taken over by the C&C's creditors who then hired them back. The Receiver installed his son, Samuel Howe, as general manager, and in June 1866 Sharp, Stewart rented their two locomotives to the Howes, releasing the Rothwell pair which eventually went to the South Devon Railway. Howe's receivership ended in August 1867 when a C&C shareholder took over and the directors resumed management. *Heron* and *Magpie* worked the line until its conversion to standard gauge (p 229), when they too went to the South Devon. Three standard gauge 0–6–0 saddle tanks were then hired from the GWR, two of which were purchased late in 1872, together with an unusual Llanelly Railway 0–6–0 goods tender locomotive *Victor*, with smokebox-mounted outside cylinders driving the rear coupled wheels : built by Fossick & Hackworth in 1864, it had originally been used by contractors on the Mid Wales Railway. The third GWR tank was purchased in 1876. The Receiver was discharged in 1878, and by C&C Act of 22 August 1881 the line and its working stock vested from 1 July in the GWR.

A CHANGE OF DIRECTION

A meeting of the Manchester & Milford shareholders in February 1864 learned that Davies and Beeston, contractors, had completed from Llanidloes to Llangurig in the east, and were embarking on $27\frac{1}{2}$ miles (44.2km) at the western end between Pencader and Pontrhydfendigaid (east of Ystrad Meurig). In September the directors postponed opening to Llangurig until a decision had been reached on the line between there and the Teifi, 'considering that the country through which it had been laid out is too mountainous and the probable expense of construction too great to afford reasonable prospect of a dividend'. This section included extremely heavy earthworks, tunnelling, and a 280ft (85.4m) high viaduct. The M&Ms internal affairs had been stormy; only a minute fraction of the authorised capital had been raised; there had been considerable borrowing; landowners and contractors had been paid in shares.

Talks with the Mid Wales Railway resulted in compromise. Entry to Aberystwyth for both companies (p 205) relied on construction of the M&M's main line. By Act of 5 July 1865 Llangurig to Alltddu was abandoned in favour of a new line from Alltddu northwards through Ystrad Meurig, thence along the valley of the Ystwyth to Aberystwyth, while a branch from Ystrad Meurig was to join the concurrently authorised Mid Wales Western Extensions over which the M&M could reach Rhayader and Llangurig (p 205), retaining access to the Cambrian system. In addition, mixed gauge was authorised on the C&C south of Pencader, with M&M running powers to Carmarthen and working agreements with the C&C, Cambrian, Mid Wales, and Swansea & Aberystwyth Junction. The last-named had been incorporated in 1864 for a railway from the Vale of Towy line at Llandeilo, via Talley, the Cothi Valley, and through the mountains to Cellan, whence it descended into the Vale of Teifi to join the M&M south of Tregaron (deviated to Lampeter in 1865). The S&AJ—a 'contractor's line'—disappeared after the Mania of 1865–6.

OPENING THE MANCHESTER & MILFORD

M&M construction, supervised by the company's engineer, James (later Sir James) W. Szlumper, was in the hands of contractors Davies and Beeston, who used on the works a Manning Wardle 0–6–0 saddle tank *Teifi*. The first section opened was the sinuous $12\frac{1}{4}$-mile (19.7km) length of single line (land and overbridges for double) from Pencader Junction to Lampeter, the line acting as chords to the river's windings. There were stations and sidings at Maesycrugiau, Llanybyther, and Lampeter; the standard gauge was extended between Pencader Junction and station. Works included Bryn Teifi tunnel, 99yd (90.5m) in the Board of Trade report, and a 78ft 0in (23.8m) span lattice-girder bridge over the Teifi at Lampeter, carrying the railway from Carmarthenshire into Cardiganshire. Colonel Yolland inspected the section in December 1865. As Pencader station required lengthening, and several other works were needed, permission to open was refused. On 24 January 1866 the colonel, with commendable restraint, reported that M&M passenger traffic had nevertheless started on New Year's Day: 'I enclose an undertaking from the contractor . . . engaging to lengthen the platforms at Pencader station within a fortnight'. As there were few trains, all worked by staff and ticket, and doubtless remembering that Pencader station had already tripped up one inspecting officer, he recommended that the opening be sanctioned.

The first service of three trains daily each way, worked by the contractors with locomotives Nos 1-3 (see later), included a road coach between Lampeter and Aberystwyth with a Manchester connection via the Cambrian which, overall, took from the evening of day one to mid-morning of day three to accomplish the journey!

July of 1866 saw the colonel inspecting the 15¼-miles (24.5km) of single line (again with provision for double) on to Strata Florida station (named after nearby abbey ruins but serving Ystrad Meurig and Pontrhydfendigaid villages). There was a passing place at Tregaron, sidings there and at Bettws (later Derry Ormond), Pont Llanio, and Strata Florida, all with short platforms and temporary buildings. North of Tregaron the railway skirted an extensive peat bog:

> In consequence of the great Heat and Dryness of the Season it will be absolutely necessary that the line should throughout be boxed up with Ballast outside the Rails as it will be quite impossible to keep the wooden keys in the chairs unless this be done.

Lampeter to Strata Florida opened on 1 September 1866. Meanwhile the third rail for standard gauge had reached Abergwili, and M&M trains commenced working through non-stop to Carmarthen from 1 November 1866, a passing loop being restored at Llanpumpsaint for this purpose.

The 14½ miles (23.3km) on to Aberystwyth, inspected in August 1867, curved sharply westward from Strata Florida to climb out of the Vale of Teifi on a ruling gradient of 1 in 43 to a short tunnel, emerging from rock cuttings high above the wooded Ystwyth Valley. Thereafter it descended for four miles (6.4km) at 1 in 41 along the eastern flank of Mynnydd Bach, past Caradog Falls (site of a later halt), and Trawscoed station, flattening out through Llanilar station to run alongside the river, through Llanrhystyd Road station to terminate, after sharp reverse curves, sandwiching a bridge over the Rheidol, alongside the Cambrian at Aberystwyth. 'The Company are to make use of the south side of the platform of the Cambrian Railways Company at Aberystwyth as a departure platform, but they have provided an independent arrival platform south of the other . . .' Strata Florida to Aberystwyth opened on 12 August 1867. The entire line, having nothing whatsoever to do with either Manchester or Milford, was complete. Soon new stations opened: north of Bettws, at Llangybi; and north of Pencader Junction at 'Cross Inn (Llanfihangel)', renamed New Quay Road in the mid-1870s and Bryn Teify (sic) in 1916. Abolition of GWR broad gauge in Wales was completed by 1 June 1872, the C&C being the last to convert.

From 1 August 1872 M&M passenger trains stopped short at Pencader, passengers transferring to the C&C. Trains—three or four daily each way—stopped at all stations (Llangybi on market and fair days only), and took about $2\frac{1}{2}$ hours between Pencader and Aberystwyth, though that was fast. The first down train, for instance, of mixed passenger and freight, left Pencader at 7.00 am, shunted about on its way, and wandered into Aberystwyth at 11.15 am. A decade later the journey time for 'fast' trains had shortened to around two hours.

One wonders why the M&M retained its misleading title; discreetly it did not blazon it on the locomotives, the only identification being a small brass plate on the frame inscribed 'M&MR'. No 1 *General Wood*, was a Sharp, Stewart 0-6-0 goods tender locomotive, built 1865. No 2, *Carmarthen*, a 1866 Sharp, Stewart 2-4-0 passenger locomotive was destroyed by boiler explosion at Maesycrugiau on 19 August 1890; apparently bits of it still lie in the Teifi. Temporarily replaced by an ex-LNWR 2-4-0 Crewe-type goods, it was superseded in 1891 by a new Sharp, Stewart 2-4-2 radial tank, No 2 *Plynlimmon* (sic). No 3 *Lady Elizabeth*, was similar to *Carmarthen*; with 5ft 6in (168cm) wheels it was the 'express' on the line. 1867 saw arrival of a Manning Wardle 0-6-0 saddle tank, No 4 *Lampeter* which proving unsuitable was exchanged in 1868 for one of the firm's 0-6-0 goods tender locomotives, *Aberystwyth*. No 5, no name, was similar to No 1 but built in 1870; No 6 *Cader Idris* was similar to *Plynlimmon*, but slightly larger and built in 1896. Nos 7 and 8 (or 1) were LNWR 0-6-0 goods tender locomotives bought in 1902 and 1904 (the latter replacing *General Wood*) and both destined to be 'Swindonised' by the GWR. Some 16 passenger vehicles and over 100 goods wagons completed the rolling stock. Some of the locomotives had already been pensioned-off and none of the remainder was suitable when in the summer of 1905 the GWR introduced a new Carmarthen–Aberystwyth service; thus three Dean goods 0-6-0s No 2301, 2351, and 2352 were loaned to the M&M and numbered 8, 9 and 10. The M&M did not prosper; a Receiver had been appointed in 1880. The line was leased by the GWR from 1 July 1906 and was absorbed by that company by Act of 18 August 1911.

DEVELOPMENT IN GWR TIMES

The C&C having abandoned Cardigan, the Tivy Side Railway was incorporated in 1872 for a Llandyssil–Newcastle Emlyn line, but not implemented. The C&C amalgamation Act of 1881 authorised a similar line, with time extended by GWR Act of 1886. This was seven miles (11.2km) long, single, with passing loop at intermediate Henllan station, and avoided major earthworks—bar a 154yd (141m) tunnel—by following the river valley, crossing the Teifi twice. Llandyssil became a passing place with new up and down platforms. Though platforms had been built at Henllan and Newcastle Emlyn the permanent buildings were not ready (completed January 1896), and wooden huts sufficed when the line opened on 1 July 1895. Concurrently loops and platforms had gone in at Conwil and Llanpumpsaint, while Pencader up platform and the loop were extended, a crossover put in and a footbridge erected. Resignalling and interlocking of these three preceded similar treatment in 1895 on the M&M, on completion of which Strata Florida, Tregaron, Lampeter, Llanybyther, and Maesycrugiau had passing loops and two platforms; Llanrhystyd Road, Llanilar, Pont Llanio, Derry Ormond, and New Quay Road were single-sided with goods loops; Trawscoed was single with a siding; and at Ystrad Meurig a connection (inspected in 1878 along with the M&M Aberystwyth harbour branch) led to a quarry. In 1905 a new passing loop went in between Llanpumpsaint and Pencader; 1911 saw Llanrhystyd Road single platform and goods loop extended. Pentrecourt Platform on the Newcastle Emlyn branch was sanctioned in 1912; halts opened in the 1930s at Pencarreg, Olmarch, Alltddu, Caradog Falls, and Felindyffryn.

In the late 1930s there were five trains daily each way between Carmarthen and Aberystwyth, plus extra ones on Saturdays. The service was reduced to three during World War II, when the line handled much south to north munitions traffic, but was increased seasonally for tourist traffic in the immediate post-war period. A feature was the up and down 'Butlin Special' between South Wales and Penychain (p 168). The older GWR locomotives were replaced during this time with Manor class 4–6–0,

2–6–0 and 0–6–0 tender types or 2–6–2 tanks, banking on the severe gradients being performed by 0–6–0 pannier tanks which also worked the branches. Pont Llanio milk depot generated considerable traffic, as did one at Felin Fach on the last of the standard gauge branches to be discussed.

RAILWAY TO ABERAYRON

Cardigan was reached from Whitland on the South Wales line in 1886. Of the harbour towns in Cardigan Bay only Aberayron, six miles (9.6km) north of New Quay, now lacked rail communication. New Quay had been passed over in early years as a possible rail and packet port for Irish traffic, and its development had been overshadowed by Aberayron. An attempt in 1886 for a Llandyssil–New Quay line came to naught; New Quay was served by a daily horse bus return trip, and from 1907 by a road motor, from Llandyssil station.

The first move to serve Aberayron came when by its Aberayron Extension Order of 13 August 1898 the Vale of Rheidol Railway Company (see later) was authorised to make a 16¼-mile (26.1km) narrow gauge line from Aberystwyth, via Llanddeiniol, Llanrhystud, and Llansantffraid to terminate near Aberayron harbour. Construction time was extended until 1905, but the powers remained unexercised. By Order of 9 October 1906 the locally promoted Lampeter Aberayron & New Quay Light Railway was sanctioned for a 21-mile (33.8km) line from the M&M at Lampeter, thence north-westward through sparsely populated agricultural country along the Aeron Valley. The engineers, S. W. & A. L. Yockney, also surveyed a 22-mile (35.4km) Llandilo & Lampeter Light Railway which, unsuccessful in 1905, was authorised in 1908 but not made.

The first sod of the LA&NQL—constructed only between Lampeter and Aberayron—was cut on 20 October 1908. In February 1909 the GWR agreed to work the line and drummed up traffic by running a bus service covering the route. The railway opened to freight on 10 April 1911. On 12 May 1911 Lt Col Druitt sanctioned use for passenger traffic which started that day. The line was noted as being 12⅛ miles (19.5km) in length, single, with ruling gradient of 1 in 41, and a half-way, two-platform passing place at Ystrad (Felin Fach). Halts at Silian, Blaenplwyf, Talsarn, and Ciliau–Aeron had single platforms, as had Aberayron terminus. Two further halts went in at

Llanerch Ayron and at Crossways. The company remained independent until the 1923 Grouping, GWR services consisting of a Lampeter–Aberayron auto shuttle four times each way on weekdays, and a daily freight.

As often happened with branches opened this century, there was a proprietorial feeling for the Aberayron line, manifested by pride of local railwaymen in immaculate permanent way, and a parochial view on operating (reversing back to a halt for a fellow villager arriving late). But with rapidly falling receipts after World War II the auto-trains became uneconomic; a coal crisis gave British Railways the excuse to withdraw passenger services after 10 February 1951 (officially 'temporary' but confirmed as final from 7 May 1951). The Felin Fach milk plant, and agricultural traffic, nourished the branch for a time, but Felin Fach to Aberayron closed completely from 5 April 1965.

CLOSURES—AND RE-OPENINGS

Newcastle Emlyn–Pencader passenger services ceased from 15 September 1952. Falling receipts which had led to this also affected the 'main' line which closed to freight between Aberystwyth and Lampeter on 14 March 1964. Following floods the Aberystwyth–Strata Florida passenger service ceased from 14 December 1964, a bus connecting with the northern terminus of three remaining trains to Carmarthen. These services were withdrawn from 22 February 1965. After reprieves, freight services from Carmarthen to Felin Fach, Lampeter, and Newcastle Emlyn ceased from 1 October 1973. Populations in 1981 (for 1971, see p 222): Newcastle Emlyn 664, Lampeter 1,972.

Anticipating closure, a preservation society was formed, with headquarters at Henllan station. When Dyfed County Council dropped plans to retain the Teifi Valley track, lifted by late 1975, the society concentrated on the Bronwydd Arms–Conwil (Cynwyl Elfed) length of the main line where track was retained, purchased by 1976, to be worked by the Gwili Railway Company Ltd. The Abergwili & Llanpumpsaint Light Railway Order of 24 October 1977—the first for a Welsh standard gauge preserved line—authorised the society to purchase eight miles (12.8km) of the former trackbed between the two places named in the Order, the intended limits of restoration. A 1939 Peckett, now named *Myrddin* on its left side and *Merlin* on its right, commenced working public passenger trains from 25

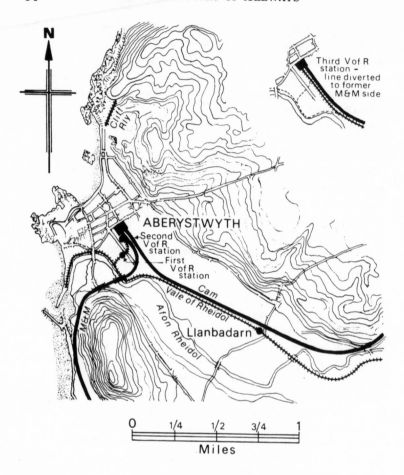

March 1978 over ½-mile (0.8km) of track north of Bronwydd
Arms, extended by July 1978 for a further half-mile to a new
halt at Cwmdwyfran. There are two more saddle tanks—a 1936
Peckett and 1942 Robert Stephenson & Hawthorn, GWR-
designed 4–6–0 No 7820 *Dinmore Manor* which arrived at Bronwydd
Arms in September 1979 for restoration, and items of passenger and
freight rolling stock. During 1979 work was in progress to extend the
line to a picnic site and new station at Llwyfan Cerrig. (See Chapter
XV.)

    Another tourist venture, the Vale of Teifi Narrow Gauge Railway
based at Henllan, agreed in 1977 to purchase nine miles (14.5km) of
trackbed between Newcastle Emlyn and Pencader, later applying for
a Light Railway Order. (See Chapter XVI.)

VALE OF RHEIDOL RAILWAY

Aberystwyth is also the main terminus of the popular Vale of Rheidol Light Railway, the 11¾-mile (18.9km) 1ft 11½in (60cm) gauge line to Devil's Bridge. Following abandonment of the M&M's 1861 Devil's Bridge branch (p 205), and a Devil's Bridge Railway Bill of 1872 over the same route, the M&M obtained an Act of 15 May 1873 for a 7¾-mile (12.4km) light railway from a point 1¼ miles (2km) north of Trawscoed station, eastwards along the valleys of the Nant Magwr and Nant Cwmnewydion to west of Pontrhydgroes, and then due north to Devil's Bridge. Time was extended in 1876 but the unexercised powers were abandoned by Act of 1880.

Built to bring lead ore and timber down to Aberystwyth for shipping, and as a tourist attraction, the present Devil's Bridge line was authorised by the Vale of Rheidol Light Railway Act of 6 August 1897, the gauge being set at 'two feet' (61cm) with provision to increase to standard. Engineered by Sir James and Mr William Szlumper, and with Pethick Brothers as contractors, the railway follows much the same route as the 1861 M&M proposal. As first constructed the V of R main line commenced on the west side of Smithfield Road, Aberystwyth, and ran south-west to the River Rheidol, where a ½-mile (0.8km) branch served the harbour. The main line continued alongside the river, passing beneath the Manchester & Milford, until meeting up with the Cambrian main line, where an exchange siding was laid. It then continued along the river's flood plain, passing over the Rheidol by a seven-span timber trestle bridge near Llanbadarn. At just over five miles (8km) it commenced a dramatic ascent to Devil's Bridge, rising nearly 670ft (204m) over its total length, at a ruling gradient of 1 in 48, with numerous curves, ledged into the valley's south face with several unnerving precipitous drops to the river far below.

While navvies released from the Elan Valley works laboured on the line, construction materials arrived by sea at Aberystwyth, carried along the works by the Plynlimon & Hafan's redundant 2-4-0 tank (p 188) and 15 wagons, with altered gauge. Track was laid throughout by July 1902, after which the 2-4-0 was renamed *Rheidol*. When Major Druitt inspected the line in August there were two intermediate tablet stations: Capel Bangor, with carriage shed; and Nantyronen where the locomotives took water. Aberystwyth boasted the headquarters office and a locomotive shed. The line opened for freight that month but a second inspection was necessary before passenger traffic started, with an additional halt at Llanbadarn, from 22 December 1902. By May 1903 stations or halts were also open at Rhiwfron, and Aberffrwd which thereafter became the locomotive watering place; Glanrafon and Rheidol Falls halts opened shortly after, and a loop went in at Aberffrwd in 1905. At Rhiwfron an aerial cable brought lead and blende from the Rheidol mine on the other side of the valley: in 1903 three mines sent up to 20 tons of ore daily to Aberystwyth by the new railway. The management set out to attract tourists who until then had visited Devil's Bridge by slow, expensive horse conveyance over a less scenic route: over 1,000 passengers travelled daily on the line during the Easter 1903 holiday. As the works' scars slowly disappeared beneath a growth of trees the ride became even more attractive (and to the nervous slightly less hair-raising), the magnificent views being glimpsed through leafy cover in high summer. From 1910 an annual army summer camp was served by a private halt and loop at Lovesgrove, three miles (4.8km) from Aberystwyth, which remained in use until 1914. Arrival of the military swelled the heavy tourist traffic, necessitating loan of the Festiniog Railway locomotive *Palmerston*, while with the intention of increasing capacity electric traction was discussed. In August 1913 the line was sold to the Cambrian, and a year later World War I put a stop to further plans. The mines closed and all traffic declined. The GWR acquired the V of R in 1922. Two years later the harbour branch closed (rails being lifted in 1930), and in 1925 the first Aberystwyth terminus was closed, the tracks being extended across Smithfield Road to a new terminus beside the main line station.

During the 1920s tourist traffic increased, closed carriages being used in winter and open ones in summer. Following the Great Depression daily passenger services were withdrawn from 1 January 1931, becoming summers-only, local people being accommodated by bus. Freight ceased completely from 26 September 1937. In 1938 the passenger stock was largely replaced with new Swindon vehicles, but the railway closed entirely from 31 August 1939 and stayed shut throughout World War II. It re-opened on 23 July 1945 with two trains daily each way and has operated seasonally ever since, for passenger traffic, though freight was reinstated until withdrawal on 1 June

1964. In 1968 the Aberystwyth terminal tracks were realigned away from the riverside to run alongside the Cambrian so as to use the former Carmarthen line platform.

The first locomotives were supplied new in 1902 by Davies & Metcalfe of Manchester: No 1 *Edward VII* and 2 *Prince of Wales*, 2–6–2 tanks based on the design of Lynton & Barnstaple locomotives. They underwent several changes of livery. Harold Macfarlane (*Railway Magazine*, September 1903) then described them as being like the 'canary-hued' locomotives on the Brighton line. From about 1908 they were in elaborately lined-out green, and in Cambrian times in that company's more sombre finish. No 3 *Rheidol* (renumbered as GWR No 1198) ceased working in 1923 and was withdrawn in 1924, when No 2 (GWR No 1213) was rebuilt to match two new Swindon locomotives, 2–6–2 tanks Nos 7 and 8. No 1 (GWR No 1212) was withdrawn in 1932. In 1949 No 1213 was renumbered 9, and in 1956 names were bestowed: 7 *Owain Glyndwr*, 8 *Llywelyn* and 9 *Prince of Wales* (re-instatement). For years they were in proud Great Western green but between 1968 and 1981 they had to suffer the indignity, for Swindon steam locomotives, of unsuitable BR 'electric blue'. (See Chapter XVI.)

CHAPTER XV

The 1980s – Investment for the 'Nineties

Fortunes of the railways in North and Mid Wales during the 1980s were varied. That some BR and tourist railways remained open was due to outside support: the EEC, Welsh Office, local authorities, tourist and development boards, and local organisations, all contributed by grant, subsidy, servicing or physical labour. Much has happened; though technicalities and minor events have not been overlooked there is not space to record them all.

NORTH WALES COAST LINE

The Chester resignalling (p 33) brought control of 55 miles (88km) of track under one new signal box in May 1984. In 1990 Chester station was to receive improved approaches and concourse, booking hall and travel centre. Except over the Britannia Bridge, Saltney to Holyhead is double track, there being only short lengths of triple or quadruple, and some of these recently removed, for instance Mold Junction–Sandycroft down slow in autumn 1987, and Prestatyn–Rhyl down slow early in 1990—though part retained as a siding. Fflint, a commuter town (population 16,454 in 1981, a 12 per cent increase in ten years), received an extended down platform and park and ride facilities in 1979. Connahs Quay closed to freight in February 1981, and Courtaulds siding at Holywell Junction in July 1985, but Mostyn Dock thrives, with new sidings, as does Point of Ayr colliery at Talacre. At Rhyl, following freight closure in June (coal in March) 1984, trackwork south of the station had gone by late 1987. The carriage shed gave way to engineers' sidings. Of the two ex-LNWR signal boxes, No 2 was taken out of use early in 1990 on pruning of the remaining through lines and semaphore signalling; it has, however, along with the station buildings, been given Grade 2 listed status. Mention can be made here of other closures: Bangor to freight and Gaerwen and Valley to coal in March 1984. Beyond Rhyl, from 1985 up and down tracks were concentrated on the up side 1885-built Foryd Bridge over the Clwyd, tracks being lifted on the adjacent 1901 structure. At Abergele & Pensarn the up and down slow lines have been retained, but as loops serving the platforms. Between 26 February and 4 March 1990 Colwyn Bay (excl) to Fflint (excl) was closed following extensive damage by storm-driven spring tides which breached the sea wall at locations between Mostyn and Abergele. Worst hit was Towyn on Morfa Rhuddlan; when completed the strengthened, repaired sea wall will have cost BR some £6.5m.

The North Wales Coast Road—or 'expressway'—first impinges on the railway after Penmaenrhos tunnel, where the new Tan-y-lan viaduct carries the track, slewed on to it in 1983. The expressway brought changes to Colwyn Bay (26,278 population in 1981—see p 26): reconstruction of the station approach and the down side booking office and waiting rooms started in March 1981, the down loop having gone the previous September. The new facilities opened on 22 April 1982, there being only two through tracks; the up loop platform and buildings, with the famous glass screen renovated, opened on 8 October 1989 as a privately developed 'Platform 3' restaurant, museum and shops, with a static display of a tank engine and coach. To accommodate the expressway beyond Colwyn the railway was moved to the north. The work, which involved cutting away part of the hillside, was completed in January 1984. For just under two miles (3km), through Mochdre, the site of railway and first water troughs lies beneath the A55, the trains running alongside on an infill of pulverised fuel ash. The junction of the Conwy Valley branch was moved ½ mile (.8km) to the east in November 1980 when the site of the former Llandudno Junction depot, reached by a new level crossing over the branch, was enlarged for a new freight terminal, the opening of which replaced Llandudno Junction and Colwyn Bay goods stations, closed in September 1981. The former junction carriage shed survives to stable dmu sets and departmental vehicles. Engineering works affected the main line, including a deviation, with sharp curves, at the west end of Llandudno Junction station. A siding was laid in 1982 for pulverised fuel ash from Fiddlers Ferry power station, and other works for expressway construction traffic continued during the decade. In February 1985 a new signalling centre was commissioned, with colour light signals, simplified trackwork, and with the original north island No 2 platform—the former up fast—being used for reversible working. Just beyond the Llandudno branch junction the expressway burrows beneath the main line to run along the east shore of the river beneath which it tunnels to avoid Conwy, surfacing at Conwy Morfa. Llandudno Junction Quay Sidings were restored to use in February 1990. Track rationalisation at Llandudno in 1978 left up and down lines merging before entering the station with three running lines and two sidings. The signal box and semaphores were retained, and the station interior remained LNWR and LMS in flavour. The roof, however, became unsafe and was demolished in 1990. At Conwy a new station, on the former station site, was opened on 27 June 1987 and for public service two days later. Another expressway works siding existed at Conwy Morfa between 1987 and early 1990. Penmaenmawr continued to dispatch crushed granite from the sidings where a new 5,000 ton stone hopper came into use on 16 October 1984. While unstaffed Penmaenmawr retained its square Thompson-style structure, Llanfairfechan lost its more homely building to the expressway in 1987. In 1988 Bangor received a new waiting room and an extended car park. Amlwch lost its loop in 1984; that year Associated Octel and Railfreight agreed on traffic which would keep the branch open well into the 1990s, the company's wagon fleet carrying chlorine westwards and ethylene-dibromide eastwards between Amlwch and Ellesmere Port, with raw sulphur coming from Mostyn Dock, and from Amlwch outward traffic of anti-knock compound. South of Valley station, reopened to passengers from 15 March 1982, the siding laid in 1962 for Wylfa Head power station traffic, also used until 1988 by Stockton Haulage for ferry services, received a southerly curve and spur in 1989 for turning of steam locomotives (p 252). At Holyhead the ferry *St David* came into service on 10 August 1981. Following B&I Line competition with Sealink, however, from 1985 only *St Columba* remained on station. During the 1980s Holyhead was a mixture of surviving departure side train shed with permanent and temporary buildings; a new terminal building and connecting footbridge to the town were largely completed by spring 1991. Holyhead locomotive yard closed and the steam shed was demolished in 1989.

In 1981 an improved timetable was introduced, giving an hourly Bangor–Chester service. Apart from the Irish Mail and four Euston–Holyhead InterCity services with air-conditioned stock, the Bangor–Manchester and Holyhead–Crewe services had until then been making do with ageing dmus and coaches. Faster two-hourly locomotive-hauled trains took over. Other trains operated seasonally to and from Leeds, Liverpool, Nottingham, Sheffield, Stockport, Stoke-on-Trent, York and Scarborough. From May 1983 the Bangor–Manchester trains were extended into the Liverpool–York/Scarborough Trans-Pennine timetable, linking Irish and North Sea coasts. Diesel power included class 40s and 45s, occasionally 31s, 33s and 47s, the last gradually becoming dominant. Variations relating to Llandudno included some reversions

Page 241 (*Top*) Conwy, looking east, with Llandudno Junction–Holyhead Sprinter, April 1988; (*centre*) Penmaenmawr at sunset, with Cardiff–Holyhead InterCity train passing Railfreight 47318 on stone train loading from hopper, April 1988; (*bottom*) Rebuilt Britannia Bridge and 1871 Nelson statue, August 1989. (*Robert H.E. Baughan, top and centre; Author*)

Page 242 (*Top*) Holyhead, with Sprinter 150115 and m.v. *St Columba*, April 1988; (*centre*) Blaenau Ffestiniog, looking west, with DMU 291, April 1988; (*bottom*) Machynlleth, looking west, with 37427 *Bont Y Bermo* arriving with Aberystwyth–Euston train while Sprinter 150125 waits to leave for Aberystwyth, 18 February 1990. (*Robert H.E. Baughan, top and centre; Author*)

to dmus on summer Saturdays. Three Holyhead–Euston services via Birmingham connected North Wales with InterCity 125 trains and the Birmingham airport and exhibition centre; two of these reverted to the quicker Trent Valley route from May 1985. May 1984 saw an evening Scarborough–Holyhead working, in the slot formerly taken by a Manchester–Holyhead boat train; the morning Scarborough–Bangor service was diverted from and to Newcastle. From 3 April 1985 an innovation in association with Dublin City Helicopters allowed first class passengers to fly between Holyhead and Dublin—thirty minutes compared with 3¾-hour ferry crossing. This enterprise, which saw the return of sleeping cars to the night 'Irish Mail', giving an 08.30 arrival in Dublin, ceased from 18 June following failure of the company's backer. From May 1985 there were through services between Holyhead/Bangor and Cardiff Central. Class 142 'Pacer' and class 150 'Sprinter' dmus were in service in North Wales from May 1986. With remaining older dmus, they replaced some locomotive-hauled trains, including the Trans-Pennines. Hull was linked with Holyhead by a two-hourly interval service of around five hours in May 1987, and a 'Welsh Dragon/Y Ddraig Gymreig' Holyhead–London service started, taking about 4½ hours; summer Saturdays saw the 'Holidaymaker Express', a morning down and afternoon up Paddington–Llandudno train. Sprinters mainly worked Holyhead–Chester services, while Holyhead–Llandudno became the province of Pacers and 'Skippers', the West Country version of this four-wheeled rolling stock which had proved unsuitable on tightly curved Cornish branches. Some two-car Sprinters were strengthened to three from May 1988, though it remained possible for crowds on Bangor station, stretched along the platform and looking expectantly towards the tunnel, to be faced, to their incredulity, with a two-car Holyhead–Hull Pacer already bursting at the seams. 'The Welshman', Holyhead–Cardiff twice-daily, however, boasted class 155/6 Super Sprinters. May 1989 saw fare cuts and improved services, including an hourly Bangor–Chester semi-fast, saving 18 minutes journey time, with Chester connections to re-routed Trans-Pennine trains via Manchester Oxford Road and Piccadilly.

As to freight, Point of Ayr colliery forwarded coal to Fiddlers Ferry power station, and occasionally to Ironbridge and to ICI at Northchurch. Llandudno Junction received fuel oil from Stanlow, domestic coal from Midlands and South Wales pits, and timber from Chichester. A daily Speedlink working from Warrington connected at the junction with two trip workings, one with chemicals for and aluminium ingots from Anglesey Aluminium, and oil for Holyhead fuelling point, and the other as required to Maentwrog Road for explosives (p 245). Anglesey Aluminium received coke weekly from Immingham. Weekly oil trains from Milford Haven ceased in July 1985 on closure of the Courtaulds factory at Greenfield. The expressway consumed steel from South Wales, sand from Widnes and cement from Penyffordd. Bangor dealt with cement from Hope, Penyffordd and Clitheroe. Twice weekly a Sellafield-Valley train conveyed nuclear flasks for Wylfa Head, connecting with a separate Trawsfynydd trip. Freightliners ran between Holyhead and Crewe, Manchester, Birmingham and London. In January 1990 Railfreight Distribution announced a new Holyhead–Dublin container service, using the Sealink terminals and Maritime Transport Services. Argument that this traffic, coupled with the advent of closer EEC ties on opening of the Channel Tunnel, demanded electrification of the Holyhead line, was stilled by Sealink's decision to close down its Holyhead and Dublin terminals from 31 March 1991. Reason: disagreement over the level of improvements required by Railfreight to remain profitable at Holyhead.

In 1989–91 there was talk of reopening to Caernarfon, a major tourist attraction with a growing population of some 10,000, and even down to Talysarn near Nantlle for rubbish landfill of the quarries, either south from Caernarfon or north from Afon Wen. On the coast line the 'open station' system (no ticket barriers) was introduced from March 1990. Track and signalling is to be upgraded to 90mph (144km) limit, with possibly more intermediate stations (Holywell Junction and Kinmel Bay have been mentioned). Class 158 dmus and an InterCity 125 service were due to be introduced on the Chester–Holyhead route from autumn 1991.

CELEBRATION AT BLAENAU FFESTINIOG

The Blaenau Ffestiniog (Central Station) Light Railway Order became operative from January 1980. On 22 March 1982 the old LNWR station closed, the first regular passenger arrival that day at the new station being accompanied on the adjacent Festiniog Railway by the first narrow gauge steam train into Blaenau since 1946, an engineer's special headed by 2–4–OST *Blanche* (p 258). Formal opening was on 30 April 1983. Blaenau freight depot officially closed by 19 June 1987.

For the National Eisteddfod at Llanrwst in 1989 a station opened nearer the town centre on 29 July; the existing station became 'Llanrwst North'. On summer Sundays in 1989–90 a passenger service ran to a temporary platform at Maentwrog Road (the old station was in private use) for a visit to Trawsfynydd power station. Opening of the 'Festiniog Link' (p 258) increased passengers on the

Conwy Valley line; some ten per cent used the service for non-leisure travel. On BR Gwynedd County Council's summer Sunday shuttle proved increasingly popular. Though Sprinters were introduced on service trains from 26 May 1986, trouble from 'wheel-screeching' on sharp curves resulted in retention of older dmus, probably until 1992, preferred by many passengers for the view through the cabs. During 1981–8 the branch carried explosives which arrived at Blaenau by road from Penrhyndeudraeth (p 246). Timber traffic from Roman Bridge to Mostyn Dock was to start in 1989. By this time uncertainty over the future of Llanrwst signal box and passing loop threatened reduction of the service to one train on the branch. This, coupled with increasing bus competition and continuing costly seasonal flood damage, gave cause for concern.

SHREWSBURY & CHESTER AND THE BIDSTON–WREXHAM LINE

The unstaffed and vandalised stations between Shotton and Wrexham were renovated in 1980–1. Wrexham Central–Abenbury closed to freight from 4 May 1981; from 1 June 1981 Wrexham Exchange became linked to and renamed as Wrexham General. From 1 October 1982 the Brymbo steelworks branch closed (p 63), followed next month by Croes Newydd yard. The final Mold branch freight through Penyffordd (p 63) ran on 15 March 1983. After tracklifting in 1985 there remained a short spur to Castle Cement works at Penyffordd. The Chester–Wolverhampton service became second class only from 1981. The S&C was singled Saltney Junction–Rossett by 5 January 1986, Rossett–Wrexham 2 February 1986 and Wrexham–Croes Newydd North Fork 16 March 1986; colour lights replaced semaphores and level crossings were automated. A Wrexham–London service may become possible after introduction on the Cambrian of class 158s, which would work in conjunction with the S&C. April 1989 saw completion of superb refurbishment of Gobowen station, the building thereafter being used for other purposes, BR's booking office now being the crossing keeper's cottage. In contrast, Chirk up side building, though 'listed', was demolished in 1987. Chipboard manufacturers Kronospan resited their Chirk siding away from that of Cadbury's, the new siding opening on 16 November 1988 for logwood from Scotland. Other S&C freight, apart from through traffic, particularly of hot rolled coil steel between South Wales and Shotton, north of Chester, included: Stanlow to Whittington BP terminal, petroleum; Penyffordd, cement by block train to Curzon Street, and also via Speedlink to Warrington; Washwood Heath to Gobowen, domestic coal; and Blodwel to Bescot, ballast (but see p 170). Bersham colliery sidings were removed in 1987. At Wrexham, Watery Road terminal was served by Speedlink from Warrington. In 1990 consideration was given to reopening the Blodwel branch to the quarries for dumping household waste; restarting freight traffic could offer opportunities for passenger working to Oswestry. Girls of Moreton Hall School campaigned during 1987–9 to reopen Baschurch, Weston Rhyn and Whittington stations, following which a trial station was planned for (demolished) Whittington in 1990. The school caused the reopening of Rossett for one day, 22 June 1989, for a Shrewsbury–York special. Shrewsbury resignalling, abolishing semaphores and replacing five boxes by solid state interlocking, located in a new control centre, has been postponed to 1996.

CAMBRIAN TRANSFORMATION

The Cambrian Coast line narrowly escaped closure, largely due to the refusal of local people to let it go. Early in 1980 piers in Barmouth viaduct were found to have been attacked by a marine wood-boring mollusc. From 25 May locomotives were banned, and dmus were reduced to 10mph (16km). Explosives traffic from Penrhyndeudraeth was limited to six vans hauled by a motor parcels unit. From 12 October the viaduct closed to passenger traffic for an indefinite period. Pwllheli-Barmouth and Morfa Mawddach–Machynlleth services operated, with a Barmouth–Dolgellau–Machynlleth bus to the Shrewsbury–Aberystwyth line, and a Pwllheli–Bangor bus ran until 5 January 1981; the explosives now went by road to the Blaenau railhead. There was also a 45-minute minibus journey, Morfa Mawddach–Dolgellau–Barmouth. Concern was voiced by the Cambrian Coast Line Action Group (CCLAG) and local authorities that the closure could herald the end of the railway north of Dovey Junction. Such was the perceived threat to local movement and the tourist industry by loss of the estuary crossing, that the Director-General of the EEC Development Fund visited the viaduct, coinciding with a BR statement that it looked to other authorities to help meet the repair costs. Meanwhile, after replacing the minimum of affected piles, BR reopened the bridge to dmus on 22 May 1981. The public responded by buying over 8,000 'Welcome Back to Barmouth Bridge' tickets, giving a day's unlimited travel between Shrewsbury, Aberystwyth and Pwllheli. Nevertheless, for some time there was no guarantee the bridge would not close again. The CCLAG was unremitting in its efforts, organising publicity, events, petitions and special trains, supported by local authorities. With no grant available, BR undertook full repairs, spreading the £1½ million costs over a number of years. Affected piles were encased in a reinforced glass and concrete shell, with stone around the base to stop formation of pools of unscoured water where it was believed *Toredo Norvegica* had lurked. Late in 1984 BR announced a £4.7 million modernisation plan for the Cambrian, including auto-mated level crossings, loop reductions, radio signalling, and class 150 Sprinters.

A special train, headed by 37426 and 37427, crossed the repaired viaduct on 13 April 1986, reopening it to InterCity trains. At Barmouth cheering crowds were reminiscent of opening scenes more than a century before. Following speeches, 37427 was named *Bont Y Bermo* (sic), 'Barmouth Bridge'.

During the modernisation programme, there was public concern about level crossings being replaced by the unmanned, ungated, flashing lights type, described by one local authority as 'death traps'. Undeterred, BR went ahead with the work, including removal of signal boxes, though Barmouth South was a listed building and permission to demolish was refused. Cemmes Road signal box and loop closed on 17 March 1984, the loop being lifted shortly after; Pwllheli loop, out of use since 1985, was reinstated from 7 June 1986 for locomotive-hauled trains; and Talerddig loop was lengthened. Caersws loop and the sidings to the old Van branch station were removed on 11 January 1987. That year the Westbury, Tywyn and Harlech loop points were converted to be hydro-pneumatically sprung, set to the left for trains either way, so that the loop might be safely run through in the trailing direction. Remaining loops, from Welshpool westwards, were converted in 1987-8. Westinghouse Signals won the contract for resignalling with Radio Electronic Token Block (RETB), between Shrewsbury and Aberystwyth and Dovey Junction–Pwllheli. The system, similar to that on the West Highland line, works with two signalmen on duty at the control box at Machynlleth, each in direct radio contact, through masts along the route, with individual trains in his own section, one being responsible for Shrewsbury–Machynlleth, where RETB came into operation on 21 October 1988, while his colleague controls the coast lines, Aberystwyth to Barmouth from 22 October 1988, and on to Pwllheli the following day. Portable cab equipment is available for visiting locomotives. Overall, some thirty boxes were closed. Machynlleth retained some semaphores, and colour light signalling down to Dovey Junction. Teething troubles included wavelength interference; in 1989 Barmouth box was temporarily reopened to control the crossing (with barriers since 1988). Eventually, the box was to be removed to the up platform.

Westwards from Shrewsbury, Hookagate permanent way depot closed in 1986. Freight closures included Newtown, Barmouth,

Penrhyndeudraeth, Porthmadog and Pwllheli in 1983 (the last four confirming their demise in 1980, sidings being lifted in 1984); Aberystwyth, Machynlleth, Tywyn, and Welshpool (coal only) in 1984; and Welshpool (freight) in 1987. Destined to lose its trackbed, moved to a new station to the south, to make way for a relief road, Welshpool station building was let to a catering firm. Aberystwyth was reduced by 1982 to one platform serving the Cambrian, with a short run-round loop, and the other the Vale of Rheidol Railway; operating problems can arise with locomotive-hauled trains. The deteriorating state of Gogarth and Abertafol halts between Dovey Junction and Penhelig, open only during term time to school trains, was the excuse for their closure from 14 May 1984, pending official sanction, though Tonfanau, in like condition, was reprieved for 'educational journeys and the occasional passenger'—known to be just one schoolboy. It remained open, later serving a development on the site of the old army camp. Gogarth and Abertafol closed 'officially' from 2 January 1985. Barmouth, which lost its footbridge in 1979, was repainted in Cambrian Railways livery and received bi-lingual signs in 1984, 'Abermaw/Barmouth' replacing 'Y Bermo'. Porthmadog, with the Welsh Highland but half a minute away and the Festiniog half a mile, has seen the former refreshment room graduate to a public house. Pwllheli had its canopy replaced, and buildings repainted as at Barmouth; the former island platform was closed on one side, on to which a supermarket impinged. Borth lost its down platform; Machynlleth was tastefully modernised, the fine building becoming available for other use. Welshpool and Caersws became unstaffed in 1988. By 1990 there remained five staffed stations: Newtown, Machynlleth, Aberystwyth, Barmouth and Pwllheli.

Following Barmouth viaduct closure, summer (SO) Euston–Pwllheli trains went to Aberystwyth, with connecting Machynlleth–Pwllheli dmus from 1981, which year also saw a Birmingham–Pwllheli (SO) service and restoration of evening trains. During 1981 services became second class only. From 8 to 18 January 1982 snow closed the coast line: three dmus became stuck in drifts, on one of which, southbound near Tywyn, passengers had to stay overnight. 30 December 1986 saw Dovey Junction, the coast line loop now gone but that on the Aberystwyth line remaining, suffering flood water to platform level and services suspended west of Machynlleth; more flooding came on 26 February 1990. In August 1982 a 'Cambrian Parcels Service' started, covering 23 stations, Holyhead–Chester–Shrewsbury–Aberystwyth–Pwllheli, and including the Festiniog Railway; the Red Star parcels service was extended to certain Cambrian stations and to the Festiniog.

Sunday 19 June 1983 witnessed an HST for the first time on the Cambrian, working a Bristol–Aberystwyth excursion. There was no Sunday service, save for summer peak single return trips, locomotive-hauled Birmingham–Aberystwyth and dmu Machynlleth–Barmouth (return to Shrewsbury), which connected at Machynlleth (down in the morning and up in the evening). For the late Spring Bank Holiday and Sundays in July and August 1983 dmus were chartered by CCLAG between Pwllheli and Tywyn, connecting with the BR train and allowing time for a trip on the Talyllyn Railway. The Cambrian saw two freight ventures in 1984, a Wednesdays-only tanker train between Stanlow and the Aberystwyth oil terminal; and timber from Scotland, up to three times a week, to Welshpool, though now finished. After trial runs in 1985, local Cambrian services went over to class 150 Sprinter operation from 17 March 1986, to the existing timetables until 12 May when up to 20 minutes were cut from some journey times. The 'Cambrian Coast Express' returned, Euston–Aberystwyth (Mon–Sats), an air-conditioned five-coach train worked by a class 37 diesel. There was a new Euston-Pwllheli InterCity service. That summer, Saturday trains had to be strengthened to up to twelve coaches, requiring double-heading. On the evening of 2 March 1987 two Sprinters collided on the Welshpool side of the Westbury loop, injuring 40 passengers. The up and down 'CCE' connected at Machynlleth with trains respectively from Barmouth dep 06.48, and to Pwllheli arr 22.22. As it was still seasonal, the September 1986–May 1987 timetable stated baldly 'NO SUNDAY SERVICE'; a helpful note might have added there was a bus operating instead, calling at all stations, dep Aberystwyth 14.15 and 17.00, and Shrewsbury dep 18.00 and 20.30. The May 1987 timetable showed the 'CCE' and another 'SO', 'The Snowdonian', Euston dep 07.40, Pwllheli arr 14.43, and Pwllheli dep 08.00, Euston arr 15.07. Success of the CCLAG trains and the Sunday buses persuaded BR to reinstate an all-year Sunday service, Shrewsbury–Aberystwyth and Machynlleth–Pwllheli, from May 1988.

Though approaching profitability, the Cambrian ended the 1980s with shortages of stock, overcrowding and poor timekeeping, belying the auguries for the new decade. Already agreed, though, was further investment including class 155 or 156 Super Sprinters, and later class 158s, giving faster services with more capacity. For Rank Organisation's Butlins Starcoast World Centre the summer 1990 timetable provided an additional overnight holiday train from Euston to Pwllheli, returning on Saturday morning as the up 'Snowdonian' retimed. Pwllheli booking office reopened in January 1990, and generally on-station retail development was to be encouraged, dissuading vandalism, with long-line passenger information at unstaffed stations. The daily 'CCE' was withdrawn from May 1991, though the famous name may well reappear on the Saturday Pwllheli trains.

'HEART OF WALES' LINE

On 20 December 1980 diesel locomotive 40030 arrived at Llandrindod with a weekend excursion from Leeds, berthed overnight on the siding and left on Sunday. The railway over which it had run from Craven Arms was in poor condition, with track renewals deferred. The class 40 was to be the last visitor for some time; from New Year's Day 1981 the maximum axle loading on the Central Wales line was reduced to 12 tons, excluding main line locomotives and leaving dmus in charge of the five daily services each way between Swansea and Shrewsbury. The twice-weekly freight, running only as far north as Llandovery, was worked by a lightweight class 03 diesel. By maintaining the track 'in a safe and serviceable condition', BR did the minimum necessary to keep the line open. With other economies, £½ million was thus saved during 1981–2. It was at this time that the railway's subtle change of name came more prominently into use; official adoption was gradual. In 1982, while acknowledging the Central Wales as a government-recognised 'social railway' which attracted a grant, BR emphasised that high renewal costs were inevitable; only by aggressive marketing, growth of tourism, and local support in promotion and finance would it survive. It was a single track, with passing loops at Llandrindod, Llanwrtyd, Llandovery and Llandeilo and was worked as a light railway (p 221).

Plans in 1983 to eliminate Llanwrtyd loop and signal box were opposed by the Heart of Wales Line Travellers Association (HOWLTA): timekeeping was already bad; leaving Llandrindod as the only passing place between Craven Arms and Llandovery would reduce operating flexibility and increase delays. HOWLTA won a reprieve, possibly because BR was planning simplified operation with minimal costs. A £544,000 investment, announced in 1984, included automated level crossings, resignalling, and the return of the Llandrindod loop into the station so that northbound trains could use the refurbished platform, no longer delaying southbound trains which had to wait at the signal box loop. Sprinters were to replace the old dmus. Though RETB was suitable for the more intensively-worked Cambrian, the Central Wales was to get a simpler signalling system which apart from obvious savings—except for Llandrindod, stations would be unstaffed—would be easier to operate for special Sunday working. In 1984, meanwhile,

Llandovery became a tourist 'Park and Ride' station; that summer a platform at Sugar Loaf Summit halt reopened seasonally for trains decanting walkers returning to Llanwrtyd. Introduced in 1987, a Sunday 'Recreation Rambler', a dmu with two vans for cyclists, attracted good support. Though it was intended to close Llandrindod level crossing loop and to remove the box, by 1986 the latter was 'listed' and might not be demolished; the new station loop opened on 2 June 1986 (see below), with the box closed and the crossing barriers operated by the train guard. The station, with two platforms again, and renewed footbridge, became home in September 1989 to the resited box as an exhibition centre. In keeping with the town's contrived Victorian image, the station acquired a cast iron canopy from the demolished Powys County Hall, and a Victorian letter box. The existing train staff and ticket system, with box to box telephone communication was changed to the novel 'No Signalman Key Token' signalling in 1986, under control of the Pantyffynon signalman. Craven Arms–Llandrindod was commissioned on 2 June, Llandrindod–Llanwrtyd 7 July, Llanwrtyd–Llandovery 10 August, and Llandovery–Llandeilo 31 August, leaving Llandeilo–Pantyffynon on train staff and ticket. The loops now had hydro-pneumatic trailing points, all semaphores were removed, and drivers used instruments at the loop platforms to deposit and withdraw metal tokens, permission being obtained by telephone from Pantyffynon. Knighton station loop was reinstated on 10 June 1990, giving greater flexibility on the previous 31¾ mile (51km) Craven Arms–Llandrindod section.

Despite the ban on locomotives, October 1981 saw a nine-coach royal train taking the Prince and Princess of Wales to Builth. On 4 January 1982 the prototype Pacer started demonstration runs, failing on the 5th and not returning before blizzards closed the line for ten days; it reopened on the 18th. On its return the Pacer worked on the Central Wales until the end of the year. From 1982 Metro-Cammell dmus appeared, giving a superior ride compared with their Swindon predecessors, some of which remained. The last freight north of Pantyffynon ran on 18 April 1983, though two class 03s cleared remaining wagons on 26 May, Llandeilo and Llandovery being by then closed to coal and freight. The locomotive ban was broken in June 1983 by a chartered train, 'The Central Welshman'. That September Llandrindod Wells staged a 'Victorian Festival', visitors being welcomed by station staff wearing hired uniforms with LNWR insignia. After some twenty years, Sunday services operated during July–September 1986, with one train each way. Though a Sprinter appeared on the line in 1986, full introduction of these trains was not expected to be until 1991–2. Following gales and flooding the three pier Glanrhyd Bridge across the Tywi collapsed beneath the 05.27 Swansea–Shrewsbury dmu on 19 October 1987. Tragically the driver and three passengers drowned. Substitute buses operated until the bridge, with single replacement span, reopened on 31 October 1988. In 1989, among various specials, including two royal trains, and a 'Welsh Prince' comprising VSOE coaches carrying American tourists to a Victorian event at Llandrindod, there appeared on four Tuesdays a land cruise train, 'The Welshman', which included sleeping cars. More important has been the resumption of some extended workings, at first to Crewe, but also to Manchester, Cardiff, Carmarthen and Pembroke Dock.

STANDARD GAUGE MAIN LINE STEAM

Since the 1968 ban on steam locomotives there seemed little hope of seeing them again in North and Mid Wales, at least not alongside the sea. Chester–Newport was an 'authorised route' in the relaxation of the 1970s, inaugural runs in 1977 between Hereford and Chester with No 6000 *King George V* and 6201 *Princess Elizabeth* being followed by continuing use of the route into the 'eighties. But there is (to this author) a heightened appreciation in steam trains beside the ocean; it happened first on the Cambrian.

On 22 May 1987 No 7819 *Hinton Manor*, from the Severn Valley Railway, worked over the Cambrian, checking clearances. Two days later it hauled a special Machynlleth–Barmouth charter as a prelude to 25 May, start of a five-day Spring Bank Holiday working, shared with SVR's No 75069. This was a BR venture, the 'Cardigan Bay Express', two trains daily each way between Machynlleth and Barmouth. Another charter ran on 31 May. The 'CBE' was repeated, 20 July–2 September, Mondays–Wednesdays Machynlleth–Pwllheli, and Sundays Machynlleth–Aberystwyth or Pwllheli, but with SVR's No 46443 replacing 75069. The train might have reappeared in 1988 but for disagreement over the programme. It was very popular, and happily in 1991 steam was again scheduled on the Cambrian, this time in association with anniversary celebrations at Machynlleth.

BR's steam enterprise next turned to Holyhead. The Valley curve having been laid (p 240), 'The North Wales Coast Express' started running on 20 May 1989, on a press 'launch', hauled by 34027 *Taw Valley*. The locomotive suffered a bent valve rod and 35028 *Clan Line* took over from Llandudno Junction. With Crewe Heritage Centre stabling and servicing the locomotives, public runs followed from 27 June until 3 September, on Tuesdays, Wednesdays and Sundays, and August Bank Holiday, calling at all main stations and Llanfairpwll. Outward, the locomotive headed the train into Llandudno, being hauled back to the junction by a diesel at the rear end before continuing to Holyhead; while for the return it took water at the junction while its train, again diesel-hauled, reversed down to Llandudno. The locomotive then followed the tender first, to couple up for the return to Crewe. There were two other 'NWCE' locomotives: 'Black Five' No 5407 and 6201 *Princess Elizabeth*. The next year's programme saw the steam speed limit raised to 75mph, with rostered locomotives also including 4472 *Flying Scotsman*, 71000 *Duke of Gloucester* and 60009 *Osprey*. For 1991 there were to be fewer stops—not to the liking of authorities who had backed the initiative two years before. It is sad to relate that the popularity of these trains was somewhat offset by the appalling behaviour of some lineside 'enthusiasts'.

CHAPTER XVI

Tourist Railways into the 'Nineties

During the 1980s the private Welsh railways thrived, many extending their lines. Space permits only an historical outline here (for Snowdon Mountain see p 106). Details of locomotives and rolling stock may be found in the annual publication *Railways Restored*.

STANDARD GAUGE REVIVALS – LLANGOLLEN AND GWILI

In 1980 the Llangollen Railway (p 147) constructed a run-round loop at Llangollen station and planned a passing loop at Pentre Felin, halfway between Llangollen and Berwyn. On 26 July 1981 a summer Sundays service started, worked by *Burtonwood Brewer*, a return trip of a mile (1.6km) to Ffordd Junction, extended to Pentre Felin Sidings from 4 July 1982. The Light Railway Order for the 7¼ miles (11.6km) between Llangollen and Carrog was made in April 1984. By then track had been partly laid to Berwyn, 1½ miles (2.4km), though work was still required on the Dee river bridge; services to Pentre Felin now included summer Saturdays, a hybrid two-coach dmu working a shuttle to the bridge at the end of the season. The first train passed over the Dee and into Berwyn station during the 10th Anniversary weekend of 29/30 June 1985; passengers had still to wait until completion of a run-round loop beyond the station. That year the Foxcote Manor Society moved its locomotive, under restoration, to Llangollen, where carriages were also arriving to swell carrying capacity. The weekend of 19/20 October saw the dmu (not needing the loop) work the first passenger train to Berwyn. The Railway Inspectorate passed the loop for passenger trains on 1 December. By spring 1987 Llangollen Goods Junction passing loop was installed, also giving access to Pentre Felin Sidings and the former goods yard. The first wine and dine train ran on 12 September 1987. Special events boosted traffic: seven coaches, with a locomotive at each end, were needed at a 'Thomas the Tank Engine' weekend that October. Sunday 27 March 1988 saw the first passenger working by newly-restored *Foxcote Manor*, magnificent in BR 1950s green. On 1 April 1989 No 7828 *Odney Manor* entered service, newly arrived from the Gwili Railway; and following commissioning of the re-erected Green Lane, Saltney signal box as Llangollen 'Goods Junction Box', the end of May saw two-train operation between Llangollen and Berwyn. With *Odney Manor*'s first passage through Berwyn tunnel on 6 January 1990 and opening of the extension to a loop at Deeside Halt, 3½ miles (5.6km) from Llangollen, complete with GWR 'Pagoda' waiting hut, on 13 April 1990, a further scenic length of the Ruabon–Barmouth route was back in use. Already the former Leaton signal box had been re-erected at the site of Glyndyfrdwy station, 5½ miles (8.4km), due to be reached in 1992, helped by a share issue to finance construction, with Corwen as a later goal. The first winter service operated in 1990/91. With 'Berwyn Belle' wine and dine trains, and occasional diesel days the railway has become a considerable attraction.

During 1979–80 volunteers on the Gwili Railway worked on the extension from Cwmdwyfran to the halt at Llwyfan Cerrig (p 234). Meanwhile, a halt opened at Penybont, 1½ miles (2.4km) from Bronwydd Arms, reached by trains on 22 May 1981, public traffic starting the following day, with an 'official' opening on 21 June. Train refreshments became available in April 1983. At Bronwydd Arms the former Llandybie signal box and crossing gates were erected, part of Llandovery box being used as a station building; a new loop at Bronwydd Arms and Llwyfan Cerrig temporary northern terminus and loop all came into use from Easter 1987, ending eight years of pull-and-push operation. Trophies installed at Llwyfan Cerrig included Caedu signal box, Gowerton footbridge, and a double slip from Swansea Docks. Among volunteer workers were pupils from Brynteg Comprehensive School who, while restoring everyday equipment, also tackled the rebuilding of an 1891 Taff Vale coach and a GWR van. *Dinmore Manor* (p 234) was sold in 1984 to the West Somerset Railway. *Odney Manor* entered service on 4 June 1988, going to the Llangollen in 1989 (see above). Traffic doubled in 1988. The need for a site for car parking and engineering works confirmed the wisdom of extending 1½ miles (2.4km) to Cynwel Elfed (the former GWR 'Conwil') where there was extensive space, a two-platform station under renovation (the house was occupied), and the former Cilyrychen signal box. Track for the extension came from singling on BR between Clarbeston Road and Haverfordwest. Tracklaying was from Cynwel southwards, the object being, when through to Llwyfan Cerrig, to transport materials to construct an engine shed and workshops at Cynwel before opening to passengers. Distant from Llangollen, the Gwili offers similar promise of extension along a lovely river valley for several more miles—breath of life to a preservation society and a contribution to the local economy. Early in 1990 a Wales Green Party scheme for reopening between Aberystwyth and Carmarthen was rejected by Dyfed County Council as 'prohibitively expensive'.

BALA LAKE RAILWAY – RHEILFFORDD LLYN TEGID

Aberdovey platform canopy was re-erected at Llanuwchllyn in 1980 (p 147). The railway enjoys a spectacular setting, and it is hoped to extend the Bala terminus nearer to the town centre. It seems there is an imposter on the line: *Maid Marion*, once thought to date from 1903, is now believed to have exchanged identities in the 1920s with the Dinorwic's original *Alice* of 1889; certainly the 'Maid's' centenary was celebrated in June 1989!

CORRIS AWAKENING

During 1980–1 the Corris Railway Society purchased Maespoeth engine shed, and obtained track for completing the ¾ mile (1.2km) between the shed and the Corris museum (p 177). An application to restore the railway south to a picnic site at Tan-y-Coed was refused. At Corris 'station' a temporary engine shed was erected. In 1983–4 tracklaying continued, as did negotiations with local authorities to extend a further two miles (3.2km) to the former and recently restored Esgairgeiliog station. On 20 April 1985 the society celebrated completion of the first stage by running its 1965 four-wheel diesel *Alan Meadan*, with two wagons and an NCB 'manrider', between Maespoeth and Corris. A section of the old tramway up to the main road was restored in 1987 for easier access for materials. It was hoped to operate public trains in 1991.

'ALL CHANGE!' ON THE FAIRBOURNE

A 1981 proposal to move the 15in (38cm) gauge Fairbourne Railway (p 187) to the Isle of Wight did not proceed. The line was bought in 1983 by the owner of the closed-down Reseau Guerledan Railway in Brittany, a 12¼in (31cm) system with equipment stored in Britain and looking for a home. It was decided to change the Fairbourne's gauge to suit the 'new' equipment. While the smaller gauge locomotives went on show, the Fairbourne's *Sian* was rebuilt to an American 'Sandy River' outline and renamed *Sydney*, while sister *Katie* continued as before but renamed *Shôn*. Pending change of gauge, the two engines worked together, rolling stock including some of the Brittany coaches on 15in gauge bogies replacing most of the old FR coaches. *Shôn* was sold in 1984, leaving *Sydney* and a diesel, *Sylvia*, rebuilt and renamed *Lillian Walter*, in charge of traffic. The new order came not in half measure. Fairbourne got a new terminus, 'Gorsaf Newydd', which won a Prince of Wales Award. The old trainshed became the workshops, set up to build new locomotives. An engine shed and ten-road carriage shed appeared. A 'Butterfly Safari' was built. South of the passing loop, the staff exchange for the two operating sections, the intermediate halt was saddled with a name to outdo all others: 'GORSAFAWDDACHAIDRAIGDDANHEDDOGLEDDOLONPENRHYNAR - EURDRAETHCEREDIGION'. Porth Penrhyn saw extension to a new terminus and 'Pavilion Restaurant' beside the estuary, whence a new ferry boat made the short trip across to Barmouth. The extension included a tunnel and sea defence works to reduce blown sand, always a problem for locomotives.

After closure for winter 1985–6 the gauge and rolling stock were converted, including *Lillian Walter*; *Sydney* was sold; and the Brittany coaches, offering three classes of accommodation, regained their 12¼in bogies. Inside the locomotive works there were transfigurations of the smaller gauge engines: a half-size Lynton & Barnstaple outline, *Jubilee*, was repainted in Southern green and became a passable *Yeo*; an 0–4–OST Darjeeling-Himalaya, *France*, which boasted a tender, emerged painted blue and renamed *Sherpa*; a half-scale NWNG 'Beddgelert' lookalike, named *David Curwen*, became a maroon-coloured *Beddgelert*; and a 2–6–4T *Elaine*, based on a Leek & Manifold design, was rebuilt to approximate a 2–6–4 copy of *Russell* of the Welsh Highland. Good Friday, 25 March 1986, saw launch of the 12¼in gauge, with special events and reduced tickets for through journeys over BR and circular trips via the ferry. August Bank Holiday 1986 produced hurricane force winds; a six-coach train standing on the loop was blown over, and it was decided to move the loop away from the sea wall. In 1987 the tunnel was lengthened. A second 2–6–2, the most powerful 12¼in gauge locomotive in existence, emerged from Fairbourne works at Easter 1990: it was named *Sandy River* at the centenary celebration in July 1990, an event which also saw shire-horse 'McDougall'—who else?—drawing a horse tram.

The company, on a different footing to other Welsh narrow gauge railways, did not become a member of the 'Great Little Trains' organisation. Not properly a 'preserved' line, the 'Fairbourne & Barmouth Steam Railway' nevertheless introduced an engaging assortment of locomotives. The line was put up for sale in the autumn of 1990.

THE FESTINIOG RETURNS TO BLAENAU

For the extension to Blaenau (p 135) the Festiniog received an EEC grant. Enthusiasm was high: tracklaying continued during the severe 1981–2 winter. After the initial foray (p 244), the first Festiniog passenger train since 1939 entered the station, a single platform linked by footbridge to the BR establishment, on 25 May 1982. The Blaenau to Tan-y-Grisiau bus link gave place to the 'Festiniog Link', 65 minutes for the 13½ miles (21.6km) from Porthmadog, bringing a 15 per cent increase in traffic. Now required to book through to many destinations on BR, the FR installed a micro-computer in 1985 which can produce any ticket in under six seconds.

Having reached Blaenau, general improvements were made to stations, rolling stock, presentation and maintenance. The Festiniog's 150th anniversary in April 1986, for instance, included the use of restored, long-abandoned slate wagons on a demonstration gravity slate train at Gwyndy Bank, Minffordd; November saw and heard (a distinctive 'roaring' sound) a gravity run from the summit at Tan-y-Grisiau: the 'Isaac Newton' special careered down the 1 in 80 ruling gradient to Boston Lodge, brakesmen slowing it at curves, momentum almost taking it to Porthmadog, reached by a push along the Cob by the crew. Works for 1987 included platform resurfacing and a new canopy at Porthmadog, a water tank at Tan-y-Bwlch, a shelter at Plas Halt, and automation from 10 May of Tan-y-Bwlch loop and signalling. In April 1988, the 125th anniversary of Festiniog steam, *Russell* from the Welsh Highland paid a visit. Early in 1989, with need for more motive power, the society decided to build a new single-Fairlie locomotive, a reproduction of *Taliesin*, dismantled in 1932, and 1990 saw a new station building and platform canopies at Blaenau. Diesel-worked 'push-pull' operation of a modern 'up market' train, mainly for off-peak services, started in 1990.

LLANBERIS LAKE RAILWAY – RHEILFFORDD LLYN PADARN

Throughout the 1980s, the railway (p 107) operated between Gilfach Ddu and Penllyn. A 1989 highlight was the return to steam of *Wild Aster*, dormant since its quarry days, and renamed *Thomas Bach*. Restricted space at Penllyn makes it a 'closed' terminus, journeys starting and ending at Padarn station/Gilfach Ddu. The halfway point at Cei Llydan, however, with its passing loop and picnic site by the waters of Llyn Padarn, with Snowdon looming beyond, is

Page 259 (Top) Llandrindod, looking south, with reinstated loop and resited signal box, February 1990; (*centre*) Restored class 5 No 5407 heading 'The North Wales Coast Express' alongside the expressway at Mochdre, August 1989; (*bottom*) Llangollen, looking west, with 7828 *Odney Manor* on train from Berwyn and 5952 *Cogan Hall* awaiting restoration, August 1989. (*Author*)

Page 260 (*Top*) Bala Lake Railway's 0–4–0ST *Holy War* passing Pentrepiod Platform at speed, August 1989; (*centre*) 2–6–2T *Russell* waiting to leave the Welsh Highland Railway's Porthmadog station, August 1989; (*bottom*) 0–6–0T No 2 *The Countess* leaving Welshpool Raven Square station with train for Llanfair Caereinion, August 1989. (*Author*)

an attractive spot to spend some time, though only to be reached on the return journey because outward trains do not stop there. At Gilfach Ddu the Victorian offices and workshops of the old Dinorwic company house the Welsh Slate Museum, a fascinating collection of machinery and relics. A siding laid into the museum in December 1982 permits the National Museum of Wales' 1905-built Hunslet 0–4–OST *Una* to take occasional demonstration freight trains along the lakeside. Beyond is the Quarry Hospital and Visitor Centre. On the lower slopes of Elider Fawr, dominating the railway, is Llyn Padarn Country Park, with the Dinorwic and Vivian railway inclines to the old quarries, and waymarked nature and industrial trails, including the famous 'Zig Zag' steps to the road above.

TALYLLYN RAILWAY – RHEILFFORDD TALYLLYN

At wooded Nant Gwernol (p 175) a footbridge across the ravine was opened in May 1980 linking the station with new footpaths on the slopes of Graig Wen, a project which won a Prince of Wales Award and an increase in passengers. Welcome was the visit of the Prince and Princess of Wales on 25 November 1982, the Prince riding the footplate of the decorated *Dolgoch* between Tywyn Pendre and Rhydyronen; 0–4–OWT *Douglas* acted as pilot. A worrying fall in passenger journeys starting in the early 1980s continued for several years, perhaps in the Talyllyn's case simply because it had 'arrived' first; elsewhere there were extensions and openings and the railway enthusiast went there instead. Changing patterns of tourist travel, however, with more through bookings via BR, and extending into the autumn, resulted in a daily October service in 1988. An annual event, recognised by the Welsh Amateur Athletic Association, was 'Race the Train', with hundreds of runners competing against a loaded train from Tywyn Wharf to Abergynolwyn and back. Restored to service in 1991 was Irish Turf Board tank engine No 7, renamed *Tom Rolt*, in memory of the founder of this premier preserved line. Seasonal use of locomotives repainted as Reverend Awdry-style characters from his fictional 'Skarloey' has offended some purists, but it brought in revenue and, importantly, captivated the children; it is just such youngsters who are the future lifeblood of railway preservation.

TEIFI VALLEY RAILWAY – RHEILFFORDD DYFFRYN TEIFI

The Newcastle Emlyn Branch Light Railway Order became effective from December 1980. Though land purchase (p 234) was completed, the Dyfed Railway Company, formed to own and operate the line,

sold the Llandyssul–Pencader length, retaining Llandyssul–Newcastle Emlyn, 6 miles (9.6km), with Henllan as headquarters, and
changed its name to Teifi Valley Railway. Clearing the trackbed
started in 1983, while at Henllan workshops, a ticket office, shop
and refreshment room were erected and a low, stone platform was
built west of the overbridge. Track to 1ft 11¾in (61cm) gauge
was laid for about a mile (1.6km) to terminate at Pontprenshitw.
Passenger trains started from 24 August 1985, ex-Penrhyn 1984
Hunslet 0–4–OST *Alan George* (regauged by the Talyllyn Railway),
hauling a coach constructed at Henllan. A 1941 Hunslet 0–4–0
diesel *Sholto* operated a two-coach train during the 1986 season,
and 1987 saw commissioning of a refurbished Ruston & Hornsby
diesel *Neath Abbey*. From Henllan a nature trail went through the
woods, and intermediate Forest Halt gave access to a campfire
site, amphitheatre, woodland walks and picnic areas; the railway's
'Tourist Guide' lists the plants and animals to be found. Good
Friday, 24 March 1989, saw the line extended by just over ½ mile
(.8km) to a platform at Llandyfriog. Despite floods in 1987 which
damaged the Teifi bridge west of Llandyfriog, the company intends
to reach Newcastle Emlyn. A bearer bond issue was made in 1988
to finance further extension.

ROLL UP! FOR THE VALE OF RHEIDOL

In April 1981 No 8 *Llywelyn* emerged from Aberystwyth depot
in unlined Great Western livery (p 237). Three engineer's wagons
from the old Plynlimon & Hafan Tramway of 1897 were returned
to the grey and black of 1902. Whatever the appearance of the
trains, however, the V of R faced an uncertain future. Peak traffic
of 179,500 passenger journeys in 1975 had slumped to 111, 900 by
1980, approaching break-even point when money was shortly to be
needed by BR for the Cambrian Coast line. Unlike other narrow
gauge railways with active volunteers, V of R staff worked under
BR service conditions; volunteers perforce confined activities to
promoting the railway. The line kept open largely due to dedication
and resourcefulness of BR staff at Stoke, Chester, and on the ground.
More passengers were essential. *Llywelyn* seemed to point the way
for 1981 saw decline in journeys almost arrested. The railway's 80th
anniversary in 1982 therefore saw No 9 *Prince of Wales* returned to
original V of R livery of line yellow ochre, funded by its builders,
Davies & Metcalfe, and the supporters' association. Next No 7
Owain Glyndwr, sponsored by Shell UK, sported lined BR Bruns-
wick green for 1983, with GWR chocolate and cream coaches, and
matching new 'Vista' saloon. Passenger journeys began an upturn;

track rationalisation had by now limited the maximum potential to about 140,000. For 1986 *Llywelyn* donned Cambrian black. The V of R, apart from its own efforts, also benefited from recast Cambrian services, Sprinters, and the 'Cambrian Coast Express'.

Rumours that BR might close the line were not wide of the mark. In 1987 BR wished to sell, but to a purchaser who would undertake to operate trains for at least five years. Despite BR staff wishing to take over, in August 1988 the Brecon Mountain Railway was announced as the preferred bidder. A special Gala Day on 5 November 'celebrated' the 'official' end of steam under BR operation, with a 'Guy Fawkes Special' and fireworks displays at each station. In fact the 'real' last BR steam-hauled passenger train ran on 18 December, the 13.30 'Santa Special' from Aberystwyth and return, headed by *Owain Glyndwr*. The line opened under BMR ownership for the 1989 season. Aberffrwd loop was brought back into use from 9 July 1990; it is expected that watering facilities will be reinstated there in place of Nantyronen.

WELSH HIGHLAND RAILWAY – RHEILFFORDD UCHELDIR CYMRU

The Welsh Highland Light Railway Order (p 110) was effective from May 1980. On 2 August *Kinnerley* and a bogie coach formed the first fare-paying train over the ¾ mile (1.2km) line between Porthmadog and Pen-y-Mount. A similar diesel, *Glaslyn*, started the July 1981 service. The first steam-hauled train for over forty years ran on 30 April 1983, hauled by *Karen*, rebuilt at the Welsh Highland works at Gelerts Farm. A four-road train shed came into use at Porthmadog in 1985. A year later the WHR reaffirmed its intention to reach Beddgelert, 'and probably beyond'. Winter 1986–7 saw platforms extended at both stations, and construction of a wooden-bodied coach in NWNG style. In April 1987, after fifty years, *Russell* was in steam again, outshopped from Gelerts Farm. An acquisition in 1987 was the body of the WHR's Ashbury 1893-built former buffet car—unique on a pre-1939 Welsh narrow gauge railway. In December 1986, in order to surmount difficulties involved with the receivership of the trackbed east of Pen-y-Mount (the old WHLR went into liquidation in 1944), Gwynedd County Council decided to seek, jointly with the WHR, a Light Railway Order for the further 1½ miles (2.4km) on to Pont Croesor. This is the WHR's attraction: it still has a way to go. Perhaps it was not surprising that the nearby Festiniog Railway, having reached its own promised land, should have made a bid for participation in possible reopening over the remaining Welsh Highland trackbed.

WELSHPOOL & LLANFAIR LIGHT RAILWAY –
RHEILFFORDD YSGAFN Y TRALLWNG A LLANFAIR

The 2¾ miles (4.4km) extension from Sylfaen to Welshpool Raven Square (p 187) opened on 18 July 1981, the culmination of four years' hard work, clearing vegetation and trees, rebuilding culverts, repairing drains and fences, dismantling and renewing track, and building a new terminus. With its large car park and connection with BR, albeit on the other side of the town, it was not long before Raven Square was booking more passengers than Llanfair; it soon sprouted a water tower, signal box and sidings. During this time the railway's famous locomotive pair was absent: *The Countess* reappeared on 16 August 1986, overhauled and in Cambrian black, welcomed at Raven Square by the Dowager Countess of Powis. *The Earl* represented the narrow gauge at the 'Rocket 150' celebration in 1980, and has been displayed at the National Railway Museum, Birmingham Railway Museum and, at the time of writing, was at Didcot Railway Centre. In 1983 staff and ticket working started between Raven Square and the Sylfaen loop; Castle Caereinion loop now sees infrequent use. At Llanfair in 1988 the workshops were extended for a machine shop to speed overhauls; a four-road carriage shed was completed the following year. The preserved railway celebrated its Silver Jubilee in 1988. Starting in 1991 Raven Square was to get a new station building, with improved facilities following at Llanfair. With its unique gauge, the W&L runs through idyllic countryside and has an exotic collection of locomotives and rolling stock.

Acknowledgements

I thank the following for their help: Roy Anderson, Terence Barry, Phil Briers, Stephen C. Edwards of the Cambrian Railways Society, Frank Harrison, John Miller, Roland J. H. Parry of Morfa, Abergele, Trefor Thompson of the North Clwyd Railway Association, Susan and Keith Turner of Port Dinorwic, Laurie Ward, and A. S. Wilson-Jones.

I am indebted to Meirion Mill Publications for information about Mawddwy, the Editor *Railway Magazine* for permission to quote from the article by Mr A. S. Wilson-Jones, and Methuen & Co for permission to quote from *Wales: A Physical, Historical and Regional Geography*, ed. E. G. Bowen.

Apart from the primary source material made available by the helpful staff at the British Library, the House of Lords Record Office, and the Public Record Office I also wish to thank The National Library of Wales, the County Archivists of Clwyd and Salop, Gwynedd Library Service, Anglesey Area Library, Clwyd Library Service, Glyndwr Area Library, Ludlow Museum, and Westminster City Library.

Finally, my thanks are due to Professor Allan J. Patmore for his most helpful advice on many aspects of the book as series editor.

For the second edition I gladly acknowledge again the contributions made by the above. A rewarding aspect of writing a book such as this, with a pitfall at every step, is the constructive, often local, criticism which is offered and which can correct and improve the text. The extensive revisions are the result of such advice and of information and time generously given in response to further questions. Old and new friends who have helped with this edition include Terence Barry of Burgess Hill; Bill Batteson of Watford; V. J. Bradley, General Manager, Llanberis Lake Railway; R. A. Cooke of Harwell who generously made available information from then unpublished sections of his excellent GWR and BR(WR) Track Layout Diagrams; Stirling B. Dickson of Bangor; Ian D. S. Hills, Director, Teifi Valley Railway; G. A. Hookham of Epsom; and Roland Parry of Morfa, Abergele. Finally, I would thank my son Robert for help with technical knowledge and photographic contribution, and my wife Anne for continuing support and encouragement.

Sources, Bibliography and Further Reading

British Library: Parliamentary Papers, Statutes, etc, railway and other newspapers and periodicals.

House of Lords Record Office: Bills, deposited plans, minutes of evidence on Bills.

Public Record Office: Railway company minutes and official records, Board of Trade Reports, public and working timetables, correspondence, etc.

Abbott, Rowland A. S. *The Fairlie Locomotive* (1970)

Ahrons, E. L. *Locomotive and Train Working in the Latter Part of the Nineteenth Century* (1953)

Barrie, D. S. M. *The Brecon & Merthyr Railway* (1957)

Baughan, Peter E. *The Chester & Holyhead Railway* Vol 1 (1972)

Bick, David E. *The Old Metal Mines of Mid-Wales* (1977)

Biddle, Gordon. *Victorian Stations* (1973)

Black's Picturesque Guide to Wales (1866 and 1885)

Boyd, J. I. C. *Narrow Gauge Railways in Mid-Wales* (1970)
Narrow Gauge Railways in South Caernarvonshire (1972)
The Festiniog Railway Vols 1 and 2 (1975)

Brewster, D. E. *Motor Buses in Wales 1898–1932* (1976)

Carrington, D. C. and Rushworth, T. F. *Slates to Velinheli*

Cartwright, Ralph, and Russell, R. T. *The Welshpool & Llanfair Light Railway* (1972)

Christiansen, Rex, and Miller R. W. *The Cambrian Railways* Vols 1 and 2 (1967)

Christiansen, Rex. *Forgotten Railways: North and Mid Wales* (1976)

Clark, Edwin. *The Britannia and Conway Tubular Bridges* (1850)

Clinker, C. R. *LNWR Chronology 1900–1960* (1961)
Light Railway Orders (1977)

Cozens, Lewis. *The Mawddwy, Van and Kerry Railways* (1972)
Daniels, Gerald, and Dench, L. A. *Passengers No More* (1974)
Dendy Marshall, C. F. *A History of British Railways down to the Year 1830* (1971)
Dow, George. *The Great Central Railway* Vols 1–3 (1959)
Dunn, J. M. *The Chester & Holyhead Railway*, and various articles on the railways of North Wales in the *Railway Magazine* and the *Stephenson Locomotive Society Journal*
Ellis, C. Hamilton. *The Midland Railway* (1953)
British Railway History Vols 1 and 2 (1954)
Greville, M. D. and Spence, Jeoffry. *Closed Passenger Lines of Great Britain 1827–1947* (1974)
Hadfield, Charles *British Canals* (1959)
Atmospheric Railways (1967)
Hughes, D. Lloyd, and Williams, Dorothy M. *Holyhead: The Story of a Port* (1967)
Kidner, R. W. *The Cambrian Railways* (1954)
Mineral Railways (1967)
Standard Gauge Light Railways (1971)
The Narrow Gauge Railways of Wales (1972)
Lee, Charles E. *The Penrhyn Railway* (1964)
Lewis, M. J. T. *How Ffestiniog Got its Railway* (1968)
MacDermot, E. T. *History of the Great Western Railway* Vols 1 and 2 (1927)
Neele, George P. *Railway Reminiscences* (1904)
Parry, Edward. *Railway Companion from Chester to Holyhead* (1848)
Prideaux, J. D. C. A. *The Welsh Narrow Gauge Railway* (1976)
Railway Correspondence and Travel Society. *The Locomotives of the Great Western Railway* (1956–66)
Rees, D. Morgan. *Industrial Archaelogy of Wales* (1975)
Rolt, L. T. C. *Railway Adventure: The Story of the Talyllyn Railway* (1961)
Red for Danger (1971)
Smith, D. J. *Shrewsbury to Swansea* (1971)
Thomas, Brian D. *The Cerrig-y-Drudion Railway*. Manuscript in keeping of the County Librarian, Clwyd
Thompson, Trefor. *The Prestatyn and Dyserth Railway* (1978)
Tonks, Eric S. *The Shropshire & Montgomeryshire Railway* (1972)
The Snailbeach District Railways (1974)
Tucker, Norman. *Colwyn Bay, Its Origin and Growth* (1953)

Turner, Keith. *The Snowdon Mountain Railway* (1973)
Turner, Susan. *The Padarn and Penrhyn Railways* (1975)
Watson, Edward. *The Royal Mail to Ireland* (1917)
Wren, Wilfrid J. *The Tanat Valley, Its Railways and Industrial Archaeology* (1968)

Further books which have proved useful or of general interest are:

Anderson, V. R. & Fox, G. K. *An Historical Survey of Chester to Holyhead Railway Track Layouts and Illustrations* (1984)
Baker, S. K. *Rail Atlas Great Britain & Ireland* (Various editions)
Baughan, Peter E. *The North Wales Coast Railway* (1988)
Beck, Keith M. *The Great Western North of Wolverhampton* (1986)
Butcher, Alan C. (Edit.) *Railways Restored* (Editions 1980–1989/90)
Casserley, H. C. *Welsh Railways in the Heyday of Steam* (1979)
Clark, R. H. *An Historical Survey of Selected Great Western Stations Layouts and Illustrations* Volume One (1976), Volume Two (1979), Volume Three (1981)
Coles. C. R. L. *On the North and West Route from Chester to Newport* (1984)
Green, C. C. *Cambrian Railways Album* (1977), Vol 2 (1981)
Hawkins, Chris & Reeve, George *LMS Engine Sheds Vol One, The LNWR* (1987)
Johnson, Peter *Rails in Wales. The Cambrian Lines* (1984)
Kneale, E. V. *North Wales Steam (1927–1968)* (1980)
Potts, C. R. *An Historical Survey of Selected Great Western Stations Layouts and Illustrations* Volume Four (1985)
Rear, W. G. *LMS Branch Lines in North Wales Vol 1 Bangor to Afonwen, Llanberis and Nantlle* (1986)
Rear, W. G. & Williams, M. F. *Scenes from the Past: 4 The Cambrian Coast Railway* (1988)
Rhodes, Michael & Shannon, Peter *Freight Only Volume 3: Wales & Scotland* (1988)
Williams, G. Haulfryn *Railways in Gwynedd* (1979)

Index

Illustrations are in italic type. Some locations and stations, and variations in spelling, are indexed together, e.g. Buckley/Jct, Conway/Conwy. Abbreviations used are: Brn = Branch, Extn = Extension, Jct = Junction, Jt = Joint, Lt = Light, Rly = Railway, Stn = Station; also some railway company titles: AWC = Aberystwith & Welch Coast, Cam = Cambrian, DRC = Denbigh Ruthin & Corwen, GC = Great Central, GW = Great Western, LMS = London Midland & Scottish, LNW = London & North Western, MM = Manchester & Milford, MW = Mid Wales, NWNG = North Wales Narrow Gauge, PSNW = Potteries Shrewsbury & North Wales, SC = Shrewsbury & Chester, SM = Shropshire & Montgomeryshire, VR = Vale of Rheidol, WL = Welshpool & Llanfair, WMCQ = Wrexham Mold & Connahs Quay. For lack of space proposed railways are not indexed.

Abbey Dolgarrog & Trefriw Lt Rly, 133
Abenbury, 168
Aber, 23, 32
Aberangell, 177-8
Aberayron, *191*, 222, 232-3
Aberdovey, 156, 159-60, 163, 171, 175, 177
Aberdovey harbour, *122*, 156, 160, 163
Aberedw, 211
Abererch, 160
Abergele, 21, 23, 26, 31, 239
Abergwili/Jct, 217, 223, 225, 229
Abergynolwyn, 171-2, 176, 261
Aberllefenni, 175-6
Abermule, 151-2, 167, 183
Aberystwith & Welch Coast Rly, 97, 138, 141-2, 155-7
Aberystwyth, 97, 148-9, 152, 155-6, 163-6, 168, 189, *192*, 197, 205, 207, 222, 224, 227, 229-30, 233-6, 246-9, 252, 262-3
Accidents: Abergele, 31; Abermule, 167; Brinkir, 98; Caernarvon, 103; Chwilog, 103; Dee Bridge, 23; Friog Cliffs, 163; Glanrhyd, 252; Llandulas, 32, 75; Llanerchymedd, 85; Menai Bridge, 94; Penmaenmawr, 32; Rednal, 42; Welshampton, 167; Westbury, 249
Acrefair, 61, 137, 145
Afon Eitha, 47, 61
Afon Wen, 97, 103, 155, 159-60, 166-8
Alltddu, 205, 227-8
Amlwch, 13, 81, 84-5, 90, 240
Anglesey Central Rly, 82-5, 90

Ardleen, 152, 185
Arenig, 131
Arthog, 144

Bagillt, 25, 32
Bala/Jct, 50, 71, *83*, *88*, 130-1, 141-4, 146, 155
Bala & Dolgelly Rly, 75, 141-4
Bala & Festiniog Rly, 129-32, 144
Bala Lake Rly, 146-7, 256, *260*
Balderton, 44-5
Bangor, *18*, 22, 26, 82-3, 85, 92, 111, 238, 240
Bangor & Caernarvon Rly, 92, 94-5, 101-5
Bangor-on-Dee, 161
Bank Pool Quay, 151
Barmouth, 141, 148, 155, 160, 164, 166-9, 246-8
Barmouth Ferry, 157-60, 187, 257
Barmouth Jct/Morfa Mawddach, 157, 159-60, 165
Baschurch, 39, 45, 246
Beaumaris, 85-6
Beddgelert, 97, 107-9, 124-6, 263
Beddgelert Siding, 124
Berwyn, 138, 145, 147, 254-5
Bethesda, 110-12
Bethesda Brn, 111-12
Bettisfield, 154, 161
Betts, Edward, 22, 24, 50
Bettws (Carmarthen & Cardigan), 229
Betws Garmon, 97, 102, 107